NOTORIOUSLY MILITANT

NOTORIOUSLY MILITANT
The Story of a Union Branch

Sheila Cohen

MERLIN PRESS

Published in 2013
by Merlin Press Ltd
99B Wallis Road
London
E9 5LN

www.merlinpress.co.uk

© Sheila Cohen, 2013

ISBN. 978-0-85036-645-7

Catalogue in publication data is available
from the British Library

The right of Sheila Cohen to be identified as author of this work
has been asserted in accordance with the Copyright, Designs
and Patents Act 1988

All rights reserved. No part of this publication may be
reproduced, stored in a retrieval system, or transmitted,
in any form or by any means, electronic, mechanical,
photocopying, recording or otherwise, without the
prior permission of the publisher.

Printed in the UK by Imprint Digital, Exeter

Contents

Acknowledgements		vii
Abbreviations		xi
Introduction	'Notoriously militant'	1
Chapter One	'You'll never organise Ford', 1900-1945	10
Chapter Two	T & G meets FMC: the birth of 1107, 1946-1959	40
Chapter Three	The sixties: From defeat to victory – and the 'upsurge'	70
Chapter Four	The seventies: high noon at Dagenham	101
Chapter Five	The eighties: storming 1107	132
Chapter Six	Nineties to noughties: the beginning of the end	163
Conclusion	PostFordism: the battle for trade union democracy	194
Bibliography		215
Index		220

ACKNOWLEDGEMENTS

The author of any history based on original research and interviews must offer heartfelt thanks to all those who have put up with the often tedious, repetitive requests that come their way. All of those individuals and organisations are, I hope, recognised here – and I apologise for any omissions which may result from my less-than-perfect records.

First and foremost in these acknowledgements must come 'The 1107-ers' – the key activists in the union branch this book celebrates, and also those who first agreed to the project and went on to give their endless and patient help in the form of interviews, fact-checking, further contacts and general help and encouragement. The names of these activists, who relaunched the 1107 branch as a more active and member-led organisation in the early 1980s (see Chapter Five), come up again and again in this book as staunch defenders – and promoters – of workplace trade union strength and democracy. Jim Brinklow, Matt Conker, Alan Deyna-Jones, Roger Dillon, Ron Doel, Rod Finlayson, Mick Gosling, Janet Marlow, Allan Martin, Mavis Martin, Alf Richards, Pete Singh, Trevor Tansley and Terry Turner; these are the 'usual suspects' past and present who lent me generous help with the work- and union-related insights which form, I hope, the basis of this account.

One name cannot be omitted from this list, although he himself is now sadly absent. Steve Riley perhaps did most of all to raise the banner of staunch workplace activism across the many years in which he represented the essential spirit of 1107 as branch secretary and later convenor in that 1107 stronghold, the Paint, Trim and Assembly plant (PTA).

Other Dagenham activists who gave enormous help are gratefully acknowledged here: Ted Amos and Frankie Bland, ex- stewards and 1107 activists in the Engine Plant; Johnny Davies, retired Engine Plant deputy convenor; Dora Challingsworth and Sheila Douglas, sewing machinists from the River Plant; Fred Creamer and Mick Hadcraft, TGWU 667 member and EPIU activist in the Body Plant; Joe Gordon, ex-convenor of the PTA; Keith Gould, PTA steward; retired PTA activist Berlyne Hamilton; AEU Body Plant activist Des Heemskirk; ex-PTA lineworker Janet Marlow;

retired River Plant convenor Bernie Passingham; and Maisie Thomas, who provided the wonderful account of wartime work experience relayed in Chapter Two – not to mention Henry Coleman, a veteran Ford worker with a memory stretching back to the construction of the Dagenham plant.

Kevin Halpin, ex-AEU activist and, in the late 1950s and early '60s, PTA convenor (see Chapters Two and Three) provided invaluable information and analysis through my interviews with him and his own recent book *Memoirs of a Militant*[1]. Eddie Prevost, another retired Ford activist, also contributed unique insights. Ken Weller, who worked at Dagenham in the late 1950s and early '60s, was generous both with his insightful recollections and with back copies of *Solidarity*, the magazine he co-edited in the 1950s-70s.

At more official level in Unite, Steve Hart and Steve Turner provided crucial background information and submitted to time-consuming interviewing despite their busy schedules. I would also like to thank Graham Stevenson, who provided me with useful historical information on TGWU/Unite. Other trade union full-timers, current and retired, provided valuable accounts of their experiences at Dagenham, including Ed Blissett and Justin Bowden from the GMB.

Many academics and other 'experts' provided me with much-needed resources and research information. First and foremost must come Dr Gregor Gall, Director of the Work and Employment Research Unit (WERU) at the University of Hertfordshire; WERU has provided me not only with an income but also theoretical 'feedback' and encouragement. Dr Patricia Fosh introduced me to Fords Dagenham via the 1986-88 Workplace Trade Union Democracy research project (see Chapter 5); this was when I first encountered the 1107-ers. I am also grateful to Professor Huw Beynon of Cardiff University (author of the classic *Working For Ford*), for his support and endorsement, and to Steve Jary, who kindly provided his MSc thesis on new technology. Darren O'Grady of South Thames College Trade Union Studies department and Roy Greenslade, Professor of Journalism at City University, have also provided helpful assistance.

Jon Cruddas, MP for Dagenham and Rainham, met me for an extended interview at an early stage, while Margaret Hodge (Barking) provided information on Unite's role in the 2010 election. Tony Benn has lent me his always generous support and encouragement.

On the Liverpool 'side', retired Halewood activist John Bohanna has patiently answered my endless questions with warmth and – of course – wit; Greg Dropkin provided a copy of his film on the 1984-5 sewing machinists' dispute, 'Making The Grade', as well as helping me with various queries, and ex-Halewood convenor Eddie Roberts was also generous with time and information.

On the archival front, both the Marx Memorial Library and the TUC deserve my warm thanks for their enormous help with the research; the Barking and Dagenham Archives and Local Studies Service at the Valence House Museum also offered aid well beyond the call of duty. Many thanks to Judith Garfield at Eastside Community Heritage, who generously allowed me access to unique interviews with Ford workers, and to the Working Class Movement Library in Salford. Bob Jones, the best second-hand bookseller in the business, also deserves a hand for his remarkable book-ferreting talents!

On the financial front, I would like to thank Marion Kozack, in particular, for her help with obtaining a small grant from the Lipman-Miliband Trust; on the technical front, Jenny Lewenstein and Mike Parker for pitching in on tasks before which I quailed. Huge thanks to Tony Zurbrugg and Adrian Howe of Merlin Press for their unstinting support.

Last but not least, my grateful thanks to *Socialist Worker* journalists for putting up with my somewhat distracted presence once a week for several months as I searched through their unique archives and wrestled with their equally unique computers! Sabby Sagall, who covered Fords Dagenham in the late '60s and 1970s, was also most helpful.

Such acknowledgements may lead readers to suspect political partisanship; in fact, I am not a member of any political party myself, but assiduous readers of what follows will probably deduce that my sentiments are closer to those of Marx than Ford.

All friends and relations who have humoured me in my obsession with this history over the last two to three years are here acknowledged, but most of all – as always – my heartfelt love and gratitude go to my husband, partner and comrade Kim Moody and to my cherished daughters Lauren and Berry – both of whom now excel in matters literary and political.

1   Kevin Halpin, *Memoirs of a Militant: Sharply and to the point*, Glasgow: Praxis Press, 2012.

ABBREVIATIONS and ACRONYMS

AAVW	Auto, Aircraft and Vehicle Workers of America
ACAS	Advisory, Conciliation and Arbitration Service
AEF	Amalgamated Engineering Federation
AEU	Amalgamated Engineering Union
AEEU	Amalgamated Engineering and Electricians' Union
AFL	American Federation of Labor
AJ	After Japan
AMICUS	Union resulting from merger between AEEU and MSF.
ANL	Anti-Nazi League
ASTMS	Association of Scientific, Technical and Managerial Staffs
AUEW	Amalgamated Union of Engineering Workers
BLMC	British Leyland Motor Company
CAD/CAM	Computer Aided Design/Computer Aided Manufacturing
CAITS	Centre for Alternative Industrial, Technological and Technological Systems
CIO	Congress of Industrial Organizations
CP	Communist Party
DRC	Divisional Review Committee
ECH	Eastside Community Heritage
EDAP	Employee Development and Assistance Programme
EEF	Engineering Employers' Federation
EEPTU	Electrical, Electronic, Telecommunications and Plumbing Trade Union
EI	Employee Involvement
EPA	Employment Protection Act (1975)
EOCs	Equal Opportunities Committees
EP	Engine Plant, Dagenham
EPA	Employee Protection Act
ETU	Electrical Trade Union
FMC	Ford Motor company
FNJNC	Ford National Joint Negotiating Committee
FJSSC	Ford Joint Shop Stewards' Committee

FWG	Ford Workers' Group
GLC	Greater London Council
GM	General Motors
GMB	General, Municipal and Boilermakers' union
HASAW	Health and Safety at Work Act (1974)
IPOS	'In Place Of Strife' (Labour government White Paper)
IR	Industrial relations
IS	International Socialists
IWC	Institute of Workers' Control
IWW	International Workers of the World
J-i-T	Just-in-Time (working)
JNC	Joint Negotiating Committee
JSSC	Joint Shop Stewards' Committee
JWC	Joint Works Committee
KD	Knock-Down plant/department
MDW	Measured Day Work
NEDO	National Economic Development Organisation
NLRA	National Labor Relations Act
NUPE	National Union of Public Employees
NUVB	National Union of Vehicle Builders
PTA	Paint, Trim and Assembly plant, Dagenham
QCs	Quality Circles
QWL	Quality of Working Life
SLL	Socialist Labour League
TGWU	('T&G') Transport and General Workers' Union
TUEL	Trade Union Education League
TULRA	Trade Union and Labour Relations Act (1974)
TUC	Trades Union Congress
UAW	United Auto Workers
Unite	Union resulting from merger between Amicus and the TGWU in 2007.
URTU	United Road Transport Union
WoD	Winter of Discontent

Introduction

'NOTORIOUSLY MILITANT': THE STORY OF TGWU 1/1107 FORD CENTRAL BRANCH

TGWU 1/1107 is no ordinary trade union branch. Though it would be wrong to call any form of trade union organisation 'ordinary', 1107's historic role as the largest union branch at one of the UK's most iconic industrial workplaces – Ford's Dagenham plant – guarantees it a place in any history of workers, trade unions and industrial conflict. This place is all the more deserved given the historic struggles carried out by 1107 against the anti-union and anti-worker culture of the company which gave its name to a whole industrial system – Fordism.

From this point of view the history presented here is of a workplace as well as a branch. Indeed, Chapter One retells the classic tale of Henry Ford's first efforts to get his 'Flivver' on the road, and the assembly line-based work process this unleashed across the world. But it also tells the immemorial story of how an oppressed and exploited workforce organised in spite of it all – in both Detroit and Dagenham – from the factory floor up rather than the trade union office down.

This story, and its sequel in 1946 – when the 1107 branch was founded in the wake of an insurgent occupation at Dagenham – is told in the first two chapters. In Chapter Three the 'action' switches mainly to the new Paint Trim and Assembly plant (PTA) with its thousands of super-exploited line workers, and documents how those workers continually fought back against Dagenham management's attempts to hoodwink and oppress them. Chapter Four, which covers the 1970s, documents how that unbeaten will to resist was expressed through occupations and even riots against the injustice of barely compensated lay-offs from work.

But it is in Chapter Five that the birth of a new 1107 – one based on principles of workplace union democracy and determined opposition to Ford's collaborationist 'Employee Involvement' policies – is recorded.

In the early 1980s, the now middle-aged branch was 'stormed' by a new leadership made up of stewards and TGWU activists. Most were from the PTA, but many Engine Plant 1107ers also rejected what had become a stale and allegedly corrupt leadership. *Notoriously Militant* – the slogan the reformed branch adopted in mockery of a scaremongering journalist – is a tribute to the spirit of that newly accountable leadership.

'A Lot of History ...'

But the best way to introduce a history of union activism at Dagenham is to allow the 1107 activists to speak up themselves – on the value of workplace union organisation and the wider political perspective offered by the reformed branch. Pete Singh, one of the many 1107 activists who contributed valuable information and insights to the writing of this book, puts it this way: 'There's a lot of history, a lot of things that have happened. 1107 on the Ford estate have been the champions of every fight that's taken place over the years, we've been at the forefront of it all ... nowhere more so than when the PTA was up,[1] because we made inroads through our punch-ups with the company, we put foundations up for other workers, we enhanced their terms and conditions as a result. There were a lot of issues where the company had to give in to the power of the union – in the 1960s and '70s, we built the foundations for other workers to enhance their terms and conditions. The '60s, '70s, '80s, into the '90s really.'

The 'new 1107' was very different from its predecessor. For branch chair Jim Brinklow, '1107 was the catalyst for everything on the Dagenham estate from the early 1980s – the shop stewards' committee carried out policies, but 1/1107 was the catalyst – nearly all the progressive decisions were from 1/1107. We used to print T-shirts for our members with "Notoriously Militant" on the back ... One of the papers dubbed us the notoriously militant 1/1107.'

As PTA steward Alan Deyna-Jones recalled, 'It was one of the best branches going – 1107 spread their wings a bit, helped other trade union members. The banner of the 1107 was always there on marches and rallies all over Britain, supporting other workers like the nurses, miners and bus drivers. They also took the lead on other issues round the world ... Other branches would say 1107 was "too far left" but the branch was concerned with every worker, all workers. 1107 was different. We stood up for what we meant. We didn't go shouting from the rafters – we were there. 1107 – we were there.'

Terry Turner, who still works in the Engine Plant, found that 'This was the place – this small classroom in Dagenham[2] was where you found out the facts – this was where you found out what was going on. You had all the stewards turning up, the deputy convenors were there – and you suddenly found out what the score was. And it was great.' Terry adds that 'Proper lay off pay, sick pay, line workers' allowance, service holidays – every one of those ideas, although negotiated at a national level, were initiated by the 1107 branch, along with ideas such as a crèche – once they started taking on more and more female workers, a crèche was essential.'

Engine Plant steward Allan Martin noted that the branch 'enabled you to find out what was going on in other plants – and that issues you were having in the plant were not unique to the plant or even industry. It enabled me to keep my members informed – gave you access to the wider trade union movement ... As an individual it really helped – educated me and helped make me a better steward. You can meet people, discuss with people with similar problems how they overcome them, you can learn from them, and also you can give your experiences and it's invaluable – you don't have to keep reinventing the wheel – someone's been there and done it before.'

Mick Gosling, who was sacked in 1989 for his union activism, was a staunch supporter: 'I felt really proud about what the 1107 did – we never worked above people or imposed ourselves on them ... We had enormous respect on the floor amongst the workers.' Mick adds: '1107 – we were just bloody different ... We just refused to bow our knee to anybody and it didn't matter whether it was the bureaucracy or the bosses – we were the 1107 and that was it.'

Nor did the 1107 activists go without appreciation on the shop floor. One part-time woman assembly-line worker commented that 'The branch was enormously respected. They were very good at getting the men to support them ... The PTA stewards [all 1107 members] really did look after their members ... they weren't people that could be bribed by the company. So you'd automatically get the tag "militant", wouldn't you, for that!' Raising the crucial issue of accountability, she added: 'Sometimes you get people in positions of power and they become like the people they're supposed to be challenging – you never got that with the 1107.'

1/1107's unusual position as a workplace branch in a movement where most branches are geographically based, covering a number of workplaces, became a source of its strength after the change of leadership. Branch chair Jim Brinklow informed me proudly, '1107 is called the Ford Central Branch. If you look at the 1107 stamp, our branch stamp, you'll see it's also designated the Ford Central Branch. And it organised over more than one section of Dagenham, but the main one was the PTA – we had several thousand members in there. There were quite a few members in the Engine

Plant and in the foundry. We had members everywhere because people left and retained their branch membership.'

At the same time, 1/1107's function as a *branch* was to extend beyond the workplace to the wider trade union at Trade Group and regional level (the '1' identifies 1107 as belonging to TGWU Region One). In an earlier interview,[3] Steve Riley addressed the issue of union branch vis-a-vis plant organisation at Dagenham: 'There isn't the sort of structure you have at other workplaces where there is only one union – here the shop stewards' committee is really the 'branch' … But branch organisation is very important. Purely trade union problems are dealt with through the branch – disputes within the T&G and so on – following through [national] trade union policies – the only way that will happen is through a branch.'

Given its workplace base, 'Until very recently, if you asked … members … what branch they were in, they would say, I think I'm in the T&G – We have even had people say I'm in the PTA.' But since the transfer of leadership 1107 activists had been working hard to increase membership involvement and education, and 'the situation has improved. The majority of people now know which branch they're in and have a very basic idea about the structure …'

An Effort Bargain?

There are many other crucial dimensions to the 'back-story' of 1107. These include the basic question of the nature of work – the labour process itself – and whatever 'reward' workers receive, a relationship sometimes referred to as the Effort Bargain. The mixture of boredom and hard graft on the assembly line conjures up Marx's phrase 'dull compulsion' in relation to the experience of job satisfaction (or the lack of it) at Ford. Indeed, the sheer monotony of the basic work process, particularly on the line, was enough to get to workers. As one wrote in a vivid description of the repetitiveness of this labour: 'Imagine bending down to tie your shoe lace. It's a simple job. But imagine doing it once a minute, 450 times during the period of a work shift … There exists a kind of "line work neurosis"… a feeling best described as being a fly under a jam jar. I have seen an operator, a man with long service who had been on lines for years, break down in tears, saying "I can't stand this job any longer". I've seen ordinary lads suddenly become stubborn, suddenly refusing to do something they have done for years … No one wants to work on a production line'.[4] The point was confirmed in an assembly-line worker's comment in the film *Ford's Dagenham Dream*: 'Going into the plant we were like the living dead. On the assembly line you had no spare time at all – same job over and over. Eventually you could do the job without thinking ...'

As this suggests, the process took an emotional toll on workers. The part-time woman worker mentioned above commented 'There was so much depression – I've seen men crying because they had to come in.' And this issue carries an interesting, and moving, counterpart in the difficult childhoods experienced by more than one 1107 activist. As 1107 stalwart Rod Finlayson recalls, 'Why did I become an activist? I had a shitty childhood. My father was a horrible bastard ... my mother was very self-centred, and I kind of grew up with a sense of justice – I always identified with the underdog.'

Depression as a result of a 'shitty childhood' and depression as a result of working on an inhuman, implacable assembly line may seem like two very different things – but they can be seen as two sides of the coin of a particularly inhuman social and economic system reaching well beyond the walls of the factory. As a young girl interviewed by the local Eastside Community Heritage project remembered: 'My Grandad working for Fords would have to do lots of different shift work, and we're very close, and I couldn't wait for him to get back from work ... When Grandad worked during the night when we used to go round there he used to be asleep. I used to try and wake him up, going into the room and patting him on the head. 'Cause I just wanted to be with him, so – Fords really had a big impact on my memories.'[5]

Yet this fundamentally inhuman system also generated some of the most human – and selfless – impulses of those unsung heroes of the working class, workplace-based activists. One woman worker commented that 1107 'really did look after their members – if the line was going fast they would get it time-checked. They were very good at doing time studies ... if the company got funny with a guy because he just couldn't manage his job the union would come down and do a survey on it – was it too much work for somebody to be doing?' – a tribute which sums up the crucial link between workplace union organisation and the fight against exploitation at work.

From a historical point of view, this link expresses itself in the whole dynamic of grass-roots trade union organisation. As shown in Chapters One and Two, effective representation at Fords in both Detroit and Dagenham was the work of grass-roots workplace activists rather than union higher-ups. And, in both cases, the explosions of conflict which forced management to accept effective shopfloor organisation were rooted in workers' long-held and burning resentment against speed-up, management surveillance and other basic expressions of exploitation and oppression at work. In this sense, the story of organising Ford is the story of organising workers everywhere.

Storming 1107

Yet the history of 1107, which rapidly became the dominant union branch at Dagenham – particularly after the establishment of the Paint, Trim and Assembly plant (PTA) in 1959 – was not one of consistent resistance. By the early 1980s, when the activists who commissioned this history seized control, 1107 had become mired in management-union collaboration and, it is alleged, serious financial corruption. Much of this tradition was rooted in the original leadership of the branch, mainly employed in the Engine Plant rather than the PTA.

The task of the 1107 reformers was far from straightforward, confronted as they were with the 'macho management' and Thatcherite anti-union laws of the 1980s. Yet, as shown, they fought at both plant level and in the wider trade union and political arena for fundamental principles of trade union solidarity, equality and justice.

Among these was the principled stand against the growing cancer of racism threatening the factory and tolerated – as documented in Chapter Six – by management. Here the reformed 1107 branch differed decisively from its 'male, pale and stale' predecessor, playing a historic role in introducing what was almost certainly the first workplace Equal Opportunities policy of the twentieth century. As 1107 stalwart Mick Gosling recalled, 'I think one of the astonishing feats of the 1107 branch was, all the way down the line, the fight against racism, sexism and elitism.'

Early battles against racism were extended to a principled stand against sexism as more women came on to the production lines in the 1980s, while in the 1990s, largely due to the courageous action of 1107-er Trevor Tansley, unions and management adopted policies securing equality for same-sex partners. The branch's radicalism in these areas shows, more than any so-called 'Diversity Policy', the crucial link between the fight against exploitation at work and the politicisation of that key layer of the trade union movement, workplace activists. As Steve Turner, previously a TGWU official for the Dagenham plant, summed up the philosophy of the branch, '1107 looked beyond its own boundaries – it was never insular. They always looked to see how they could support other workers in struggle. There are some achievements there that should be recorded – fantastic achievements. They never gave up.'

1107's strong awareness of the wider political and economic environment became crucial in the face of the 'globalising' trend asserting itself across industry from the early 1980s. In car production – perhaps at Fords more than any other company – this meant increasing duplication of production in different countries, with the Fiesta being produced in Spain and Germany as well as at Dagenham from as early as 1976. One 1980s survey of the car industry argues that 'plant-based trade union organisation [had] been outflanked'[6] by such trends; but the 1107 activists countered this with various moves towards international information-gathering and organisation. A 1982 study of robotisation at Dagenham notes that 'The stewards at Dagenham are extremely aware of the fact that the Sierra is also manufactured at Genk, and it is in response to the threat of any lost production at one plant being made up at the other that the Ford unions worldwide have been seeking to form an "international combine" so that this cannot occur'.[7]

This international awareness saw 1107 play a central role in organising a global conference of Ford workers in 1985. As leading 1107 activist Mick Gosling enthused, 'Via the branch, we started putting pressure on about forming an international unofficial combine – then we said "That's not enough – we want more than that – we want an official international Ford workers' combine." And we pushed for that and that was when there was the first worldwide international Ford Workers' Combine meeting in 1985' – a gathering which attracted Ford activists from Japan, Malaysia, South Africa, the United States, Mexico and Brazil.

'In the Back of My Cortina ...'

On a wider level, the significance and the achievements of 1107 reflect the place in history of the plant itself. As Jon Cruddas, MP for Dagenham and Rainham, put it, 'Ford Dagenham is a landmark to industrial working-class history in this country. They talk about the South Wales valleys or the Jarrow marchers, but if you think about what's happened in terms of the Ford Dagenham plant, it quite rightly has a key role in that history of the British working class. The historic turning points of the late '70s pay rounds and the role of the Ford plant in the strike that broke Callaghan's incomes policy...The women's fight for equal pay – Dagenham was in the lead of that and that is a historic turning point for equality in this country in terms of gender and working class women's voice ... These things are landmark moments in British post war industrial history, economically and sociologically – the whole role of the history of Fords in terms of Taylorism and Fordism.' Writer Graham Turner makes the same identification between Dagenham as a place and as a symbol of working-class experience and struggle: 'In a town like Dagenham ... everybody is ... working class, for solidarity's sake'.[8] As the young Dagenham resident quoted earlier put it, 'Ford work is like the working man's job really. I think there's a class thing that's related to Fords and Dagenham being quite a poor area and lot of people going for jobs round there ...'

In fact, the Dagenham area contained many other factories and workplaces like Chloride, Excel, the pharmaceutical company May and Baker, and the Bata Shoe Company – where, in 1952, Ford workers carried out solidarity action after Bata sacked a number of its workers and tried to evict them from their 'company' housing.[9] But, as was sadly indicated when the PTA finally closed its doors in February 2002, Ford's had always been the main manufacturing plant in Dagenham, with its closure having an enormous knock-on effect on related workplaces and local businesses – not to mention a long-established working-class culture.

As distinguished journalist – and ex-Dagenham resident – Roy Greenslade wrote in early 2000, responding to the first rumours of closure, 'Ford is not just a run-of-the-mill multinational. It is a global super-brand, an icon of capitalism. Talk of Dagenham to anyone anywhere and you can be sure they will mention Ford ... Ford of Dagenham has a peculiar place in the British imagination. In its Essex heartland, it is embedded in the culture'.[10] As were the cars it produced. Greenslade quotes the lyrics of Ian Dury, raised in nearby Upminster:

'Had a love affair with Nina
In the back of my Cortina ...'

In this sense and many more, this book has to be more than the story of 'just' a union branch. It is a story of early industrial exploitation under the umbrella of those twin employer strategies that have become legendary – Taylorism and Fordism; a story of trade union organisation and workplace resistance against the impact of those strategies and the savage anti-unionism that accompanied them; a story of the working-class community that grew up in the shadow of the massive Dagenham factory, and the impact on that community, three quarters of a century later, of brutal plant closure when the global corporation that had industrialised a rural enclave of Essex 'deindustrialised' it just as capriciously.

As all these varied aspects show, we will be following many threads in this story. But the force that unites them all, as it did tens of thousands of workers, is that 'notoriously militant' union branch, 1/1107.

NOTES

1   As described in Chapter 6, the Paint, Trim and Assembly plant was closed in early 2002.
2   For many years after its inception in 1946, 1107 branch meetings were held in the local Marsh Green primary school.
3   My first contact with the branch was in the mid-1980s, when it was one of

a number of organisations included in a study of workplace trade union democracy: see Sheila Cohen, *You Are The Union: Trade Union Workplace Democracy*, Workers' Educational Association Studies For Trade Unionists Volume 14, Number 53, April 1988, and Patricia Fosh and Sheila Cohen, 'Local Patterns of Union Democracy' in Patricia Fosh and Edmund Heery (eds), *Trade Unions and their Members*, London: Macmillan, 1990.

4 'On the Track at Ford: if you don't go off sick, you go off in a box', A Ford Worker, *Socialist Worker* 30 May 1970, p. 4.

5 Interview for the Eastside Community Heritage Project (see Acknowledgements), 1999.

6 David Marsden, Timothy Morris, Paul Willman and Stephen Wood, *The Car Industry: labour Relations and Industrial Adjustment*, London: Tavistock Publications, 1985, p. 156.

7 Steve Jary, 'New Technology: The Union Response at the Local Level' MSc thesis, Imperial College of Science and Technology, University of London, 1985, p. 85.

8 Graham Turner, *The Car Makers*, Harmondsworth: Penguin, 1964, p. 13.

9 Henry Friedman, 'Multi-Plant Working and Trade Union Organisation', WEA Studies for Trade Unionists, Volume 2, Number 8, December 1976, p. 9.

10 Roy Greenslade, 'The Town that Will Not Die', *Guardian* 7 April 2000, p. A2.

Chapter One

'YOU'LL NEVER ORGANISE FORD', 1900-1945

Part I

To begin the long story of a flourishing trade union branch founded at Ford's Dagenham plant just after the Second World War, we must go back to the turn of the century in America, and to an individual still the byword for a brutal industrial system: Henry Ford himself.

This story begins with Henry's early struggles to develop his Model T, which were greeted with scepticism in his Detroit neighbourhood. As local urchin Little Abner reports to his mother in Sinclair Lewis' *The Flivver King*,[1] 'There's a feller down the street says he's goin' to make a wagon that'll run without a hoss.' Mom's retort, 'He's crazy' probably reflected the feelings of most contemporary Americans.

But the young Ford persevered, using the wide roadways of Detroit to road-test his invention. On June 4 1896, the attempt was finally successful; in Henry Ford's own words, 'I set the choke and spun the flywheel. As the motor roared and sputtered to life, I climbed aboard and started off … '.[2]

The Ford Motor Company was formed In 1903; its first plant, in Detroit's Mack Avenue, was followed in 1910 by Highland Park and later 'the Rouge', which eventually became a centre of union organising at Fords. From the beginning, Ford's ruthless regime ramped up production by leaps and bounds – from 1708 cars in 1903 to 200,000 ten years later and, by 1915, half a million, reaching over two million by the early twenties. As Huw Beynon writes in his classic *Working For Ford*, 'Ford had made it. He had broken into the mass market for automobiles. And he was rich … '.[3]

Runabouts and Roadsters

As early as the 1920s, the name already engraved in flowing script on the front of Ford's cars became part of a wider term – 'Fordism' – used to describe the standard methods of production becoming common in the twentieth century. The phrase stuck, and before long was being twinned with 'Taylorism' in a double reference to the two giant shadows then cast over work and industry. Frederick Taylor, nicknamed 'Speedy' by resentful workers, was as dedicated as Ford to squeezing maximum labour out of the industrial workforce. This was particularly true in the growing motor industry: 'Car workers were always the laboratory rats of the Taylor theory because this was a brand new industry where to be as efficient as Henry Ford was a life and death issue'.[4] In this sense, although Ford and Taylor never met or expressed much admiration for one another, 'Fordism' and 'Taylorism' are routinely linked.

Meanwhile, Fordism gained increasing expression in the huge factories and snaking conveyor belts that now littered the 'land of the free'. The assembly-line-based, fragmented work process which came to typify production in the twentieth (and even twenty-first) century was rooted in Ford's leaning towards standardisation, which also applied to the design of his cars; as he wrote in his autobiography, 'Any customer can have a car painted any colour he wants so long as it is black'.[5] For many years he refused to produce the more elaborate designs constantly urged on him; and the policy paid off, meaning 'runabouts and roadsters' rather than luxury cars dominated the growing market. With even its most expensive model selling at $750, the company's course was set: fortunes were made and did not stop flowing. In 1906, Ford sold more than five times as many cars as in the previous year.

Ford production was simplified still further with the company's focus on only one model, the Model T or 'Flivver'. As one history puts it, 'Offspring of the assembly line, cheap enough for a skilled workman, the Model T was a living legend ...'[6] Offspring of the assembly line it was. Yet neither Ford nor his company actually pioneered this process; Ford claimed that he 'got the idea ... from the "disassembly lines" found in Chicago's and Cincinnati's slaughterhouses'[7]. When Ford management tried to integrate the process into car production, the effort was clumsy, even comical; 'They put a frame on skids and pulled it from one end of the building to the other with a rope.' Ford's senior production manager Charles Sorenson recalled 'The idea [then] occurred to me that assembly would be easier, simpler and faster if we moved the chassis along ... One Sunday morning [we] put together the first car, I'm sure, that was ever built on a moving line. We did this by putting the frame on skids, hitching a tow rope to the front and pulling the frame along ... '.[8]

The impact of the assembly line on productivity was jaw-dropping; 'Within three months, the assembly time for the Model T had been reduced to one-tenth the time formerly needed ... by 1925 [Ford was producing] almost as many cars in a single day as had been produced ... in an entire year'.[9] But the impact on the workforce was less positive. As Henry Ford himself observed, 'Some of the operations are undoubtedly monotonous – so monotonous it seems scarcely possible that any man would continue so long at a job'.[10]

The new conditions brought mass desertion by workers who preferred to work in almost any other plant in the city, none of which had yet introduced the dreaded 'line'. Ford was already unpopular amongst Detroit workers, and with the introduction of the assembly line 'their ranks almost literally fell apart ... Ford admitted later that his startling factory innovations had ushered in the outstanding labour crisis of his career'.[11] At one point he complained bitterly, 'How come every time I want a pair of hands I get a human being?'.[12]

By 1913 the company was losing $3 million a year in hiring and training costs. Yet out of this crisis came Ford's famous 5-dollar day. If you could not give your workers job satisfaction – in fact, the exact opposite – then you could 'motivate' them, as Ford's counterpart F.W. Taylor argued, with money.

Not Marx But Ford?

The idea of paying Ford workers $5 a day – then a significant amount – did not start with Henry. It was his business manager, James Couzens, who first raised the idea as a possible answer to Ford's labour turnover crisis. Couzens' light-bulb moment came on a bitter winter night in 1913, when the hard-headed manager was struck by the fact that 'outside his warm house he could see men walking hunched into the cold'.[13] The insight hardly turned Couzens into a socialist, but it prompted him into musing on Ford workers' salaries, at that time a meagre $2.50 a day.

Ford himself was open to the idea of some kind of reform. A few days earlier, he had been walking through the plant with his young son Edsel when he noticed a worker 'glower' at the boy. As Ford described it to Couzens, 'He was saying "Look at Henry Ford's boy! What has mine beside him?"'. But this moment of empathy did not move Ford to accept Couzen's suggestion; at most, he would agree to $3.50. Couzens' response was 'No, it's five or nothing ... A straight five-dollar wage will be the greatest advertising any automobile concern ever had'.[14] That clinched the deal.

The offer was, of course, irresistible. The morning after the announcement, several thousand men gathered in the bitter cold outside Highland Park; as they waited, a riot broke out and police doused the would-be workers with high-pressure hoses in a foretaste of the brutality later shown towards union activists. Meanwhile, the publicity was everything the company could desire; the New York *Globe* enthused that the $5 day had 'all the advantages and none of the disadvantages of socialism.' The conservative unions of the American Federation of Labor were just as impressed. 'Not Marx – but Ford!' was the slogan coined by the then AFL leader, William Green.

Turning Out Better Men ...

But Ford's 'generosity' created another fear in his eccentric brain; his workers' newfound affluence might lead to moral depravity. This bizarre concern led to a new project known as the Ford Sociological Department, aimed at supervising the behaviour of Ford workers and encouraging their 'morality'. Staff employed by the Sociological Department visited homes and enquired into family customs. In this way, Ford perhaps hoped to 'turn out better men the way the assembly line allowed him to turn out better cars'.[15]

But the Department soon became little more than a spy network as the 'sociologists' turned into a kind of morality police force. Workers were required to produce bank books and – to prove they were not living in sin – marriage certificates; the investigators gave out a pamphlet called 'Rules for Living' which urged employees not to spit on the floor and not to take in boarders in case their wives started sleeping with them. And, before long, Ford's 'moral' concerns were transformed into an openly brutal spy regime led by the notorious Harry Bennett.

Bennett had joined Fords as a shop floor worker in 1917, just as head honcho William Knudsen began to see the need for someone 'tough enough' to keep an eye on watchmen he suspected of stealing materials. One worker suggested 'just the man for you – an ex-champion of the Navy named Harry Bennett.' Bennett's slightness and 5' 6" stature – he became known as the 'Little Fella' – failed to impress Knudsen, who said scornfully, 'I thought you were going to bring me a prizefighter.' But shortly afterwards Bennett came to the notice of Ford himself for beating up a thug who had assaulted a worker, and after a number of similar stunts he was rewarded by being made head watchman at Ford's massive new River Rouge plant.

Before long, the innocent word 'watchman' had gained a more sinister meaning. Bennett and his henchmen soon dominated a newly-created Service Department set up to maintain order within the plant – a task carried out with a level of discipline more like a prison than a workplace. Bennett's men followed workers into washrooms to prevent them talking about anything subversive like – in particular – union organisation. While workers were at the lines their lunch pails and overcoats were searched for union literature, and any meeting between two workers was seen as evidence of 'conspiracy'. Even beyond the plant, Service men skulked around the streets and taverns of Detroit, listening for any conversations which might include the dreaded word 'union'.

'Organization Failed, and ... The Workers' Movement Grew'

Ford himself was fanatically anti-union – not to mention anti-Semitic. As he delicately put it, 'Unions are organized by Jewish financiers, not labor. A union is a neat thing for a Jew to have on hand when he comes around to get his clutches on industry'.[16] Nor was he alone in his hostility to trade union organisation. In the early twentieth century, 'Detroit was the open-shop capital of the country'.[17] Even the cross-union International Workers of the World (IWW), which had organised thousands of workers in the early years of the twentieth century, was unsuccessful in the Motor City.

Yet, as so often, it was dedicated activists who – beginning decades before victory – played a central part in organising the apparently unorganisable. One early attempt at a union for auto workers, the Auto, Aircraft and Vehicle Workers of America (AAVW), established a tiny group at Fords who put out a newsletter, *The Ford Worker*. In 1920, the AAVW joined the Communist Party-led Trade Union Education League (TUEL), and in February 1928, the TUEL held an autoworkers' conference in Detroit with the aim of bringing together all possible forces in a drive to organise the unorganised car workers. According to Phil Raymond, secretary of the AAVW 127 'local' (branch) at Ford, the speed-up and brutality intensifying even now in the plants was changing the mood of the workers, making it more desperate and more militant.

Meanwhile, the Depression was hitting Detroit in no uncertain fashion. In March 1929, over 122,000 were employed at Ford's; by August 1931 the numbers had crashed to 37,000 in a reflection of similar disasters repeated all over America. And yet, as the Great Depression took hold in the early 1930s, radical activity on behalf of workers was on the increase. In March 1932 a Communist Party-organised 'March on Hunger' mobilised many thousands of Ford workers, their families and supporters. As the march neared its goal – the Ford River Rouge plant – police used tear gas and water cannon to disperse the demonstrators, who nevertheless broke through and began to throw bricks at the plant. Their anger was directed at Bennett, who was showered with debris as he went out to address the crowd.

Ever-resourceful, Bennett used one of the Communist organisers as a human shield, while police opened fire on the unarmed marchers. Three were killed, along with the organiser 'protecting' Bennett. Yet Henry Ford's anxiety was all for his henchman; as one onlooker reported, 'It was like it was Edsel [Ford's son] lying there ... there were tears in his eyes'.[18] Encouraged by his employer's apparent devotion, Bennett rapidly ramped up his anti-worker arsenal, stockpiling tear gas and even constructing machine-gun emplacements at strategic points in Dearborn, the Detroit suburb that now housed Ford's headquarters.

Yet only a few years later, a real push to organise began as part of a massive wave of militancy involving workers across America and particularly in the mid-West, hub of the auto industry. This upsurge of struggle was based on an unexpected boost from the powers-that-be: President Roosevelt's 1935 National Labor Relations Act (NLRA) offered workers a positive right to trade unionism as part of his 'New Deal' policy. Workers flocked to the existing unions, all affiliated to the American Federation of Labor (AFL). But they faced a hostile reception; the mainly skilled Federation did not welcome semi- and unskilled labour into its ranks, partly due to their growing levels of militancy. As Daniel Tobin, head of the AFL-federated Teamsters' union, sniffed, 'We do not want the men today if they are going on strike tomorrow'.[19]

As a result of this cold-shouldering approach, a bizarre (but not unusual) thing happened: 'Factory workers ... extract[ed] their most substantial concessions ... *before they were organized into unions* ... Strikes ... and sit-downs spread during the mid-1930s despite existing unions rather than because of them'.[20] In this sense the impressive organising wave of the 1930s in America was very much a rank-and-file affair, taking place in spite of rather than because of the existing trade unions; and this pattern was repeated in Detroit. In January 1933, five hundred Briggs Bodies workers walked out over their pay, and returned less than five days later having won almost all their demands, including 40 cents an hour, restoration of a 20 per cent pay cut, grievance machinery and no reprisals.

The Briggs Bodies victory was so spectacular that within two weeks 10,000 more Briggs workers had walked out, along with 5000 workers from other Detroit parts plants. Their action had an unprecedented outcome: the Ford Motor Company itself was forced to grind to a halt. This was an amazing event to Ford workers, indeed workers throughout the country. Ford had often boasted that no worker action would force him to shut down. Now it had happened – even at one remove.

Fearing exactly this impact on its workers, the company posted notices offering a 25 cents an hour rise; but the workers refused to accept the bait. Instead, the following Monday morning 6,000 Ford workers gathered in front of all the main plants and roared 'Down with the 25 cents!' At the Highland Park plant, thousands of workers, many of whom had never previously walked a picket line, paraded up and down before the gates, singing the old IWW anthem *Solidarity Forever*. Predictably, the police broke up the demonstration with tear-gas and batons, but the workers had gained an unforgettable glimpse of their collective power.

Birth of the CIO

Meanwhile, the American trade union movement was experiencing its own dramatic transformation. In 1935 the leader of the coal miners, John L. Lewis, socked the AFL carpenters' leader in the jaw in true American fashion, and the breakaway Congress of Industrial Organizations (CIO) was born. This federation, at least in its early years, was much more aligned towards the needs of the millions of unorganised semi- or unskilled workers in America who now made up the main flank of worker resistance as the Depression rolled on. The same year, the newly-formed United Auto Workers (UAW) was formed, with two 'locals' set up in Detroit. The CIO was now fully established as a radical alternative to the AFL, with organising for the auto industry put in the hands of Walter Reuther.

By 1937, the wave of sit-down strikes had brought unionisation to even the massive General Motors in nearby Flint, Michigan. This was a crucial piece of the puzzle to be knocked out before Ford could be won. Yet UAW membership still numbered only a few thousand, and the AFL was doing little to help build it. Determined to push forward, the activists decided to choose a specific company as an organising target; the one they selected was Kelsey-Hayes, later to manage the wheel plant at Dagenham. Activists staged a dramatic *coup* by mobilising workers to turn off the power in the plant at an agreed time. At 11.15 the 'pin' was pulled, bringing the works to a grinding halt. The Kelsey-Hayes strike lasted thirteen days; it was followed by similar uprisings in Fisher Body, Cadillac, and scores of small metal shops.

But where was Ford? By this time a Ford branch of sorts had been set up, but by a union organiser distrusted by the rank and file, one Homer Martin. When UAW officials obtained a permit to distribute leaflets in front of the River Rouge plant in May 1937, their efforts ended in a brutal going-over by 'Bennett's Boys'. UAW president Walter Reuther himself was dragged down the 36 iron steps of the overpass. After the attack, Henry Ford denied the whole thing, despite photographic evidence[21]. The largely symbolic 'Battle' made little difference to conditions or union membership, and Martin himself was soon caught red-handed with his (not-so-red) hand in the local's till.

The hard core of Ford activist-organisers applied to the AFL for affiliation; but the federation's response was lukewarm, requiring as always different 'locals' for different trades, while the activists insisted on 'One union for all'. Undaunted, the activists formed a new branch which later became Local 600, famous within the CIO's United Auto Workers. Activists set about recruiting, but were instantly stymied by Ford stoolpigeons who ensured workers were sacked the moment they joined up.

'Nothing had seemed more impossible ...'

Finally, in February 1941, events turned in the Ford workers' favour – though the boost came from above, in the form of a ruling by the Supreme Court that the company was guilty of 'unfair labor practices' as defined within Roosevelt's 1935 National Labour Relations Act. Legally, Ford was now obliged to recognise the union. In response, workers stampeded by the thousands into the UAW offices, picking up their union cards and pinning on their union 'buttons'.

But, incredibly, even this was not enough. The newly-elected Ford shop stewards found themselves shifted to other parts of the plant, well away from the workers they had been elected to represent. Meanwhile, workers who had confidently lit up cigarettes (smoking had previously been forbidden, though not for health and safety reasons) were pounced on by Bennett and his henchmen, rushed to the office and sacked. Shortly afterwards, Bennett fired eight shop stewards.

It was the last straw. Finally, the long-suffering Ford workforce had had enough. Three thousand workers sat down, and as a direct result the eight shop stewards were reinstated within an hour. But the impetus was now unstoppable. As the news spread of Ford's attack and the workers' victory, sitdowns spread all over the enormous plant; by the end of March, over 15,000 Ford workers had joined the action. The spontaneous grass roots wave of organising – independent even of the new CIO regime – galvanised the Ford workforce. On 2 April 1941 the entire plant shut down.

There was only one group of workers less sure of their stand. The brutal racism which characterised America was, of course, more than evident in Detroit; yet an 'exception' had been made by Ford in the early years of the company, when his agents had travelled to the southern cotton plantations and lured thousands of Black workers, grateful beyond words for the 'opportunity', to Detroit.[22] Their loyalty proved a tough nut to crack when the sleeping beast of Ford's labour force finally began to stir in earnest; about 3000 Black workers remained in the plant, undermining the full success of the action.

Yet their conditions as workers finally outweighed any gratitude to a less-than-generous 'benefactor'. On the afternoon of 2 April, CIO organiser Michael Widman shouted through the fence at the strikebreakers that they had 'nothing to be afraid of'; in response about 1000 marched out and, before long, enough had joined the strike to assure its success. As another historian puts it, '[Ford's] attempts over the years to form an anti-union bulwark of the doubly-exploited Negro workers proved useless. Out of 10,000 in Ford, less than 1,500 remained in the plant ...'.[23] Despite scouring the city, Bennett was now unable to find a single scab prepared to break the strike. The Ford workers recognised their power with jubilant scenes, beating on drums and waving union flags.

The site of the mass picket line was the same as that of the doomed march in which four young workers had been shot down nine years before. From what had once seemed an impossible fantasy, a vast workplace had been organised virtually overnight. The final upsurge, and its accompanying total victory, perhaps shows the unexpected truth that 'the company is the union's best organiser'.[24] As Ford historian Herndon reports, 'A sagacious union leader once told me, "We could never organize a plant if it weren't for the cooperation of management." He was referring to inadvertent cooperation, the harsh practices which organizers can promise to eradicate or alleviate. Bennett's labor policy invited unionism; he strove with bloody and effective means to keep the unions out. [His rule] was one of the most sickeningly brutal episodes in industrial history …'.[25]

Whatever the cause – and many activists can back up Herndon's point – Ford USA was now, conclusively, unionised. Charles Sorenson insisted that the strike had been provoked by 'union terrorism', Henry Ford himself suggested arming the non-strikers, and Bennett was 'eager to use his Service Department in a pitched battle …'. And yet on 11 April Ford finally agreed to let the union in. Sorenson commented later that this was, for Ford, 'perhaps the greatest disappointment he had in all his business experience'.[26]

The state had helped through the provisions of Roosevelt's National Labor Relations Act and its accompanying Board, whose pro-union objectives have now long disappeared in America. But the real job, as always in history, was done by no one else but the rank and file activists and workers of Ford USA themselves. The impossible had become possible; Ford had finally been organised – by its own workers.

Part II

'Little to Rely Upon but Themselves … ' Ford crosses the Atlantic

On the other side of the Atlantic, a similar story was repeated over a very similar period – decades of anti-unionism and repression culminating in a burst of resistance which achieved the apparently unachievable: organising Fords.

As early as 1903, the year the Ford Motor Company was first formed in the US, two Ford cars were exported to Britain – and in 1904 a Ford sales organisation was set up in London. Although Ford himself was 'deeply anti-British', having been offended by Winston Churchill's contempt for his ideas on farming,[27] his friendship with an aristocratic Brit – Perceval

Lea Dewhurst Perry, First Baron Perry – led to the setting-up of Ford's first overseas branch in London. Perry had paid £50 for a five-year franchise to sell Ford cars across Europe, and this grandly-named individual was to stick to Ford UK for many years.

Also in 1904, the new Model A Ford made its British debut at a Motor Show in the now-defunct Agricultural Hall in Islington, meaning that, as historian David Burgess-Wise proudly points out, 'There were Fords on Britain's roads before Austin, Rover or Rolls-Royce …'.[28] And in 1908 the Model T, advertised as 'the car that put the world on wheels' made its world debut at London's Olympia motor exhibition. All this before a single car had been built in Britain. But in 1911 – long before Dagenham – the company established a plant in a disused former tram factory on the Trafford Park industrial estate, and it was here that the first British-built Ford car was produced, on 23 October 1911.

At first, the cars were made using 'classic' craft techniques, but in 1913 the factory adopted mass production methods, featuring Britain's first moving production line. Output rapidly expanded, putting Ford UK well to the fore. As Dagenham historians Friedman and Meredeen comment, 'the successful transplantation into Ford (England) of mass production techniques, inspired by the "scientific management" movement[29] and perfected by Ford in Detroit, was demonstrated by the fact that the Manchester Works, producing 150 cars a day, outstripped the entire production of the next five largest firms taken together'.[30] The *Financial Times* later summed this dynamic up in terms of 'Ford's introduction at the outset of "Fordism", a combination of standardised flowline production, rigid division of labour and pyramid management [which] was to have a profound impact on factories throughout the UK'.[31]

A skilled worker from the nearby Vulcan car factory, John Woods, recalled that cars were built by hand at that time for wealthy customers, using skilled craftsmen: 'They were all fully-skilled tradesmen … turners, drillers, capstan-gear cutters … smiths, strikers, moulders. There was no welding, everything had to be brass-brazed.' Not for the impatient Henry: 'From the moment that Henry Ford set up a new kind of car factory at Trafford Park in Manchester, in 1911, the days of the Vulcan car … were numbered'.[32] In 1914, the company built about 8.300 cars, equivalent to the combined output of the next five biggest British manufacturers.

The transAtlantic influence did not stop there; not long after his spectacular introduction of the $5 day, Ford suggested a similar rate at Trafford Park. Workers at the new factory were paid a minimum wage of 1s and 3d (about 6p) an hour, as against the industrial average in Britain of only 7d, about half that amount. Yet serious unrest had already broken out in the plant. Baron Perry sniffed that 'Manchester is ... the hot bed of trade unionism'; from 1912 to 1913, he had had to deal with 'an annoying series of strikes which seriously curtailed production'. In February 1913, sheet metal workers had walked out at both Ford and a nearby (unrelated) body plant. Perry argued that the body plant strike was 'being used by the [Ford] metal workers as a lever ... to force us into settling the dispute within our own works.' The entrepreneur was 'deeply distressed', writing to Henry Ford that 'The recent labour disputes have almost broken my heart'.[33]

In response, Ford lieutenant Charles Sorenson rushed over from America, coming to the heartbroken Perry's aid by making promises of job security and higher wages to the skilled engineering workers most likely to support trade unionism. This tactic both ended the dispute and successfully 'broke the union power at Ford-Manchester'. By April 1914, Sorenson could be assured that 'in the past six months there has been no sign of labour trouble. The unionism which has always been cropping up heretofore has been absolutely broken up'.[34]

Sorenson was all the more triumphant given that other plants in the Trafford Park area were continuing to see disputes in this historically militant period.[35] As the American manager gloated, Ford was now the only employer in the area 'who is not obligated in some manner to labour organizations ... '.[36] Ford had now taken over the body plant involved in the earlier 'trouble', and the merged factory took off as a centre of motor manufacturing, closely supervised by Detroit.

Yet Trafford Park always remained a sore point with Henry Ford; as Wilkins and Hill put it, 'The Manchester plant was repugnant to him because of the labour troubles encountered there, its ugliness, and its grim climate.' Not only that, but the area was seen as too small for successful expansion: 'Ford of England could be a giant, and no giant could be contained in the Trafford Park area'.[37] Ford himself suggested that Cork, in southern Ireland, might be a good alternative; but Perry rejected the location as too remote.

However, before a clear decision could be made, the thunderclap of the First World War broke over Europe. Rather unexpectedly, Henry Ford was opposed to the conflict – a position in stark contrast to his quasi-Fascist sympathies during the Second World War. Yet pacifism was not to interfere with Ford's profits; only two weeks after war broke out, Perry was working to obtain government orders for Ford chassis to be used for ambulances and other military purposes. By late September 1914 the War Office had ordered nine 'van ambulances', and Trafford Park soon went over to wartime production, with Model T troop carriers, water carriers, ambulances and munitions trucks supplied to the government.

Britain urgently needed to grow more food to beat the German blockade, meaning more tractors; the ever-industrious Perry, now appointed Assistant Controller of the government's Agricultural Machinery Department, persuaded Ford to build a tractor factory in Cork, southern Ireland. In fact, the Cork factory was unable to begin production until after the war, so all the 'Fordson' tractors used in the war came from Henry's American plants; yet the plant was indeed built, and remained in operation until the early 1930s, with many of its workers later coming to Dagenham to work in the Foundry.

After the war, Ford was determined to develop the Cork site. His concern was unusually personal; Cork had been his grandfather's county. But there were limits to Ford's sentimentality. Although part of the company's deal with the city of Cork was a promise to employ 2000 workers, under the postwar depression the plant eventually employed only 1600 men. The city threatened to cancel Ford's lease if at least 400 additional workers were not employed, but Ford 'announced that he would close the plant down if the city didn't get off his back, immediately stopped new production and laid off 500 men ... He had no more trouble with Cork'.[38] Yet the Cork factory was soon 'hanging about [the company's] neck like the ancient mariner's albatross'.[39] In November 1932 Ford took the decision to close down the plant for good, despite the fact that there were still 2,000 workers employed there in this chronically depressed area. For the business-like Mr Ford, profits would always prevail over family feeling.

Of course Cork itself was never considered as the site for a major Ford plant in Britain, any more than was Manchester. Southampton (which later, of course, did 'gain' a Ford plant) was another possibility. During the decision-making, the energetic Mayor of the city, Florence Welch, 'was on hand to urge the advantages of her city as the hub of Ford operations'; in fact she appealed to Mrs Ford to persuade her husband to favour Southampton, commenting, 'We women must stand together.' 'We certainly must,' Clara Ford replied, 'but Mr Ford himself must decide about the site. I have nothing to do with that'.[40]

The Best Labour in London

By the late 1920s Ford – both the man and the company – had definitely shifted focus towards Dagenham. On 10 July 1923, a Mr Grace, taken on by the company to investigate suitable locations, wrote to Edsel Ford, 'I wish to state that we have thoroughly investigated England, and both Mr Gould and myself confirm the recommendation which I made to you during my recent visit to Detroit; that is, that the most suitable place for the future plant is in the London District ...

'After looking up and down both sides of the Thames we came to the conclusion that the best place would be on the northern side of the river, somewhere in the neighbourhood of Dagenham. We found a site which particularly suits our requirements ... The location is about 10 miles from London Bridge and is served by frequent railway accommodation ... It has sufficient water to accommodate the largest steamers which are leaving every day from the port of London to all points in the world ... It is also closely situated to East and West Ham where the best labour in London can be secured, as well as on the opposite side of the river. Also there is a very good property in the village which no doubt would become a residential place for our man ...' That 'man' was clearly not a shopfloor worker.

In 1924, 294 acres of land were bought in Dagenham for the then bargain price of £150,000. That evening, London news vendors were shouting 'LATE EXTRA – GREAT FORD FACTORY FOR LONDON'.[41] Henry Ford's rather timid son Edsel, who died in early middle age after a lifetime of domination by his father, was given the task of digging the first spadeful of boggy soil from the new site in the Dagenham marshes. Soon, 'a spectacular new manufacturing facility began to arise on the banks of the River Thames in Essex'.[42]

In 1928 Ford revisited England, paid a visit to Dagenham and duly indicated his enthusiasm. The next step was to form the Ford Motor Company Ltd (FMC), in order to bring together all Ford's western European operations; in an agreement signed on 7 December 1928, the new FMC Ltd acquired the Ford Motor Company of England, including the Manchester plant, Henry Ford & Son of Cork, and a controlling interest in Ford companies in nine western European countries, including France, Germany, Italy and Spain.

At this point 'the 500-acre area, a low, water-soaked tract overgrown with coarse grass, looked highly unpromising. These were the Essex marshes which Dickens had vividly described in *Great Expectations* ...'.[43] More than 22,000 piles had to be driven into the swampy soil to hold up the buildings scattered over the huge site. Yet four large structures were soon erected: a foundry and machine shop, manufacturing and assembly plants (the Paint, Trim and Assembly plant would not be built for another 30 years), and office buildings. Displaying his usual on-and-off 'social conscience', Henry Ford brought in an innovative powerhouse connected to a refuse-preparation plant which would burn up to two thousand tons of London rubbish a day.

Blood and Tears ...

Henry Coleman, a lifetime Ford worker now in his 90s, started working on the site in 1928 at the age of 13 ½ – illegal even then: 'I was still at school, but there were three million unemployed. A man came round looking for labourers, but you had to be 14. Mum said "He *is* 14". I was excited – everybody was out of work. When we started it was more or less on the beach. It was just marsh then. We were pile-driving for the foundations ... putting all the mains in, all the drains ... It took three years to build'.[44]

According to Wilkins and Hill, 'The whole workforce was aware of the importance of its task and was prepared to push ahead briskly. "It was easy to build Dagenham than to get my house painted," recalled [the] project manager ... "Everyone was keen and eager"'.[45]

But 'keenness' was not the only factor pushing this early workforce. As Henry Coleman recalled, 'Blood and tears went into it ... Accidents happened every day when they were building the site. Men fell off scaffolding, got crushed by machinery, drowned in mixed concrete, and the work never stopped. They simply loaded the dead into handcarts to carry them away to the nearest road ... There were no health and safety investigations, no compensation. I was still a lad when I watched five men die in a shaft that was being dug to bring water from the Thames into the plant's power station. Four were overcome by fumes. The fifth was still alive, but as they hauled him to the top the rope snapped and he fell back'.[46] This horrifying anecdote might spur twenty-first-century critics of 'elf and safety' to think again.

By September 1930 'the great plant was no longer foundations, but roads, walls and half-completed buildings ... It was as if at the muttered words of an incantation the north bank of the lower Thames had been incredibly remade'.[47] The press referred to Dagenham as 'a magnificent gesture of faith in Britain's commercial future ... a lighthouse of hope in a storm-tossed sea of industry.' Yet due to various difficulties with roads, drainage etc, opening the plant was delayed until March 19 1931, and even then Ford UK experienced some unforeseen difficulties. The taxes on Ford's new car, the Model A, were higher than those on than the smaller Model T, and before the Dagenham plant was finished the impact of the Depression had taken its toll on the prosperity of the middle class, Ford's potential consumers.

The first Ford vehicle, a 30 cwt Model AA truck, left the line at precisely 1.15pm on 1 October 1931; the hard-pressed workforce was soon producing two vehicles every minute. But almost immediately Perry wrote to Ford that Dagenham 'faced financial disaster unless it could have a light car to build.' A 33 per cent tariff on motor imports introduced during the war had been continued under the 1931 national government; this policy galvanised competition within the British car industry, and Ford's UK rivals, Morris and Austin, were threatening to 'run away with the market'.[48]

Almost as serious was the disappointing reception of the Model A, which used too much petrol and was too large for the narrow British roads – not to mention that, as one Ford executive put it, the British were 'somewhat unfriendly to American automobiles'.[49] In response, Dagenham was tooled for a new Model Y, which became known as the Baby Ford and soon became highly successful, outstripping its British rivals. As one twenty-first-century commentator put it, 'Dagenham ... was the American Dream, imported from Detroit. Henry Ford wanted to sell to the British scaled-down versions of American cars – dreams that were accessible'.[50]

The assembly line was, of course, an integral feature of the new plant; 'At Dagenham the cars moved as they did at Ford's plants in the United States, slowly carried forward by a moving chain ... Where before gangs of men had worked on each car together, they were now spread out along the track, obliged to follow the speed of the line'.[51] British car companies followed suit: Morris almost immediately transformed its main assembly plant at Cowley, installing four moving lines for its four different models.

Though half the size of the Rouge, Dagenham was still the largest manufacturing plant in the whole of southern England. To justify its size, the new English Ford company obtained the exclusive right to manufacture, assemble, market and distribute Ford cars, Fordson tractors and any other Ford products in the area. The English company also set up the Industrial Estate of Dagenham and encouraged other companies to lease and build on the land; this was how Briggs Motor Bodies, one of the union organising forces in Detroit, came to set up a subsidiary on the Dagenham estate alongside the Kelsey-Hayes wheel plant – also familiar from Detroit struggles.

A Social Experiment ...

Yet the 'Dagenham Dream' was something of a nightmare for Ford employees, especially those still employed at Trafford Park. In 1931, when the Manchester plant closed, about 2,000 workers were transferred to Dagenham, most travelling on special trains hired by Ford. Fred Harrop from Manchester was given the 'opportunity' to move south at short notice, to say the least: 'I went into work as usual on the Monday morning, and in the early afternoon the foreman came down the line and told me, "Oh, you will finish work here tonight and you'll report to Dagenham, at eight o'clock on Thursday morning". So ... on Wednesday we came down on a discounted ticket which had been arranged by Ford'.[52]

In this way about 4,500 Northerners settled in the area; and in 1933, Irishmen also began migrating to Dagenham to work in the Foundry. As one account points out, 'There were therefore wide differences within the working population which were made worse by the housing situation. Only the East Enders could rent council houses; the remainder went into lodgings until they could buy a house. This created a division between "owners" and "renters" ... [T]here was very little evidence of total integration into a community [with] a common purpose ...'.[53]

The new plant also changed the lives of those already living nearby. Until then, Dagenham was no more than 'a small village, complete with cottages and fields of corn.' Yet 'within a decade 20,000 houses had been erected to sustain a working-class population'.[54] By 1932, the area had increased its population by an eye-watering 879 per cent. The Ford plant could be seen as part of a new kind of industrial development in Britain in which the state and the local authorities played an important part, from assisting with the draining of Dagenham's marshlands to the building of houses for the first few thousand workers who started at the Ford plant.

Yet Aldous Huxley's 1932 classic *Brave New World* parodied both Ford and the standardisation of living conditions seen as part of Fordism. As one character comments, 'Our Ford [Huxley's version of 'Our Lord'] himself did a great deal to shift the emphasis from truth and beauty to comfort and happiness. Mass production demanded the shift. Universal happiness keeps the wheels turning steadily; truth and beauty can't ... Our civilisation has chosen machinery and medicine and happiness'.[55]

Humans became Robots ...

The Ford Dagenham plant was effectively the pioneer for all the most advanced production and work organisation techniques then available. Such processes had already begun in Manchester under one Thomas L. Nuttall; unfortunately for the Dagenham workforce, Nuttall was transferred to the new plant and there carried on his work, which was extended into Time and Motion Study, influencing the layout of the plant and the timing of machine operation. So much did Nuttall excel in his chosen role that when the American Chief of Time Study visited Dagenham in 1933 he commented, 'I have learnt more about time study than I ever thought possible!'.[56]

From this point of view the UK company's rapid rise was not obtained 'without some sacrifice in the field of employer-employee relationship' as Wilkins and Hill delicately put it.[57]

Dagenham had by now been nicknamed a 'little Rouge' for more reasons than one; the incessant drive for lower costs and higher volume made working at the plant a grim experience. As Henry Coleman recalled, 'When a line started moving, everyone along it had to work in perfect synchronisation. Humans became robots. Ten seconds to pick up your components, 10 seconds to walk to the car, five seconds to get into position. After one minute and five seconds, the car had moved on and you had 15 seconds to prepare for the next one. You worked on the same small section, in the same way, over and over for eight hours a day, every day. Fixing exactly the same type of nuts and bolts, driving in exactly the same screws, with no variation. In an eight-hour shift, a worker would have two half-hour breaks, opening their flasks and sandwiches on the assembly line. Your toilet break would be supervised by the foreman. Any longer than two minutes and he would be tapping his watch and shouting a warning …'.[58]

An undated Communist Party pamphlet from the period, *Men and Motors*, comments that 'Ford studies with … energy and minuteness the exploitation of human beings', quoting a Dr Feioler as commenting 'In some of the Ford shops I witnessed terrible exploitation of human beings by the conveyor system'.[59] As in Detroit, Ford strenuously avoided piecework, which allowed workers in other companies a certain amount of control over the effort/reward relationship. For Dagenham workers, the pace of work was determined solely by the 'conveyor' or assembly line.

Yet monitoring and surveillance was also pervasive, not only by 'service' men patrolling the factory like a marginally less sadistic version of Harry Bennett, but also other spies disguised as sweepers, janitors etc. – not to mention noticeboards. One feature which even workers in today's high-tech Dagenham plants might recognise is that 'in order to maintain the "Minute Cost" charts are displayed in conspicuous parts of the factory'. Andon boards, anyone?

Finally, *Men and Motors* exposes the widely-held illusion that Ford paid high wages by pointing out that the total absence of overtime pay during the period reduced the comparatively 'generous' basic rate to a miserly pittance compared with take-home pay in other factories. Added to disciplinary layoffs as a punishment for talking (yes, talking), this grim picture amply justifies the pamphlet's conclusion that 'Fords is not the Eldorado it is claimed to be'.

A 'Staggering Lack of Organisation'

Nor, at the time, was there much chance of Ford workers turning to a union to protect them against these conditions. As far back as 1924, when the Dagenham project was first announced, Henry Ford had threatened to pull investment from the UK if trade unions 'interfered' with his project.

In the beginning, there seemed to be very little that could be done about it. The Transport and General Workers' Union had begun to recruit car workers in early 1927, and in 1929 the Workers' Union, formed in 1898 with the aim of organising 'lower-skilled' workers, merged with the TGWU. As a result 'a large section of Workers' Union members transferred into the T&G's new Metal, Engineering and Chemical Trade Group, leaving the union well placed to grow in ... modern industries when the economic upturn eventually arrived'.[60] Yet, as distinguished industrial historian G.D.H. Cole wrote at the time, 'In most old-established industries Trade Unions have now secured full recognition ... [but] this is by no means the case in the newer industries such as motor manufacture ... Many of the big motor firms refuse to recognise any sort of combination'.[61] During the same period one Jack Jones, then a young TGWU organiser, reported the 'staggering lack of organisation' when he first went to the major car industry centre of Coventry. At the time 'the employers' policies varied from the anti-union "paternalism" of the Morris companies to the outright resistance of Fords.' And yet, 'With little ... to rely on but themselves, the motor workers began to force their organisations into the plants, and in the most up-to-date of 20th century industries ... re-enacted a battle for organisation that had been fought many times over by earlier generations'.[62]

As in America, the – ultimately successful – struggle for union organisation of Fords Dagenham is an illustration of how to achieve the apparently unachievable. But, of course, this 'miracle' did not take place by itself. It came about as a result of those unsung heroes and heroines – so-called ordinary workers – who never gave up the struggle for organisation and justice. In itself, this is an important indication of the real nature and process of trade union organisation.

There's a Star Man waiting on the Line ....

As shown above, when Ford began operations at Dagenham, the plant was totally dominated by management; the organisation of work, let alone pay and hours, was entirely the company's prerogative. Any worker who dared to attempt union organisation risked instant dismissal. Supervision was intense, based on a system of foremen themselves watched over by a higher level of supervision known as 'star men'. Unpaid lay-offs, still familiar to Ford workers even in the 1970s (see Chapter Four) were a constant hazard. Workers could be kept on the premises without pay or told to report back to complete their shift; either way, they were only paid for the actual time they worked. Given the massive unemployment in the 1930s, management could play on workers' desperation to mastermind 'numerical flexibility' in a way that would make today's post-Fordist managers proud; the workforce could fluctuate between 12,000 and 24,000 according to the time of year and the demand for production. Every summer the whole plant would close down, throwing thousands of assembly-line workers on to the mercies of the 'Public Assistance Committees' of the time.

Years later Bob Lovell, an AEU activist central to the unionisation of Ford, described the seemingly hopeless task of organising the plant: 'In Dagenham in 1930 trade unions and shop stewards were neither recognised or tolerated ... Arbitrary dismissals were a frequent occurrence. A non-uniformed staff of men were employed to keep observation on those thought to be militant.' Nor was the general environment encouraging for workplace resistance; politically, it was a bleak period throughout the country. In 1926, the historic nine-day General Strike had been betrayed by the TUC, and the years of unemployment which followed 'strengthened industrial tyranny'. At Dagenham 'Fascist elements inside and outside the ... factories were showing their ugly heads, and the Economic League was distributing anti-Communist leaflets and holding factory gate meetings ... Very little official trade union activity took place to counter this gloomy atmosphere and propaganda'.[63]

During the same period Ford brought in wage cuts of 3d per hour, claiming that they were necessary because of the 'crisis' posed by the Great Depression. These reductions were all the more damaging following the introduction in 1933 of a new pay structure which placed Dagenham employees into three grades – skilled, semi-skilled and unskilled. The cuts were brought in department by department in order to split the workers, with skilled workers the last in line.

'The Balloon Went Up'

Yet during this early period an organised nucleus of factory militants was beginning to build up at Dagenham around activists who had come down from Trafford Park: 'Underground activity was ... taking place among the skilled engineers in the Toolroom and Machine Shop, led by Ernie Lathorne and Jack Longworth, both AEU toolmakers.' And when Ford announced its pay cuts, in March 1933, 'the balloon went up ... the call was given and ... department after department stopped work until the factory was at a complete standstill...'.[64]

As Jack Longworth wrote in his own account of these events, he was transferred from Trafford Park to Dagenham in 1932 and was 'ready to carry on the good work at Dagenham'. One of the advantages of the Dagenham plant for activists was its layout – 'open shops, no walls round' – meaning 'it was possible to get around if you were careful.' In 1933, management itself provided an organising opportunity for the activists, 'present[ing] just the issue by imposing wage cuts'. At the time 'there was considerable and growing resentment in the works,' according to Longworth. 'When the notices of wage cuts went up ... everyone was up in arms. We held a short meeting there and then and decided to call a mass meeting in Barking Park that Sunday ... We expected 500-600 workers ... To our surprise, thousands turned out, including a big proportion of the production workers, most of whom weren't in any union. We decided there and then to strike ...'.[65]

Violent conflict erupted; according to another writer, 'The struggles on the picket line were sharp – the confusion was so great, owing to the mass picketing with flying squads, mounted police, firemen with hoses, barricades, buses, cars jamming the entrance that the company chairman Sir Percival Perry had to close the factory'. That Monday morning, strikers massed on the bridge to the factory, asking any workers coming in to turn back and using, literally, strong-arm tactics to stop any scabs: 'When cars tried to drive through, the workers lifted the back wheels and turned them around ...'.[66]

Although Longworth contacted Dagenham's chief Labour Officer to ask management to receive a deputation, the request was refused; the strike continued, and after four days was becoming even more solid despite a hostile press and interference by local religious bodies (many Ford workers, particularly those who had come to Dagenham from Cork, were strong Catholics). Before long, 'the management capitulated and met us'.[67]

In the face of the workers' unity and determination, management agreed to restore the wage cuts and not to attempt any others; they would look into shiftwork and overtime conditions and recognise a works committee. Yet, although the strike was 'a bit of a turning point ... hundreds joined the union', the company still refused to recognise trade unions, 'for all even the TUC could do'.[68]

The strike committee itself stayed in existence as a Ford Workers Committee, which issued its own regular bulletin *Ford Worker*. It was clear from this publication that the workers saw the strike not only as a victory on wages but also, ultimately, the principle of collective bargaining. Nine issues of *Ford Worker* were produced, and soon indicated increasing concern with two issues familiar to Ford workers decades later – lay-off and speed-up. As the July 1933 issue put it, 'It's hell inside in every sense. The continuous drive of the company for lower minute costs ... brings out the Stop Watch on the piston line ... Ford's are getting more production with 6,132 men [than with] the 8,000 of last year and fear of the lay-off is used to the fullest extent.'

Perhaps to undermine the activists' efforts, in 1933 a Ford ferry was established to transport workers from South London to Dagenham (this 'generous' benefit was removed in 2004). Along similar lines to Ford's remaining plants in the twenty-first century, a Sports Club was set up, and various other fringe benefits such as pensions (1935), paid holidays (1937), death benefits, free (pre-NHS) medical treatment and a Boys' Training School were introduced in the same decade. Yet none of this could stop the organising.

'Before any formal union organisation existed ... '

Following on the 1933 strike, the activists stepped up their underground trade union recruitment, and soon a number of new AEU branches were formed. As Lovell recalls, 'the other unions and the TUC played little part in it.' Yet 'the TUC was finally forced to reconsider its official position (which was to "leave Ford alone") and to start a recruiting campaign in Essex', which of course included Ford. Trades Councils also pitched in, and 'many new branches were formed by the various unions whose officials made efforts to gain recognition'[69] – although the TGWU seems not to have been involved at this stage.

Elsewhere, however, the union had begun to make inroads, stimulated by rank and file action; in 1934, a historic strike at Pressed Steel in Oxford achieved the TGWU's first entry into the motor industry. The original action, like so many, was a pre-recognition outbreak of conflict by workers driven beyond endurance by management pressure. One account describes how 'to the astonishment of Pressed Steel management ... the spontaneous explosion happened ... 180 workers in the press shop walked out.' This uprising ultimately led to recognition of the TGWU, but not before the workers had organised themselves: 'After some ... discussion among the unorganised workers someone proposed that a provisional strike committee be elected. Thus the traditional form of strike organisation was created before any formal union organisation existed'.[70] Shades of the rank and file upsurge in the US during the same period ....

The Pressed Steel strike lit a spark across the industry; among many other factory meetings and collections, mass meetings were addressed at Fords and Brigg's Bodies, where the strikers received strong support. While the AEU and National Union of Vehicle Builders (NUVB) declared the action 'unconstitutional', the TGWU won its first major stronghold in the motor industry with the Pressed Steel workers' victory. The potential for long-overdue organisation elsewhere was helped by a respite from the

Depression in 1936-7, when Dagenham management began recruiting all available labour, including agricultural workers from what was left of the Essex countryside. The number of workers at Dagenham virtually doubled between 1935 and 1937 – and, not surprisingly, this worked to strengthen the position of the activists already operating in the factory.

Crying Out For Organisation ...

In 1936-7 an official Ford organising campaign was launched with a TUC-backed joint union leaflet distribution and propaganda campaign; following on this, a semi-clandestine network of shop stewards began flexing its muscles with a series of stoppages against not only engineering and motor manufacture employers but the TUC itself. This was based on the fact that the TUC, along with of course the employers, was still refusing to recognise the stewards' 'unofficial' workplace organisation.

Although, as 1107 stalwart Jim Brinklow recalled later in an interview, 'One of the first areas of unionism was Briggs Motor Bodies' – where many skilled workers were AEU activists – it is clear from a poignant letter written during this period that Briggs Bodies as a whole was still unorganised. In 1937, twelve Briggs workers wrote to TGWU General Secretary Ernest Bevin listing their urgent concerns and appealing for help: 'One poor fellow was crushed to death last night owing to the anarchy prevailing in methods of work. Men and women are so afraid of losing their bread and butter that they dash about here and there without any regard for the safety of themselves or any others, this was how the man was killed, he was crushed by an overhead crane, the crane man had to hustle so fast, that he had no time to look out for anyone who might be in the way. We are crying out for organisation ...'.[71]

Bevin sent the letter on to the Trades Union Congress, and Vic Feather, who had just started work in the TUC's Organising Department, persuaded the then General Secretary Walter Citrine to organise a conference of unions interested in organising at Fords, Briggs Bodies and Kelsey Hayes. Yet nothing came of the TUC efforts because Ford, predictably, refused to have anything to do with any union.[72]

In general, although trade union full-timers were now consciously carrying out 'new industry' work, organising in the growing field of car production remained difficult. Before 1939 cars were still mainly produced to individual customer order; this meant not only seasonal employment but periodic lay-offs throughout the year. 'Troublemakers' would be the last to be taken on and the first to be laid off. According to Dick Etheridge, retired convenor at British Leyland's Longbridge plant, 'Many trade unionists thought that Austin, Morris and Ford would never be organised under this regime'.[73] Yet, by contrast with Ford, three British car companies – Austin, Morris and Standard – had all been unionised by the time the Second World War broke out.

Convenor-to-be Sid Harroway, who started work at Dagenham in 1940, later recalled that 'the toilets were the hotbed for two main illicit activities – smoking and trade unionism'.[74] It was in that ominous period that 'another long campaign began to organise the plant' according to a later pamphlet by the Joint Ford Shop Stewards' Committee. Yet 'Wartime conditions caused difficulties. Many of the members of the organising committee were drafted into the Forces. Some were transferred to other factories ...'.[75]

'Be Back at Work in a Minute ...'

In fact the war actually provided union recognition opportunities at some of Ford's other factories. Due to government nervousness about industrial conflict during wartime, Ford was forced to recognise the unions at the 'shadow factory' it had established in Manchester to produce Rolls Royce engines for fighter planes, and at another new factory at Leamington, Warwickshire, set up for production of V8 engines. Both plants came under the supervision of the Ministry of Labour (presided over by TGWU leader Ernest Bevin) which encouraged unionisation in order to regulate and control conflict in any workplaces involved in direct war-related production.

Dagenham lacked the same 'war effort' role and was therefore not pressurised by the government on the union front. The German army was less concerned with this distinction; on 26 July 1940 a high-explosive bomb landed near the factory, though it did not score a direct hit, and on 18 September 1940 the first Ford worker was killed by a more 'successful' attack. On the twenty-first, 284 bombs fell on the factory, starting 40 fires. One Ford history notes that 'right from the start the Luftwaffe had Dagenham marked down as a major target ... It was the target for 1200 bomber attacks lasting a total of more than 2,150 hours'.[76] As the war became ever more ferocious, management established a system of alarms and built steel-proofed shelters beneath the floors of the building to which, as Wilkins and Hill report approvingly, 'employees could retire quickly and ... be back at work in a minute'.[77] In general, Ford management was not happy with any disruption of work caused by attending to preserving the lives of its workers. Another account records that 'Some 200 bombs fell on Dagenham, 41 workers were killed and several hundred injured. Yet the plant continued production ...'.[78]

Although in 1940 the factory was stopped for twenty-six days altogether by the raids, the powers-that-be managed to work out that employees monitoring the bomber planes from the roof could identify their destination; most were not headed for Dagenham, and this meant that workers could stay at their jobs for much longer periods. Even more usefully, an 'Alarm within the Alert' system was adopted in January 1940 which restricted alarms to occasions on which the factory itself was in danger, and the workers agreed to stay at their posts unless this kind of immediate threat was posed. Thus, throughout 1941, less than four days' production was lost despite the terrifying intensity of the conflict. In 1944 the introduction of flying bombs increased time away from the job to 114.59 hours as opposed to 15.07 hours in 1943, but overall management could feel that the demands of wartime production, intensified by the 'patriotic' need for vehicles, were being satisfied as well as could be expected.

In fact, during the war speed-up was intensified, and the official working week was increased, first to 44 hours (in 1941) and later to 48 hours. The period also saw the workforce at Dagenham steadily increase during the war despite workers leaving to join the armed forces; 4,259 workers enlisted before the end of the war, and 144 never returned. The gap, as is well known, was filled by women.

'The Women Kept England Going ...'

Women had been employed at Dagenham in the 1930s, but not in the numbers now made necessary by enlistment; as Wilkins and Hill put it, 'increasing production demanded more men and, since men were not easily procurable, women'.[79] By September 1941 these numbered 1100, helping to swell a workforce that had risen from less than 12,000 in 1939 and would total 34,163 by the spring of 1945. Burgess-Wise sums it all up: 'Over 2000 women worked at Dagenham, carrying out a variety of jobs that it had previously been thought could only be carried out by men'.[80]

One of those newly competent women was Maisie Watson, interviewed roughly 60 years later for this history. As she recalled, 'If not for women Ford would have closed down ... When I started at Fords there was no tea breaks, only half an hour for lunch. I worked on the lathes ... The night shifts were bad – There were thousands of workers in there – they were all smoking ... and it was smelly – the smell was from the burning of steel and oil. My star-man said "I'll be glad when my men come back." Then when the men came back he said "I wish I had my girls – men can't do two things at once" – not like we could.

'The women started to go into the foundry canteen and bring their tea back in a billycan – Fords thought we were wasting time so they brought round tea trolleys to give us tea. There was no smoking before – then the women changed that by just doing it. We improved the conditions just by being there ... we weren't going to be put upon. The women workers changed conditions by saying "I wouldn't do it that way".'

Bernie Passingham, later convenor of the River Plant, confirmed this: 'During the war it was through the women, quite honestly, that we gained a lot of the advances – rest periods, washing facilities, all that sort of thing – because they wouldn't put up with what the men used to put up with. You never got much from the company in them days, and bearing in mind that it was a filthy job – dust and everything – I think actually it was through the women, their insistence, that we got greater protection. It was women that really started putting their foot down on the question of safety, protection etc – and very slowly these things came in....You didn't have Health and Safety law then. We got aprons and all that to get more protection – gloves – and I think mainly that was through the assistance of the women.'

'Inspired by Political Motives'

In fact it was during the war, in 1941, that a 'comparatively minor' dispute blew up which was to have a significant impact on the struggle for unionisation. By this time the number of workers at Dagenham had increased by nearly another quarter with the full employment stimulated by the war, strengthening union influence and worker confidence in the factory. When a Briggs Bodies shop steward was dismissed for using 'hasty words' in defiance of a supervisor's authority, TGWU activists contacted their union leader Ernest Bevin, now Minister of Labour in the wartime coalition government. Bevin set up a Court of Inquiry under Sir Charles Doughty into the industrial relations situation at Briggs, resulting in an agreement to 'permit engineering employees to elect ... representatives to negotiate on their behalf with management ... and to define the position and responsibilities of elected representatives.' The 1941 report of the Doughty Inquiry recommended that Briggs 'should adopt the normal procedure for ... settling disputes, which necessarily involves the recognition of ... unions to fairly ... represent their work people'.[81]

This was a major step forward. But, while the 'normal procedure' for settling disputes in the British motor industry was set out in the 1922 Engineering Industry Procedure Agreement, Ford had never been party to the Engineering Employers' Federation (EEF) or thereby to that agreement. As one historian comments, 'For years Ford, Vauxhall and Morris Cowley stayed outside the Engineering Employers' Federation so as to avoid the unpleasant necessity of recognising any trade union';[82] and Briggs, of course, followed loyally in its sponsor's footsteps. So workers and management were left to find their own way towards any joint agreement. Briggs workers had shown that they could organise and thus establish negotiating relationships with management without help from union officials, while Briggs management felt obliged to comply with Doughty's recommendations or be penalised under the wartime regulations discouraging disputes. Yet management still stubbornly refused to behave as if it was dealing with a unionised workforce.

In January 1944 both TGWU and AEU stewards occupied the works manager's office and forced the TUC and Fords to reopen their 1930s talks on organising. Meanwhile, strikes against speed up and for reductions in hours continued despite the ups and downs of the war, although they increased as victory became more certain. During this period the split widened between stewards and their members and the official unions. In the summer of 1944 one Sweetman, a TGWU shop steward at the Dagenham foundry, was sacked along with Lynch, an AEU steward at Briggs Bodies. They received great support not only from Sweetman's fellow-Irishmen in the foundry, who had become 'pillars of the union at Fords', but from the trade union movement as a whole. Yet the TUC's Vic Feather, arguing that the shop stewards were 'inspired by political motives' (code for Communist Party membership) agreed with Fords that stewards should not be accredited by the union even if they were recognised by workers.[83]

This denial of meaningful representation led to sustained conflict, including a sitdown by shop stewards in the main Dagenham plant; the militancy resulted in a further agreement in April 1944, signed by the TUC, which set up the Ford National Joint Negotiating Committee (FNJNC), still in existence today. Yet at this point, and for more than two decades to come, the committee's 'union side' was made up entirely of full-time officials, going over the heads of the very stewards – now elected in many departments despite management's refusal to acknowledge them – who had fought so staunchly for organisation and trade union recognition. Both stewards and workers were up in arms over this deliberate attack on workplace organisation.

Yet, although strike action was threatened, district union officials effectively prevailed upon the workers to refrain from taking any action that would weaken the fight against fascist Germany – a stance reflecting the 'anti-strike' position of the Communist Party during the war in defence of their beloved Soviet Union. In fact, while the *Daily Worker* reported the 'victory' in glowing terms – 'After prolonged negotiations the great Ford combine has at last agreed to recognise trade unions ... one of the last great bastions of non-unionism in Britain has fallen' – the article continued, apparently without irony, 'The joint press statement issued by the unions and the Ford company states that the agreement has not been negotiated in consequence of any discontent with working conditions in Fords.'

Yet the paper was forced to acknowledge that 'the recognition accorded by the firm is of a limited character. The right of the district or national officials to negotiate on behalf of their members is recognised, but there is no similar recognition of the right of shop stewards. Nevertheless, the fact that the principle of recognition has been conceded in one of the largest anti-union firms will inspire all workers who are struggling for similar aims elsewhere. If the Ford workers continue to display the same solidarity as they have done in recent months, recognition of the stewards cannot be long delayed …'.[84]

Probably because of the exclusion of shop stewards, the spectacular feat of unionising Fords did not prevent the company from imposing its harshest conditions; in fact the end of the war saw hundreds of workers sacked. When Bernie Passingham returned to Dagenham in 1945, problems cropped up 'mainly when we started organising the trade unions. It was the old men there who knew about trade unions, but they didn't take the [stewards'] jobs for themselves, they used to get us to do it, become a steward … which we did – it's one of them things you learn I suppose when you come in a factory like that.' Yet organising 'came slowly … There wasn't much trade union there at all except for skilled workers – they always kept their trade union. For assembly workers and all that it was a question of persuasion as it slowly went on. Because after we came back from the war it got well organised – and that was how I became a shop steward.'

The way 'it got well organised' is examined in the next chapter – along with the birth of what was to become the Notoriously Militant 1107 TGWU branch.

NOTES

1 Upton Sinclair, *The Flivver King: A Story of Ford-America*, Chicago: Charles H. Kerr, 1984, p. 3. Early Fords were known as 'Flivvers'; *The Flivver King*, a parody of Ford and Fordism, was written in the 1930s to boost the drive for union organisation at the company.
2 Quoted in Peter Collier and David Horowitz, *The Fords: An American Epic*, London: Futura, 1987, p. 10.
3 Huw Beynon, *Working For Ford*, London: Penguin, 1973, p. 1.
4 Paul Mason, *Live Working or Die Fighting: How the Working Class Went Global*, London: Harvill Secker, 2007, p. 257.
5 Henry Ford, *My Life and Work*, New York: Doubleday, 1923, p. 72.

6 Mira Wilkins and Frank Ernest Hill, *American Business Abroad: Ford on Six Continents*, New York: Cambridge University Press, 2011, p. 59.
7 Greg Grandin, *Fordlandia : The Rise and Fall of Henry Ford's Forgotten Jungle City*, London: Icon Books, 2010, p. 34.
8 Charles E. Sorenson and Samuel T. Williamson, *My Forty Years With Ford*, London: Jonathan Cape, 1957, pp. 117-118.
9 Harry Braverman, *Labor and Monopoly Capital: The Degradation of Work in the Twentieth Century*, New York: Monthly Review Press, 1998, p. 101.
10 Ford, *My Life and Work*, p. 93.
11 Keith Sward, *The Legend of Henry Ford*, New York: Russell & Russell, 1948, p. 48.
12 John Rees, *The Algebra of Revolution*, London: Routledge, 1998, p. 221.
13 Peter Collier and David Horowitz, *The Fords: An American Epic*, London: Futura, 1988, p. 65.
14 Collier and Horowitz, *The Fords*, p. 66.
15 Collier and Horowitz, *The Fords*, p. 67.
16 Collier and Horowitz, *The Fords*, p. 156.
17 Collier and Horowitz, *The Fords*, p. 65.
18 Collier and Horowitz, *The Fords*, p157.
19 Frances Piven and Richard Coward, *Poor People's Movements: How they Succeed, How they Fail*, New York: Vintage, 1979, p. 117.
20 Piven and Cloward, *Poor People's Movements*, p. 96 (italics in original).
21 Booton Herndon, *Ford: An Unconventional Biography of the two Henry Fords and their times*, London: Cassell, 1970, p. 172.
22 The full story of Black involvement in these early struggles is told in August Meier and Elliott Rudwick's excellent *Black Detroit and the Rise of the UAW*, New York: Oxford University Press, 1979.
23 Art Preis, *Labor's Giant Step: Twenty Years of the CIO*, New York: Pioneer Publishers, 1964, p. 104.
24 Quoted in Peter Rachleff, *Hard-Pressed in the Heartland: The Hormel Strike and the Future of the Labour Movement*, Boston: South End Press 1993, p. 19.
25 Herndon, *Ford: An Unconventional Biography*, p. 171.
26 A. Nevins and F.E. Hill *Ford: Decline and Rebirth, 1933-62*, New York: Scribners, 1962, p. 164.
27 Collier and Horowitz, *The Fords*, p. 178.
28 David Burgess-Wise, *Ford at Dagenham: The Rise and Fall of Detroit in Europe*, Derby: Breedon Books, 2007, p. 15.
29 'Scientific Management' was the name given to the work efficiency techniques associated with Taylorism.
30 Henry Friedman and Sander Meredeen, *The Dynamics of Industrial Conflict: Lessons from Ford* London: Croom Hill, 1980, p. 22.
31 Charles Leadbeater, 'Dagenham's decline is Ghenk's gain', *Financial Times*, 30 January 1989, p. 10.
32 Peter Pagnamenta and Richard Overy, *All Our Working Lives*, London: British Broadcasting Corporation, 1984, p. 218.
33 Mira Wilkins and Frank Ernest Hill, *American Business Abroad: Ford on Six*

Continents, New York: Cambridge University Press, 2011, p. 49.
34. Wilkins and Hill, *American Business*, p. 49
35. 1910 to 1914 saw the 'Great Unrest' in Britain during which both strike numbers and trade union membership grew as never before.
36. Wilkins and Hill, *American Business*, pp. 49-50
37. Wilkins and Hill, *American Business*, p. 58.
38. Booton Herndon, *Ford*, pp. 150-1.
39. Wilkins and Hill, *American Business*, p. 237.
40. In fact Clara Ford's influence on her husband was sometimes considerable, as in the final decision to recognise the union in Detroit in 1941; in Ford's own words, when he reached home after telling Charles Sorenson to close the plant rather than sign a union contract, 'Mrs Ford was horrified …. She said if that was done there would be riots and bloodshed … And if I did that she would leave me … She insisted I sign the agreement … What could I do? Don't ever discredit the power of a woman' (Irving Bernstein, *Turbulent Years: A History of the American Worker 1933-1941*, Boston: Houghton Mifflin 1969, p. 75). And on this sexist note, we must indeed acknowledge the contribution of Clara Ford to the history of the American labour movement.
41. Wilkins and Hill, *American Business*, p. 143.
42. Friedman & Meredeen, *Dynamics*, p. 22.
43. Nevins and Hill, *Ford*, p. 54.
44. Interview with Henry Coleman; additional interview material from Eastside Community Heritage.
45. Wilkins and Hill, *American Business*, pp. 199-200.
46. Dennis Ellam, 'Ford's Dagenham car plant: 80 years of a British giant', *Sunday Mirror* 1.3.09, p. 24.
47. Wilkins and Hill, *American Business*, pp. 206, 236.
48. Allan Nevins, *Henry Ford: The Times, The Man, the Company*, New York: Charles Scribner, 1957, p. 564.
49. Wilkins and Hill, *American Business*, p. 31.
50. Chris Arnot, 'When the Wheels Came Off the Dream', *Guardian* 25.2.09.
51. Pagnamenta and Overy, *All Our Working Lives*, p. 224.
52. Ibid.
53. As late as 1952, one manager reported of the workers originally from Manchester, 'A couple of weeks ago they held what they call a Mancunian Dance – even after all these years all the Manchester fellows and their wives get together – and they have that every year', T.H. Carr, *O! Brave New World – The Ford Motor Company at Dagenham*, (nd) p. 37.
54. Peter Ackroyd *London: The Biography*, London: Vintage Books, 2001, p. 724.
55. Aldous Huxley, *Brave New World*, London: Penguin, 1963, p. 179.
56. T.H. Carr, *O! Brave New World – The Ford Motor Company at Dagenham*, (nd), p. 35.
57. Wilkins and Hill, *American Business*, p. 192.
58. Quoted in Dennis Ellam, 'Ford's Dagenham car plant: 80 years of a British giant', *Sunday Mirror* 1 March 2009.
59. Ford Communist Party, *Men and Motors* (nd), p. 16.

60 Andrew Murray, *The T&G Story: A History of the Transport and General Workers' Union 1922-2007*, London: Lawrence and Wishart (2008), p. 56.
61 G.D.H. Cole et al, *British Trade Unionism Today: A Survey*, London: Methuen (1945) p. 108.
62 Denis Butt, *Men and Motors* (1960). Vol I/Part 3 *New Left Review*, May/June 1960.
63 Bob Lovell, 'Fords – the Victory for Union Recognition', *Daily Worker*, 18 November 1968, p. 2.
64 Lovell *op cit.*
65 Jack Longworth, 'Rebellion and Breakaway", in R.A. Leeson, *Strike! A Live History 1887-1971*, London: Allen and Unwin (1973), p. 126.
66 T.H. Carr, *O! Brave New World – The Ford Motor Company at Dagenham*, nd, p. 37.
67 Longworth in Leeson (ed.) *Strike!* (1973), p. 127.
68 Longworth in Leeson (ed.) *Strike!* (1973) p. 127.
69 Lovell *op cit.* (1968).
70 Dudley Edwards, 'How Trade Unionism Came To Pressed Steel', *Militant Pamphlet*, London: Cambridge Heath Press (1979), p. 5.
71 Letter, 6 November 1937, held in TUC library.
72 As implied earlier, Fords was prepared to allow unionism for a minority of highly-skilled employees, but this carried no implications for the mass of workers.
73 Quoted in Richard Croucher, *Engineers at War 1939-1945*, Merlin (1980), p. 58.
74 Charles Leadbeater, 'Dagenham's decline is Genk's gain', *Financial Times* 30 January 1989, p. 10.
75 *What's Wrong at Fords* (n.d: early 1960s), p. 3.
76 David Burgess-Wise, *Ford at Dagenham: The Rise and Fall of Detroit in Europe*, Breedon Books (2007), p. 70.
77 Wilkins and Hill, *American Business*, p. 326.
78 Herndon, *Ford* (1970), p. xiv.
79 Wilkins and Hill, *American Business*, p. 327.
80 Burgess-Wise, *Ford at Dagenham*, p. 72.
81 Friedman and Meredeen, *Dynamics*, pp. 23-4.
82 Roy Hattersley, *Borrowed Time: The Story of Britain Between the Wars*, London: Abacus 2010, p. 264.
83 Richard Croucher, *Engineers*, p. 316.
84 'Ford Victory', *Daily Worker*, 18 April 1944, p. 1.

Chapter Two

T&G MEETS FMC – THE BIRTH OF 1107, 1946-1959

The Balloon Goes Up Again ...

In spite of talk of 'homes fit for heroes' after the end of the Second World War, both Fords and Briggs Bodies were doing their best to get back to pre-war conditions of employment, using the unconvincing argument that 'the war effort had created special or unique bargaining conditions which would need re-negotiating.' The dire situation for the workforce after the war is vividly remembered by Maisie Watson, the no-nonsense Ford worker quoted in our previous chapter:

> It was 1946 when the men started coming back and that's when it exploded because they were Bolshie – they had had years of being shouted at by sergeant majors and the rest of it and they wanted their freedom back. Six years of square-bashing, being told what to do and how to do it, not being let out after curfew – they came back and they said "We're going to do what we want now" – and they wanted more money. The wages weren't as good as before the war [and] after the war money didn't go as far. No homes, no food, no clothes. They just wanted a normal life.

Yet even the most reasonable demands would come up against the rigidly top-down management stance of both Briggs Bodies and Fords. The company's New Year message to its workforce called upon them to 'work harder in 1946'; in October 1945, Briggs made 440 workers redundant, 'and the firm did not miss the opportunity of dismissing those workers they considered troublemakers'.[1] ie. trade union activists. In line with this aggression was the continued refusal of Ford, at least, to recognise or negotiate with shop stewards. As three former Ford employees, O'Connell, Sweetman and Donagher, pointed out in a letter to the *Dagenham Post* on January 25 1946, 'Trade Unionism was built up in the Dagenham works as a result of a long and bitter struggle. [But] the [1944] Agreement leaves a lot to be desired, because recognition of the workers' representatives, namely the shop stewards, was not achieved.'

Trade union organisation was, of course, the main casualty. Although, as shown in the last chapter, management had finally signed a recognition agreement with trade union officials in 1944, that agreement kept the workers' chosen representatives at arm's length by excluding shop stewards from the negotiating table. Despite their members' dissatisfaction with this system, the TUC and full-time union officials did little to change it. Yet the 1944 agreement was set to expire on 17 April 1946; and as early as March that year, to use Bob Lovell's phrase, the 'balloon went up' again.

'Difficulties' Arise

As the TGWU *Record* reports curtly in its April 1946 issue, 'A dispute took place at the Ford Motor Company's works at Dagenham on March 6. The Joint Negotiating Committee immediately met and advised a resumption of work in order that discussions on the matter in dispute could be held. Difficulties arose ...' The dispute referred to was a walkout by grinders and cutters in the machine shop seeking both improved wages and 'greater shop floor representation'.[2] As with so many other supposedly 'trivial' episodes of working-class conflict, this was a spark which lit the flame of genuine workplace-based trade union organisation at Dagenham. The following day over 11,000 Ford workers came out in support of the machine shop workers' demands for better pay and – more significantly – shop floor representation.

The dramatic conflict that followed, which included an occupation and mass demonstrations, was rooted in the same joint demand for shop steward recognition and higher wages – including an end to the hated 'merit pay'. As AEU activist Kevin Halpin put it: 'Ford operated merit money on the basis of personal recommendation by your supervision. So if you wasn't a good boy you didn't get any...' To eliminate this injustice and even up wages across the company, the strikers claimed a new across-the-board rate of 4 shillings as opposed to the current mixture of anything from 2 shillings and 7 pence to 3 shillings and 11 pence.

But the issue of workplace union representation was even more important. Although by this time over 90 shop stewards had been elected in the Ford factory and endorsed by their respective unions, TUC Assistant Secretary Vic Feather had written to the General Secretary, Walter Citrine, that the left-leaning stewards elected were 'totally unsuitable from any point of view ... for appointment as shop steward'.[3] Not surprisingly, Ford management was in agreement; the stewards were denied recognition or credentials for negotiating with management. As much as pay rates or merit money, this refusal to recognise workers' own chosen representatives had brought the whole huge factory to a standstill.

The company's response was equally 'militant'. While union officials advised a return to work 'so grievances could be dealt with', workers' stubborn rejection of that suggestion forced the officials to pull out of negotiations. In response, management's next step was to threaten a lockout, posting a notice in the factory which proclaimed: 'The Company hereby gives notice that on and after 16 March 1946, the factory will be closed until further notice to all factory hourly paid employees except those engaged on essential services … no wages will be paid to employees who have not worked or do not work after 2.30 pm of that day.'

The following evening, Tuesday the twelfth, shop stewards and departmental representatives convened in the hall of the local Marsh Green primary school (later to become the regular meeting-place of the 1107 branch). A delegation which had met Dagenham MPs earlier that day reported to the meeting, expressing what was then a widespread belief that the plant would be nationalised by the post-war Labour government. As the *Daily Worker* reported the following day: 'The retort of the strike committee to the management threat to close Dagenham works was that the workers will ask the government to take over the factory.'

A Union Before the Union Got There …

But workers took the opposite course; they occupied the Dagenham plant. According to the *Dagenham Post*, 'Every morning since Friday the 12,000 employees have "clocked in" but have just stood around their machines and attended meetings in the departments …'.[4] The *Daily Worker* reported the same event with a dose of 1940's sexism: 'Yesterday, the men clocked in as usual and then moved to their places in the canteen, the women taking in knitting and books…The workers, organised and unorganised, are solid together. They are "staying-in" on strike, and are controlling the factory'.[5] The occupying workers mirrored the classic features of grass roots struggles throughout industrial history by setting up a directly accountable strike committee of 200 departmental representatives, including those from departments previously lacking a shop steward. In addition, the occupation had elected a Strike Leadership Committee consisting of ten workers of whom only half were already in the union and the rest – at that point – still non-unionists.

This committee had now met trade union district officials to discuss the occupation and the outstanding grievances; they reported that all the workers, union and non-union, were involved in supporting the action and 'the morale all over the plant was excellent'. Workers had employed their practical skills to impressive effect: 'Picketing was operating efficiently ... the canteens had been taken over for meetings, the tables were being used for filling in trade union recruitment forms. Departmental social activity was in progress, a Ford's "Happidrome" had been formed and much excellent talent was available, a fund had been opened to assist cases of distress and regular contact was being maintained with the district officials'.[6]

The new authority of workers in – at least temporary – control of capital was also on display. As the *Daily Worker* reported, 'The jetty-master asked permission [of the strike committee] that a ship for Holland be loaded with 15 cars. The strike committee, on learning that the ship would return to Holland with food for the country, gave permission for the ship to be loaded ...' Within the occupied factory itself, workers were 'allowing essential work such as the power house ... to proceed under the control of the strike committee.' It was a classic example of the 'dual power' exercised by workers in situations of direct class conflict.[7]

By this stage of the occupation, 95 shop stewards had been elected, and the workers' demand for representation was beginning to receive some support from the 1945 Labour government, whose Minister of Labour intervened to arrange a meeting between union officials and management for 15 March. The stewards led a mass march out of the factory on that date as a show of defiance against the lockout notice. The meeting resulted in a 'basis of agreement' by the union officials with management; this was reported to the stewards, who found it acceptable, and 'a resumption of work was agreed upon'.[8] The occupation continued through the weekend, but on Saturday 16 March it was announced that the workers had won a new agreement, signed by Ford management and executive members of 11 trade unions, which gave the unions the right to appoint up to 75 shop representatives. With this, the strike – and the occupation – were over. The workers had won the key demand for effective workplace representation; as always, industrial action had worked where 'negotiation' had failed to beat the stubborn anti-unionism of this most reactionary of employers.

As the *Daily Worker* reported, the agreement provided for the withdrawal of the Ford rule that three months' notice must be given of any intention to vary an existing agreement: 'This means, in effect, that Ford are prepared to discuss at once with trade union officials the removal of those regulations which are peculiar to their company' and 'discuss with the unions any points they might wish to raise, including revision of the procedure agreement so as to provide for direct representation of trade unions at factory level.' Translated, this meant that Fords had finally given in on the crucial question of direct workplace trade union representation. The one disappointment was that, with typical bad grace, the company had agreed to only 75 stewards instead of the 90-plus demanded by the workforce. Yet, as one J.R. Scott of the AEU commented, 'I regard the Ford settlement as one of the greatest advances that has taken place in trade unionism for a good many years'.[9]

On 30 April 1946, the details of the agreement were drawn up and signed between twelve trade unions and the Ford Motor Company. 'Among other important questions,' Lovell reports, the agreement 'gave full recognition to the ... shop stewards' – those shop stewards being the same individuals, chosen by the workers, who had been condemned by management and union officials alike as 'totally unsuitable'.[10] One effect of Fords' obstinacy in coming to a meaningful negotiating and procedure agreement was the unusually large number of trade unions involved on the official Ford National Joint Negotiating Committee (FNJNC), an issue which was to cause both the company and the unions endless problems in future years. As so often, they had brought these difficulties upon themselves.

1107 Is Born ...

But before this final agreement was signed, another historic event had taken place amidst the excitement and upheaval of the occupied factory. Although the workers' candidates for shop steward had not yet been officially recognised, the right to workplace union representation as such had been conceded, and in this environment 'all trade unions began to recruit rapidly'.[11] The TGWU 1/667 branch, which became dominant in the Briggs Body and River Plants, was growing fast and would eventually, by June of that year, have accumulated 500 members. But far outpacing 667 was what would one day be referred to as the 'Notoriously Militant' 1/1107.

No minutes have survived, and the newspapers of the time (even the *Daily Worker*) were silent on the issue, but Colin Pond's indispensable thesis on the Dagenham plant provides us with a definite date for the beginnings of 1107: 'At Fords a new Branch 1/1107 was commenced on the 6 April 1946, and had over 2,000 members'.[12] Appendix 8 of the thesis backs up the numbers, with a scrawled list of dates and membership figures headed '1/1107'; the numbers for June '46 were 2,003. Next to the heading 'Secretary' is written 'New Branch 6/4/46 1/1107'; by December of that year, after a short slump to 1,776 in September, membership had risen to 2,022, and in March 1950, the latest date on the list, it was 3,757. The first branch secretary was a Mr H. Miller, while the post of Organiser was held by Messrs Higgins, Lucas and, lastly, S. Fanjoy.

Representation shall be Geographical ...

Yet workplace organisation at Dagenham – and TGWU 1107 was, from its beginnings, a *workplace branch* – saw ongoing obstacles. Even after its unwilling recognition of shop stewards, the company did not 'suffer' trade unionism gladly. The formal procedure agreement signed between Ford's Dagenham management and 'certain trade unions' on 30 April 1946 specified on its first page that 'all employees, including Shop Representatives, shall carry out the rules of the Company and the instructions of the Management at all times, including the period during which a matter or complaint is being dealt with ...' - a kind of *status quo* clause in reverse. It also allowed for the transfer of employees 'from one job or department to another as may be desirable', and emphasised the company's unilateral right to 'discharge any employee, should he be unsuitable or no longer necessary ...' Yet it did include the crucial clause that 'The Trade Unions concerned shall appoint their own Shop Representatives'.

Now that the workers had won the hard-fought right to choose their own shop stewards, this apparent suggestion that selection of a shop steward would be made by full-timers was probably a gesture aimed at the union leadership, rather than reflecting shopfloor reality. In fact the Procedure Agreement did its best to come down on the side of bureaucracy; the company was still entitled to question the appointment of any specific steward, and restrictions on workers' choice of their representatives included age (over 25) and length of tenure (12 months).[13] There were strict limits on movement around the plant, and a complicated set of procedural steps for the conduct of disputes; workers were not allowed to raise a grievance with the steward until after discussing it with the chargehand or foreman, and even then were only allowed to discuss it with the shop steward during a break in working time. The employee was to remain at work while the steward negotiated with the superintendent, Personnel Manager, etc, as the grievance made its stately way through Procedure.

But the Procedure Agreement did include one important clause which specified that, with the exception of skilled trades groups, 'representation shall be on a departmental and/or geographical basis.' This meant that unskilled and semi-skilled workers could be represented by a shop steward from any trade union, as long as s/he was part of the work group. While obviously not the company's intention, in practice this clause led to a kind of 'class' system of representation in which a union's formal identity was in one sense irrelevant – with important implications for shop-floor democracy and the accountability of stewards, who would answer to their work group rather than the union hierarchy.

In the words of Steve Hart, who worked at Fords in the 1970s and later became Secretary of TGWU Region One: 'The critical thing that needs to be understood about industrial relations at Fords is that each shop steward is elected by a multi-union group, which meant that no shop steward was subservient to a union officer or the union branch - they were relatively autonomous because they could always say that they were representing people from other unions – so no one union could [dominate] – although shop stewards were responsible to the branch in rule, really their first loyalty was to their members and to the shop stewards' committee, which was multi-union. And that developed quite specifically in order to prevent over-control by union officers. The multi-union membership of Ford was to an extent contrived by the left in [the workplace] ... there was a spread between T&G, GMB and the AEU and NUVB, early on, among the semi-skilled – precisely in order to ensure that no union branch could take a decision that would say "You will do this" in the workplace.'

This multi-union shopfloor structure was initially more effective at Briggs. As PTA convenor-to-be Kevin Halpin recalled,

> When I started work at Briggs Bodies in 1949 we had a very good Joint Shop Stewards' Committee which comprised the General and Municipal, Woodworkers' Union, AEU, T&G and a few more ... and the members were represented by the shop stewards on a departmental basis, not on a union basis. If the AEU had members or the T&G had members in the shop, you might finish up with a transport steward or an engineering steward, a sheet metal worker steward. It was a very progressive position, one of the rare positions in car factories ... I used to go to Vauxhall's, and the transport union had a separate office and the AEU had an office ... they never spoke together.

At Briggs in particular, by comparison to the main Ford plant,

> we stopped the idiocy of going through separate unions and we went for a joint organisation which [eventually] worked throughout Fords – a Joint Shop Stewards' Committee and a National JSSC – based on people being from shop stewards' committees without any concern for which union they were in. You might finish up with a transport steward, an engineering steward and a sheet metal worker steward – it was a very progressive position, one of the rare positions in car factories – they usually split up.

'Probably the Most Advanced in the Country'

Yet Halpin pointed out that even after full union and steward recognition at Fords, 'The Main Plant agreement was very different [from Briggs']. Only in a strike situation did shop meetings and mass discussions take place there; the only ideas reaching the majority of the employees were what the Management or the media told them.' In sharp contrast to the on-site, weekly report-back meetings at Briggs, 'Fords shop meetings could only be held after the shift outside the plant …. The difference between the two trade union structures was that in Fords any issue went to national officials whereas [at Brigg's] if the management and the 'seven' [chief stewards] could not agree, the matter went to District [rather than national] level.' Indeed, for Colin Pond it was this 'local autonomy' that meant 'in some ways Briggs Bodies membership were more progressive and developed more quickly than the Ford membership'.[14]

Henry Friedman, who was Senior Convenor at Fords from 1962[15] and an impressive left-wing intellectual, comments that the 'rank and file movement' within Briggs 'was probably the most advanced in the country' by the early 1950s. This tradition was particularly strong in the Briggs River Plant, which employed 400 toolmakers with a particularly militant tradition; among their number was Alec Geddes, 'a stalwart of the World War I Clyde Workers' Committee … who had known Lenin personally'.[16]

The shopfloor trade union structure at Briggs had developed on the basis of the 1941 Toolroom Agreement agreed in the wake of the Doughty Inquiry into the sacking of Briggs toolroom shop steward John MacDougall (see Chapter One). This agreement specifically set out that all issues – ranging from wages to working conditions and welfare – would be negotiated by the shop stewards in the plant, rather than by full-time officials. As Friedman puts it, 'Eventually, full-time Trade Union officials were allowed to assist with the solution of problems, but this outside intrusion was confined to the district level'.[17] The arrangement at Briggs stood in sharp contrast to the Ford National Joint Negotiating Committee (FNJNC) with its full-time national trade union officials.

In this way, as Friedman puts it, 'There were two plants, barely one mile apart, securing trade union recognition based on two fundamentally different Agreements: one specifically designed to inhibit rank-and-file development (Ford) and the other (Briggs) promoting it'.[18] Yet even at Ford itself, almost 40 strikes and go-slows took place under the new workplace union regime during the three years from the beginning of 1946. In many cases these centred on Ford's continued insistence on paying its workers by 'time rate' instead of piecework, still the system at Briggs' Bodies. Yet even before the later merger of Ford and Briggs 'links between their stewards were close because of geography, competition in the same labour market, and the dependence of one plant on the other'.[19] These links were to become increasingly important in the coming years, with Briggs' comparative militancy influencing workers at Ford's rather than the other way round.

Yet the different development of trade unionism at Briggs and Fords became particularly clear when both companies used the 1947 fuel crisis as an excuse to lay off hundreds of trade union activists in both plants. After management refused to re-hire 200 workers, Briggs employees staged a 4,000-strong protest strike; as the *Dagenham Post* reported, 'the men claimed that ... an assurance [had been] given that all employees would be reinstated [but] management ... stated that there were a number of reasons why all the men could not be taken back; among them being the fact that they were trade union militants'.[20] Yet at Briggs, thanks to its independent plant-based union organisation, 'trade union consciousness was quickly rebuilt' after this disaster, while at Fords 'the adverse effects were much longer lasting'.[21]

Yet only the next year a strike at Fords won an agreement which reduced the major differentials that had existed between different groups of car workers since the war; Standard Motors in Coventry, for example, had introduced a new wage structure and payment system in 1948 which placed its workers at least 20 per cent above other car companies. The 1948 Ford strike was, according to the syndicalist publication *Red Notes*, 'the first sign that the skilled workers ... who had been a leading presence in the first 15 years of Dagenham's history ... were losing the initiative. The initiative began to pass to the lineworkers ...' Yet at the same time, in a hint of the grading struggles to come, 'another gulf was opening ... the wages of the lowest grade, comprising only women, were only a half of the skilled male workers' rate'.[22]

The Horror ...

Athough the 1946 strike had forced the company to finally recognise the existence of shop stewards, 'for the next twenty years it was to be involved in a conflict over what such stewards could and couldn't do'.[23] At the heart of this conflict was, from the mid to late '40s onwards, the issue of speedup. As one worker commented, 'What really caused the trouble was the speed-up. We used to have a works standard man come round, and he'd time you with his watch. Then the foreman would come and say, "Well, you've got to produce faster." You felt you were working and sweating hard enough as it was ...'.[24]

In the late 1940s, the Ford factory was indeed a grim place to work. Sociologist Phyllis Wilmott recorded her impressions of a visit to the plant in October 1948: 'Seeing these masses of men fixed to the assembly line [and] the inhuman vastness of the power transformer, it is impossible to believe that [conditions were] worse when factory conditions were first in full swing .... The shuffle alongside of the moving belt, now this way, now that to fix one screw or add one further bit of superstructure .... The noise – The massiveness – The horror!'.[25] That 'horror' was the price, for its workers, of Ford's position as the highest-volume and most profitable car manufacturer in Britain, trebling its production levels between 1946 and 1950.

Following on their final acceptance in 1946, the Ford stewards found themselves involved in a more or less daily war with management as they attempted to defend their members from ever-increasing attempts to increase the pace of work. Yet not all worker representatives were consistently on the side of their members; Kevin Halpin recalls that 'in the late 1940s the convenor at the main Ford plant[26] was opposed to militancy, and he developed a large group within the factory, particularly within the car assembly part of the plant where he had a terrific following amongst the stewards'. The comment is an interesting reflection on the later divide between TGWU 1107 in the Chassis/Engine plant and the form the branch eventually took in the PTA (see Chapter 5). As Halpin emphasised, the period he was referring to was 'pre-PTA – the car bodies were shipped down [from Briggs] to the chassis plant down Fords ... and the cars were built there until the PTA. It was the biggest Dagenham plant – they had about 15,000'.

Halpin also spoke of the various religious groups influencing Ford workers at the time, including the right-wing Moral Rearmament movement:

> There was a big Catholic Action following at Fords as well at that time through the Irish Catholics [employed at Dagenham after the Cork plant was shut down]. When we were having a strike Father Rory told the parish at the main Mass that the strike was the fault of Communists and they should get shillelaghs and drive them out of the factory. And the reaction was - people walked out, and by the following Monday he'd been removed from his position owing to protests .... The attitude was "Well we're militant – we don't need Communists – we can fight for our wages without them - we're not being duped." They were Catholic Action on the basis of their religion, but that didn't stop the militancy.

Women workers, in particular, had been activated by their experiences during the war. As future River Plant convenor Bernie Passingham recalled, 'They were militant on the conditions …. In the [Briggs] Body Plant there were 10,000 workers and the shop stewards' committee divided the plant into 2,000 zones. We would hold mass meetings. Of the zone convenors at one stage, two out of five were women. There were quite a lot of Transport and General women stewards in different zones, in the Trim Shop and places like that. There was still a position then where women were expected to leave when they got pregnant or got married – a disgrace really. But even ten years after 1945, women were still working in the factory, and they were stroppy, yes. We had a position where a shop meeting could move a vote of no confidence in a steward at any time – and each steward was elected by the shop every 12 months. The national union officials didn't like our way of carrying on - they weren't keen on having shop meetings because they wanted to control things.'

The Fifties

Following on from postwar austerity and controls, the 1950s brought new horizons for carmakers; as industry expert Graham Turner reports, 'By 1950, the production levels of 1946 had been trebled…'.[27] Yet, of course, such massive increases did not come without enormous pressure on the workforce and its efforts to improve conditions. At this point, there was still a divide between Brigg's and the main Ford plant in terms of shopfloor militancy and effectiveness; despite the overwhelming victory on steward recognition in 1946, Ford continued to fight back – and fight dirty.

In fact the 1950s were difficult times for car workers throughout the country. As Dennis Butt relates in his survey of the decade, 'The latest phase for the motor workers … was punctuated by the two recessions of 1951 and 1956. Between the closing down of munitions production and the [later] rise of the motor car a time lag occurred during which the gains both in membership and earnings were threatened. Many workers, drafted only for the duration [of the war], left the industry altogether … taking their union membership with them … Add to this the tremendous intake … of workers from all areas of Britain and abroad, many of them … with no experience of trade union membership, and as a veteran trade unionist observed: "We started with virtually a new labour force. The drive for organisation had to begin again, though from a much stronger position than before the war".'[28]

The Ford factory, in particular, was still lagging behind Briggs in terms of effective shopfloor organisation. A June 1950 issue of *Ford Worker* ('Official Organ of the Ford Shop Stewards') is crammed with letters detailing the less than satisfactory conditions in the plant: '[Management] are not concerned if we starve on [our] wage, that would be sentimental thinking'; 'Despite negotiations covering one year and five months, no attempt has been made by management to improve our working conditions…No provision is made for exhausting fumes, which at times are unbearable …'

An interesting sidelight is cast on the role of the Communist Party, which at the time dominated workplace union organisation: 'Dear Sir, Why should we work harder? That is the question most of us are asking. If we ask one of the 'Party' men they give us facts and figures which sound all right. But when I get home, and my wife "taps" me for more money, that is also a fact, and lately that fact is staring me in the face quite often …' The same letter questions the effectiveness of the Ford joint negotiating committee, still weaker than its counterpart at Briggs: 'Through our Shop Steward we voice our plea for more money. He in turn puts into … channels for negotiating …. But when it gets into the J.N.C. something goes wrong …' Ironically, in view of the previous comment on 'Party men', the letter concludes, 'there comes a time when people come to the end of their tether, and when they start to demonstrate they are accused of being Communist troublemakers ….'

A Union within the Union …

Being brought to the 'end of their tether' was almost certainly a question of work intensification. By the 1950s, speed-up was becoming a core issue. Between 1948 and 1959 the output of the British car industry increased by 180 per cent with an increase in the workforce of – incredibly – only 18 per cent.[29] Not surprisingly, the key struggles of the decade centred on speed-up; as Beynon records, 'The post-war period produced a struggle over the "effort bargain" within the car plants. A struggle over who does what, for what pace, for what price, and with whom. These were the issues of the 1950s …. The battle for control in the car plants was fought with greatest ferocity in those owned by the Ford Motor Company. In the 1950s at Dagenham and later in its new plants at Halewood…'.[30]

Kevin Halpin echoed this point: 'It was one of the big issues – speed up the line and get more cars out from the workforce. The line speeds would be put up without any consultation. The machinery for that was in management hands – the rheostat which turned the lines off and on ….' He emphasised the continuing distinction between Briggs and Fords in this respect: 'In piecework plants like Austin, Morris, Standards and Rootes in the Midlands and, at Dagenham, Briggs, workers were in a stronger position to bargain on a day-to-day basis with management. But at Fords there was no protection from the rate because the rate was fixed, there was no bargaining in the plant .... The [Ford] plants were the company preserve and the "right" to manage unilaterally had been bequeathed by Henry Ford to his executives.'

Even at the better-organised Briggs, when Kevin Halpin was first taken on in 1949 'It was all battles' over speed-up. The parties in the class war seem to have been better matched, however; as one near-contemporary study of shop stewards commented, 'unions have almost completely lost their influence with shop stewards and strikes have persistently taken place against union advice ... such cases ... include Briggs Motor Bodies in the mid-1950s'.[31]

The stronger confidence and militancy of the Briggs workforce was, of course, like a red rag to the bullish Ford. As one worker-friendly historian writes, 'Ford management, traditionally hostile to union organisation of any kind, had agreed to recognise shop stewards .... Yet the bosses remained hostile to the shop stewards' committee.' By contrast, 'The 10,000 [Briggs] Body Plant workers were represented by 160 shop stewards ... [They] had a well organised committee which elected a convenor as overall coordinator of union organisation on the Dagenham site ...'.[32] Indeed, the Briggs workplace trade union organisation is described by convenor Henry Friedman as 'a rank-and-file movement ... which in the early 1950s was probably the most advanced in the country .... The Briggs Shop Stewards' Committee was highly politicised ... It was based on a workshop democracy which is not generally prevalent even today'.[33]

Direct Democracy

The many methods of ensuring membership involvement, including weekly lunch-hour shop meetings to report back from the Joint Shop Stewards' Committee, meant 'everyone in the plant knew in great detail what the union was doing. This close and intense membership involvement created a loyalty to the Joint Shop Stewards' Committee ... which transcended all other craft and union loyalties ... this rank-and-file movement was the most advanced model of genuine industrial unionism at the plant level in Britain at that time'.[34] And not only 'industrial unionism' but direct democracy – the side of trade union democracy that differs from the more widespread 'representative' variety, where workers elect representatives who act on their behalf without the immediate accountability then seen at Briggs. Within this context shop steward organisation at Briggs' Bodies, particularly in the late '40s and 1950s, represented a particularly strong and effective form of such direct democracy and accountability to the grass roots.

This crucial distinction between formal unionism and the 'grass-roots' variety directly tied to workers' needs and interests was only too well understood by the 'powers-that-be'. Over the next ten years, two separate government inquiries into industrial relations at Briggs and Fords would refer disapprovingly to the 'union within the Union' at Briggs' Body and River plants. It is clear that formal, 'full-time' relations between union officials and management were fundamentally more acceptable to both industry and government than the immediate representation of raw conditions-based struggles on the shop floor.

Yet the fact that this criticism of a lack of formal union 'discipline' was made with reference to Briggs rather than the main Ford works also indicates the greater degree of subordination within the main plant, which may explain River Plant convenor Bernie Passingham's comment that the 1107 branch in its early years was 'a bit soft ... [they] made agreements we never would have made.' Any 'softness' can be explained not by the lower calibre of 1107 activists but by the far more orthodox negotiating arrangements in the main plant, where union leaders on the FNJNC ('the Union') held sway rather than stewards and activists ('the union'). In this sense, through no fault of the committed activists working as stewards and branch organisers in the main plant, a formal structure dominated which, for at least another decade, explicitly excluded steward influence. As the 1957 Cameron Report later commented, 'At the neighbouring Ford plant ... though physically separated from the Briggs plant by less than one mile, relations of management and men have been, at least in recent years, markedly different and more harmonious'.[35]

'They knew the issues backwards ...'

Many of these issues came to a head with a major strike at both Briggs Bodies and Fords in the summer of 1952. The strike, which lasted a month and resulted in 247,000 working days lost, began at Briggs over redundancies and wage restraint, but soon spread to Fords after 600 workers there were laid off. On the afternoon of Tuesday 24 June, almost 9,000 workers at Briggs stopped work and walked out of the factory; this was their third action in less than two weeks, and was the latest move in their protest against management's rejection of their claim for a 9d an hour wage rise – more than double any previous wage increase. Assembly line workers at Fords laid off by the Briggs action also walked out on a series of one-hour token strikes; less than a week later a mass meeting of Briggs and Ford workers at Princess Corner, Dagenham, voted for joint strike action – a historical first. Yet the same meeting highlighted the sharp differences of approach between the union leadership at Briggs and Fords; the FNJNC trade union officials speaking at the meeting clearly disapproved of any unofficial action, with the TGWU District Official telling the meeting that 'so far as his union was concerned ... there could be no negotiations ... until the [Ford] men returned to work'.[36]

Despite the joint action, the strike was conducted by two separate Shop Stewards' Committees which liaised only occasionally; mass meetings were also held separately in the Briggs and Ford plants. This was partly a result of anti-Communist paranoia on the part of the union leaders still dominant at Fords; as Friedman explains, 'At this time, the "Cold War" was at its height and some national trade union leaders, Arthur Deakin [TGWU] for example, saw "Reds" under every Shop Stewards' Committee's bed.' In this heated environment, TGWU Assistant General Secretary Harry Nicholas spoke to a mass meeting of Ford workers in the second week of the strike. Despite addressing them as 'Comrades', he condemned the unofficial action and ordered a return to work: 'He succeeded to such an extent than many Ford workers literally ran down the road towards the Ford works...'.[37] At Briggs, on the other hand, the workers held a mass meeting on the same day and voted overwhelmingly to stay on strike; in fact, they stayed out for another week, only returning after extracting a commitment from the company for a wage rise which, though less than they had asked for, was an acceptable compromise.

Despite the symbolic importance of this joint action, the 1952 strike showed the still significant gap between the man plant and subsidiary in terms of their levels of experience, organisation and strength. As Colin Pond writes, 'The Briggs workers were solidly behind the strike, they had been to dozens of meetings and they knew the issues backwards .... The Fords strikers joined the strike partly ... because some had been laid off by the lack of bodies from Briggs ... [but] one thing the strike brought out was the weakness of the internal structure of trade union organisation under the Ford Main Plant Agreement, and the lack of regular contact between the shop stewards and the ordinary union members'.[38]

'Stopping the Briggs wage drive ...'

After this strike, which ended in mid-July, the Ford NJNC unions reconsidered the terms of the 1946 recognition agreement with a view to placing greater control in the hands of their national executives. Yet, when the membership was asked to vote in the new agreement, ratification 'proved hard to get .... It became apparent to Fords that shop steward resistance was the cause'.[39] The opposition was not shared by management at Briggs, which for some time had been looking wistfully at a negotiating structure similar to the parent company to tackle the constant 'disruption' in their plants. Yet even the union leadership had no illusions about the difficulty of full-time officials suddenly taking control at Briggs when their members had been used to negotiating their own wages and conditions at shop level for years.

But management in both plants was determined to get its way; and the end of the 1952 strike was followed in short order by negotiations for the historic merger between Fords and Briggs Bodies. As Kevin Halpin recalled, 'We went in with Fords in '52 when Briggs Bodies had a dispute and Fords were unable to get the cars – that forced them to combine ... [Fords] didn't want to be beholden to [Briggs Bodies]. So we then cooperated with the Fords plant down the road – [though] we had a different philosophy.' Other commentators agree; according to *Red Notes*, 'Ford's 1953 takeover of Brigg's Bodies was intended to stop the Briggs wage drive spreading to Ford',[40] while convenor Henry Friedman comments that it was 'following the 1952 strike [that] Ford in Detroit decided to take over Briggs'.[41]

Management-prone authors provide more technical explanations; Ford loyalist Burgess-Wise suggests that 'the move was made at least partly to pre-empt [takeover] action by Chrysler, which in the US at least was Briggs' biggest customer'.[42] The low priority put by management on worker militancy as a factor is summed up by Wilkins and Hill: although the takeover of Briggs Bodies 'brought with it a bevy of industrial relations problems ... more importantly, it gave Ford a new and significant degree of integration'.[43]

But whatever the company's motive, in taking on Briggs the Ford Motor Company was taking on trouble. As one car industry analyst notes, 'Ford acquired Briggs Bodies of Dagenham – and thereby took on a fine body-producing plant and also a legacy of strikes and stoppages which was to cause the company abundant heartache and no little loss of production'.[44] It was also to boost workplace trade union organisation in the merged company – and contribute to the eventual domination of TGWU 1107 at Ford.

'They first had to break Fordism ...'

At first, it was clear that ex-Briggs workers were still in the lead of shopfloor struggle at the merged company. Of the more than 600 unofficial strikes that took place in the four next years, culminating in the 1957 'Bellringer' crisis (see below), the vast majority took place in the ex-Briggs Body and River plants. Added to that, in the wake of the 1952 strike Ford was more than usually determined to bring back management control – over the whole of the now merged company. The company was using aggressive anti-union strategies like isolating militants and severe workplace discipline, as well as bringing the Ford shop stewards as much as possible under the control of the full-time officials on the FNJNC.

Yet Ford activists were beginning to look to the Briggs tradition as a more effective way of organising. In April 1953, less than a month after the takeover of Briggs on 30 March, discussion at the Ford Combine Shop Stewards' Committee centred on the workplace union structures still in place at the ex-Briggs plants. The Committee minutes include the comment by one Bro Mitchell that 'to divert from Briggs present agreement would be to compromise, the fact that management had now realised the fact that they had backed the wrong horse proved the advantages the [Briggs] workers had in the present agreement.' To this Bro O'Keefe, the Committee Secretary, 'agreed, but felt it only right to mention that when Ford workers set out for a T.U. agreement they first had to break Fordism ....' He added that 'although the present [Ford] agreement left much to be desired, it was to [Ford workers'] credit they had gone so far ....'

The minutes add that 'the point [O'Keefe] wished to make was that now Fords had gained control of Briggs Plants he felt they would seek to bring the Briggs T.U. agreement into the orbit of the [Fords] JNC.' In the light of these (accurate) comments, Bro Cusick moved the resolution that 'We seek a mandate to press for an overall procedure agreement *on the basis of the present Briggs agreement* to cover all workers in the Ford Combine...'.[45] It was agreed at this meeting to send two delegates from the ex-Briggs plants to Fords meetings and vice-versa.

On 27 October a special meeting of the Ford Shop Stewards' Committee was highly critical of the behaviour of the FNJNC trade union officials in delaying their response to stewards' comments on the current pay claim. Stewards on the Joint Works Committee (JWC)[46] had met the officials as long ago as 28 August and submitted their claim, yet a date for a joint meeting had still not been set. The stewards' comments on the claim had centred on conditions in the Ford plant, where 'production had increased to an all-time high' while (taking inflation into account) pay had fallen far behind its pre-war levels: 'In pre-war days employees' wages averaged £4 a week of 40 hrs ... today employees average £10 a week of 45 hrs ...'. Meanwhile, 'Ford's annual profits ran into £11 million' – quite a sum for the early 1950s. 'Pre war meant a well-paid job but today our wages lagged behind those of the other motor firms,' the stewards noted, providing an early glimpse of the 1960s and '70s parity disputes.

That December, the *Daily Mirror* reported 'Pay rises at Fords set them talking'; increases of 8s and 4d to 9s and 1d a week (about 44-47p) had been accompanied by a cut in hours from 45 to 44 a week. As the *Mirror*'s Industrial Reporter put it, 'This is the reward for breaking all output records. The co-operation and effort of all employees during the past year is acknowledged by the firm.' Yet the ex-Briggs stewards whose Minutes Book contained this cutting have made their own connection between 'productivity' and its less positive side; a red arrow is drawn from an article in the next column featuring a 16-year-old injured in a shipyard accident to the phrase 'This [the Ford pay rise] is the reward for breaking all output records'.[47] Productivity, the hasty scrawl is telling us, is not always the positive factor it is made out to be.

Meanwhile, Briggs workers continued to defy Ford management in the wake of the merger. Kevin Halpin reports a typical incident 'in about '55 … when they sold the afternoon tea break - and we decided on the lines that we were going to stop. And they had to admit that they were wrong eventually and reinstate the tea-break. If you're working on the line continuously, and I do mean continuously, not to have a tea break would be a disaster … Yeah, we fought that and won.' This – typical - action was both incisive and justified. As Butt points out in his overview of the car industry, 'Post-war experience … not only confirmed the pre-war lesson of the need for local initiative; it … established the role of the shop floor leader, in this industry at least, *as the only feasible arrangement*'.[48]

'Strikers Pouring Out Like Water …'

Yet management at Fords was equally determined to knock such 'local initiative' on the head, and in the wake of the Ford-Briggs merger they worked hard, along with the national trade union officials, to bring procedure agreements and workplace union structures at Briggs into line with the parent company. In 1955, conflict blew up over a proposed new Procedure Agreement which still refused to recognise the shop stewards' committees at either Briggs or Fords, although it finally allowed shop stewards to play a role in defending their members during the grievance process. As one writer spells out the problem, 'In 1955, shop stewards were to be given formal recognition – at last – but only within prescribed limits …. The Dagenham Joint Shop Stewards Committee was denied negotiating rights, and trade union leaders still controlled wage negotiations at Fords'.[49] In fact, as Colin Pond notes, 'The 1955 Procedure Agreement was designed to formalise the understandings the Ford Motor Company had developed with the national leadership of the trade unions on the need of Ford management to tame the "unruly" shop floor organisation'.[50]

Unruly it was – particularly in the ex-Briggs plants. Between early 1954 and summer 1955 there were almost 300 stoppages of work at Briggs, almost all seeing workers walk out without informing management or abiding by 'procedure' of any kind. As one manager recalled the sight of a Briggs walkout, 'The strikers poured out of the building like water – it was terrifying in its scale'.[51] According to Ford loyalist Burgess-Wise, one proposed sports car design, the '105E sports project', incorporated what its designer described 'the first lift-off "Targa top" ', inspired by the uncertain labour relations in the Briggs River Plant: ' "Ford was constantly being held up by industrial action in the trim shop," he recalled, "so instead of using a sewn hood, I incorporated a lift-off roof panel. For the same reason I also used slush-moulded slabs for the seat instead of the sewn seats"'.[52] The soon-to-be-famous sewing machinists (see next chapter) had clearly already used their industrial muscle more than once.

The 1955 Procedure Agreement was therefore tilted as much as possible towards involvement of the full-time union bureaucracy, with whom the company had developed an 'understanding' on the need to avoid strike action and other unrest, rather than that of shopfloor activists. The revised agreement, finally signed on 23 August 1955, centralised negotiations in the managerial offices away from the plants and thus consciously widened still further the gap between union leadership and shop floor organisation, despite the fact that it formally recognised shop stewards and specified both their formal duties and their role in the procedural structure.

But although the new agreement produced some of the hoped-for 'peace' at the main Ford plant, at Briggs 237 stoppages took place in the next 18 months. Overall, 'between February 1954 and March 1957 there were about 600 "incidents" at the Body Plant'.[53] These strikes and walkouts were rooted in serious problems - working conditions, pay and management policy. Yet the response of Fords, as always, was repression and formalisation rather than any attempt to explore the basis of workers' actions and organisation.

In March 1956, Ford warned the FNJNC unions that 'it would be forced to take drastic action' over the continuing militancy; when another strike took place less than two months later on 17 May, with 26 paint-sprayers walking off the job in protest at fumes and bad ventilation, the company sacked all 26, while telling them it might be prepared to re-employ them if they agreed to observe procedure in future. Only days later, workers in the Chassis Department walked out; in response the company posted a notice warning all employees that 'deliberate and flagrant' breaches of the procedure agreement would lead to disciplinary action.

Yet in July that year ex-Briggs workers struck again when the company announced a massive 2,400 redundancies at the Body Plant as a result of a strike at the British Motor Corporation. Their resistance meant that, miraculously, no discharges were 'necessary'; in fact, negotiations with union officials led to a pledge by the company to consult the FNJNC whenever redundancies might be in the air. In spite of this apparent concession, stoppages continued throughout August, prompting the company to meet union officials on 4 September and repeat yet again its determination to 'obtain discipline'.

Although the company agreed the following week to put off the threat of redundancy until the New Year, workers were still on a four-day week, and the company was now also demanding mobility of labour between day and night shift workers and indeed between the Body and Chassis plants. Shop stewards were becoming increasingly concerned that the shared offensive against Fords and ex-Briggs workers was a step nearer to full standardisation between the two companies. As well as its other unwelcome aspects, this would mean replacing plant bargaining and piecework pay at Briggs with the national bargaining and time rates imposed at Fords.

Another major sticking-point over standardisation was night work. Many Briggs workers refused to do night shifts, yet they had now received letters from the company to sign to indicate their willingness to do so. Adding insult to injury, management had posted notices in the factory informing workers that 'The Trade Unions have [agreed] that the question of whether an employee signs for day or night work, as required, is a matter to be decided solely between the company and the individual employee'. Ford management claimed that 5000 of the 6,500 letters sent out had been signed and returned by workers and that nearly 100 per cent had accepted the 'day or night, work anywhere' terms.

For different reasons, stewards and activists themselves were unhappy during this period with their own workplace union structures, still largely separated between the ex-Briggs and Ford plants at Dagenham. As stewards worked to bring them together into a Fords Joint Shop Stewards' Committee, the 1107 branch played a leading role. Kevin Halpin recalled that 'The leading people in 1107… were quite progressive – and we stopped the idiocy of going through separate unions etc and went for a joint organisation which worked throughout Fords'. The organisation was extended outward to the various other Ford plants cropping up around the country – 'There was a Joint Shop Stewards' Committee and a National JSSC which we got together as a combine based on people being from JSSCs without any position of which union they were in…The NJSSC began about '56.'

The activists' drive to coordinate workplace organisation went further. According to one analysis of the motor industry in this period, 'During the mid-1950s an "unofficial" attempt was made to link up the various federal committees in the car firms through a forum for the interchange of views and information at industry level. A body called the "Big Six" (so called because it consisted of representatives from stewards' committees in BMC, Standard, Ford, Vauxhall, Rootes and Rover) arranged to meet quarterly, and in fact organised three large conferences – at Birmingham, Coventry and Oxford. These conferences were substantial ... affairs, arranged by a special steering committee and attended by around three hundred shop stewards apiece'.[54]

'Just Like That ...'

And yet, once again, Ford's particular aggression ended such promising developments – for the time being, at least. It was with the infamous 'Bellringer' dispute of 1957 that all these issues – shopfloor democracy, workplace solidarity, bureaucratic incompetence and, yet again, Ford's single-minded anti-unionism - came to a head. The threatened sacking of a steward at an ex-Briggs Bodies plant was to lead to a government inquiry, the final full integration of Briggs with Fords, and – for the time being – success for the company's mission to destroy the 'union within the Union'.

Not for the first time, this workplace union crisis was triggered by external events - in this case, the Suez crisis of late 1956. As Kevin Halpin recalled, 'At the time of Suez there was a fuel shortage, a petrol crisis, and that stopped the cars selling...[So] they sacked half the factory on the simple basis of "all those on the left hand side come forward from each track and you're sacked – those on the right carry on working." Just like that.'

The company identified 1,729 Briggs workers to be 'discharged' along with all engineering craftsmen over 65 and a small number of labourers. On top of this, as the *Dagenham Post* reported on 28 November, 'At the Ford main plant, 20,000 workers were put on short time, and at Briggs main and River plants 9,000 out of the 12,000 workers on a four-day week. Yet at a meeting in London between national union officials and Ford management on December 5th, it was agreed to "cooperate" and thus "mitigate the effects of the redundancies".'

After a further FNJNC meeting the following week, the company agreed to put off the threat of redundancy until the New Year – yet the four-day week continued, and the company was now also demanding mobility of labour, not only between day and night shift workers but also between the ex-Briggs and main Ford plants. Although the Briggs Shop Stewards'

Committee put a set of counter-proposals at a joint meeting, these were – inevitably - turned down; stewards became increasingly concerned that the joint offensive against Fords and Briggs workers was a step nearer to Ford's objective of standardising employment and wage agreements between the two companies.

On 17 December, Fords, Briggs and Kelsey Hayes stewards met district union officials and management; it was finally agreed that because of the 'trading difficulties' caused by the Suez crisis, three-day working and an 'alternative shift basis' would be introduced from 31 December 1956. Yet even these measures were not seen as sufficient to deal with the crisis, and any final decision was put off until a further meeting on 4 January 1957. It seemed as if workers' jobs were at least safe until the New Year; yet at the same time stewards estimated that about 3,000 jobs could be lost at Briggs and some, though not as many, at the main Ford plant.[55]

In fact dismissal notices were issued on Tuesday 8 January 1957 to 1,280 workers, while 250 over 65 were 'retired', 200 'absorbed in Fords' and 'of the rest approximately 200 were women'.[56] The announcement finally saw action; 1000 workers (gender unspecified) came out on strike, and 227 men in the Glass, Trim and Upholstery Department refused to work and were sent home, stopping the paint and metal lines and resulting in a further 950 men laid off. As the local paper reported, 'When the night shift started the same thing happened; 650 men refused to work [and] these together with 1200 men made idle were sent home. For a few days the place was in turmoil'.[57]

Yet despite all the resistance, when union officials met the company again two days later they were informed that more redundancies would be announced in addition to the 350 already sacked. At the same time, because the three-day week was 'uneconomic', the works would return to four-day working from the 21 January. The following week a further 1,420 employees were sacked.[58] And it was then that the 'Bellringer' crisis broke.

'Once you are out of the Gate ...'

This saga, culminating in a government inquiry and the victimisation of a respected activist, revolved around the actions of a steward from a comparatively privileged section of the workforce – skilled engineering workers and members of the AEU. Yet, like all such crises, it had a far-reaching effect on union organisation and activist confidence right across Fords.

The story began when two senior stewards – Henry Friedman and a Mr Moore, the then convenor of the River Plant - invited AEU steward Johnny

McLoughlin to come with them to a meeting of the FNJNC on 24 January 1957, which would clearly have been discussing the layoffs. In fact, Moore and Friedman were refused permission to attend the meeting, and when they nevertheless took time off to do so were suspended for three days.

This left only McLoughlin to deal with the devastating threats posed by the crisis and the company. The Jigs and Fixtures department he represented had a policy that if any worker was dismissed or suspended all other workers were to be immediately summoned to a shop meeting by means of ringing a handbell. Already 'devastated' by the suspension of his fellow stewards, McLoughlin 'went straight to where for many years a handbell had been kept by the workmen to stimulate interest in their meetings .... Taking the bell, he went to the main aisle ... and, in defiance of his foreman ... proceeded to ring it'. At this, his 200 fellow-workers stopped work and gathered for a meeting, but the sound of the bell had galvanised McLoughlin's foreman, Ted Martin. 'Absolutely raving', Martin forbade the meeting. Although McLoughlin tried to pacify him – 'Leave it alone, Ted, give yourself a rest'[59] – the foreman returned with his senior and McLoughlin was immediately suspended. On the 28 January the steward was discharged by Briggs management, leaving him to pass into Ford history with the lasting label of 'the Bellringer'.

In response, workers at the Briggs Body and River Plants struck the following Monday, the twenty-eighth; the walk-out was followed by a mass meeting which decided on strike action. The (unofficial) action continued until the thirtieth, when a further mass meeting was held to decide on action over McLoughlin (Friedman and Moore were, ironically, reinstated at this point). Engineering workers, balloted on whether to take official strike action if the company refused to reinstate McLoughlin within 48 hours, voted 1,118 to 429 in favour.[60] Meanwhile, predictably, the company was appealing to the FNJNC trade union side to deal with the dispute in accordance with official procedure. The following day, following an appeal from AEU officials, the company agreed to consider McLoughlin suspended (rather than sacked) pending the final outcome of negotiations under the procedure agreement.

Briggs stewards were unimpressed by this official union intervention; at a mass meeting early the following week they gave their officials 48 hours to gain McLoughlin's reinstatement, an ultimatum which was – predictably - ignored. It was not until a week later, by which time McLoughlin had been suspended for almost three weeks, that the decision was made to hold a ballot for strike action. This was successful, with a clear majority (1,118 to 429) in favour; the AEU now called an official strike, as it was obliged to.

But it was at this point that Parliament intervened (indicating the growing political importance of industrial action during this period). Dagenham Labour MP John Parker called on the Conservative government to set up a Court of Inquiry into the dispute; his proposal was accepted by the Minister of Labour and more importantly by the union, which called off its own strike. An additional sweetener was provided by Ford management concessions including a return to full-time working and the reinstatement of 'most of' the 1,750 Briggs workers who had been made redundant.[61]

The main purpose of the forthcoming Inquiry, chaired by one Lord Cameron,[62] was seen from the start in terms of investigating 'industrial relations' at Fords and particularly Briggs, rather than reinstating McLoughlin – who indeed never got his job back. As labour historian Allen Hutt sums up the debacle, 'Of victimisation disputes in the 1950s the most celebrated was the 1957 strike at Briggs Bodies ... in defence of steward John McLoughlin; the day was only lost because the A.E.U. executive accepted a Court of Inquiry'.[63]

An Attitude of Mind ...

In fact the only benefit that can be seen of this exercise is the light it sheds on the thinking of the overlords of law and government and their concerted refusal to see anything from the point of view of exploited and oppressed workers. Key points from the Cameron Report include, for example, that official procedure 'was ignored because an attitude of mind had grown up which prompted the workers to believe that the only way to get results was to use the method of the unofficial stoppage'. The fact that this 'attitude' was firmly rooted in everyday reality was, of course, ignored. Instead, the Report falls back on the much-used term 'anarchic' to justify its condemnation of the AEU's 'tolerance' of unofficial action. Explaining his refusal to consider McLoughlin's reinstatement, Cameron comments that such a 'concession' to the union 'could be interpreted as a gesture of appeasement of the extreme elements in the shop stewards' organisation'.[64]

Class warfare *par excellence* resounds throughout Cameron's judgement. Even his twenty-first-century 'namesake' would find it hard to outdo the ferocity of the noble lord's condemnation of a conscientious, down to earth shop steward who was simply standing up for his members and fellow-activists. The sinister issue of 'Communist Influence at Briggs' was seen as central; fingering Berridge, the decidedly moderate AEU Divisional Organiser who had accepted an Inquiry instead of a strike, as 'a member of the Communist Party from its foundation', Cameron comments 'I was left far from clear that Mr McLoughlin ... is not a Communist also.' Indeed, he was. And yet, and yet ...'all the evidence in this case establishes that the major responsibility for the dispeace out of which so many unofficial stoppages and finally the present dispute arose lies within the ranks of the workers whose immediate representatives are the shop stewards'.[65] Cameron could not more clearly have expressed the grass-roots basis of the dispute.

The victimised steward himself, when hauled up before the inquiry, based his action on the general atmosphere of 'wind-up' in the factory after the recent mass sackings; his own awareness of the urgent need for action was based on the knowledge that 'once you are out of the gate you have had it'. The general atmosphere of intimidation and insecurity in the embattled factory is further illustrated by the various workplace incidents cited by Cameron as examples of 'unreasonable' behaviour, most of which were a rational response to extreme ill-treatment and, in many cases, threats to workers' safety. In the Press Shop, for example, 'numerous protests had been from 1953 onwards about panels dropping over the aisleways from the conveyer hooks overhead due to overloading'. Labelling this reaction as 'extreme' and 'unreasonable' can only be defined as a sterling example of 'extremism' in its own right. Yet, with the privilege of state power, Cameron was able to seal the fate of one worker – McLoughlin – whose painfully accurate assessment that 'once you are out of the gate you have had it' had spurred him to organise immediate solidarity on behalf of two threatened fellow-activists.

According to one commentator, the impact of McLoughlin's dismissal 'seemed to produce a calmer atmosphere at Dagenham for a time ... but the situation soon deteriorated again. In 1958, Ford recorded 25 stoppages; in 1959, forty-four; in 1960, seventy-nine, [with] in the second quarter ... only three days free from a stoppage of one sort or another'.[66] Yet in 1958, undeterred by any threat of increased militancy, Fords introduced a Standardisation Agreement to bring Briggs' conditions of employment fully into line with those of the Ford main plants at Dagenham. One central issue here was the crucial difference in payment system between the two companies – until then, Briggs workers had been paid on piecework rather than time rate. Briggs' incorporation into the Ford Motor Company was followed by a long and finally successful offensive to bring Brigg's conditions into line with those of Ford in what was called a 'harmonisation' campaign.

The 1958 agreement also 'gave management power to operate whatever internal mobility they thought necessary'[67] – a serious blow to workers moved from job to job at the will of management. As sympathetic writer John Mathews puts it, 'Management was free to operate job transfers at will. The tight political organisation of the line was broken up ....' But perhaps most importantly – and damagingly – 'from now on all negotiating rights would be vested in the NJNC – a committee exclusively composed of Company and full-time Trade Union Officials ... "Service conditions" as well as wages, were now to be negotiated by union officials'.[68] It was a brutal blow against the 'rank-and-file movement' cited by Henry Friedman as 'probably the most advanced in the country' in its adherence to workplace union democracy.

Pulling the Plug on Fords?

Yet shopfloor conflict continued. Eddie Prevost, who started work at Dagenham 'just after Johnny McLoughlin rang the bell' recalled that 'while I was there there were several strikes - the one I remember most vividly was where a bloke was encouraged by the chargehand to not pay his union [subs] and that led to a strike. It was rumoured that ETU [Electrical Trade Union] members had threatened Ford that they'd pull the plug on Fords - shut the plant for six months if they didn't [discipline] the foreman – so in the end Fords caved in. We marched back into the plant as an organised body and everyone was chanting – the atmosphere was so electric, it felt like a lynching ... I think the film *The Angry Silence* was based on that strike.[69]

'So by the late '50s the union was very strong, and they'd ostracise anyone who wouldn't join the union. Someone from the union used to time the line every day because the company was always trying to speed the line up – and the union would come round and say How many did he say do an hour? and you'd say, and he'd say No that's a nonsense, he's put the rate up again ....'

'The Answer Was Issues'

In 1959 a major new plant – Paint, Trim and Assembly ('the PTA') was opened at Dagenham. This was part of a £75m plant redevelopment project which increased floor space at the site by 50 per cent and effectively doubled production. Fords moved 2,500 workers from the (ex-Briggs) Body Plant into the PTA, in part to 'press home the point that Briggs was now a part of Ford's'. Yet if this action was intended to cure the Briggs malaise it clearly failed; by the following year 'the joint shop stewards' committee at Dagenham ... was the most powerful unofficial body in the country'.[70]

Eddie Prevost's recollections provide some reasons for the export of the 'Briggs malaise' to the new plant: 'When they opened up the PTA we'd occasionally go over there and be on rub down, something like that – that was absolutely boring, smoothing down the paint, working away in the middle of the bloody night smoothing down – it was the most depressing thing .... It was such a boring job being on the line, soul destroying really.

People occasionally stopped the line, put a nail in it and then the chain would break and you'd have to get an engineer over to fix it - just for your own sanity.'

But compensations could be found through contact with this mixed and experienced workforce: 'As a young person you were picking up all sorts of information you hadn't known about previously. A toolmaker called Fred used to run classes on Marxist economics in the dinner time – which was great, really – The excitement of being a young bloke in a plant listening to Marxist economics being explained and marvelling at how suddenly I've found a philosophy that can explain all this ....'

More, the unceasing efforts by management in the merged Ford plant to keep down militancy were largely ineffectual in the late'50s: 'That was a good period for the labour movement – it was really beginning to acquire a certain amount of power .... Fords wouldn't negotiate with the shop stewards ... So in those days you would have unofficial strikes – most of the strikes were unofficial – it was only later that many of them were made official. The stewards would hold shop floor meetings within the plant – on the job...The management were always seeking to undermine the union – you had a closed shop there and they were trying to undermine it all the time ... but they weren't successful.'

As a semi-skilled worker on the line, Eddie would almost certainly have been a member of TGWU 1107. For Kevin Halpin, an AEU activist but by now a strong supporter of 1107, the opening of the PTA 'accelerated recruitment and organising opportunities for the branch. We initiated for the first time a shorter week with less pay...on the basis that it would keep the workforce together. And that put the workforce in quite a strong position – because previously in the car industry, after the Motor Show in September, the management would just sack all those they didn't need – they casualised the industry. We stopped that.'

As he records in his later memoirs, 'At first management wanted to hand-pick who went over [from Briggs' to the PTA] but after some skirmishing it was agreed that every worker would be transferred if their job was transferred. The remaining 2,000 were made up from new recruits. They were mostly in their early twenties, having just finished National Service. Their military training hadn't, as management hoped, made them more obedient. On the contrary ...'.[71]

Kevin himself became convenor of the massive new plant 'in about 1959, 1960', and was committed to rebuilding shopfloor strength. The failure to reinstate the Bellringer 'was a setback' but in the wake of this disaster 'We picked it up again. It knocked the militancy back for a bit – we had to build it up again.' How? The answer was 'Issues …. The company helped you because they would lead the attack on working conditions. You'd only got to sit tight and you were away again.'

In fact, the 1958 standardisation of all its Dagenham plants, so sought after by Fords, had one 'unexpected effect …. Over a quarter of the Body plant workers (2,500) were shifted into the new Paint Trim and Assembly plant in 1959. They took with them their traditions of autonomy, and soon the Assembly plant became the focus of militancy at Dagenham'.[72] Another history agrees, arguing that standardisation 'produced the most sustained shop-floor challenge to Ford's right to manage, in the form of a running battle of constant short stoppages over workloads'.[73] The story of that resurgent militancy – increasingly involving TGWU 1107 – is told in the next chapter.

NOTES

1 Colin Pond, 'The Growth of White-Collar Unions at Ford Motor Company', Middlesex Polytechnic, BA Business Studies Final Year Project, Manpower Studies, 1982-3, p. 27.
2 *Dagenham Post* 'The Ford strike: How the trouble began', 14 March 1946, p. 5.
3 Bob Lovell, 'Fords – the Victory for Union Recognition', *Morning Star*, 18 November 1968, p. 2.
4 'Strike Paralyses Fords', *Dagenham Post* 13 March 1946, p. 1.
5 *Daily Worker* 13 March 1946, p. 4.
6 Lovell, *Morning Star*, 18 November 1968, p. 2.
7 Sheila Cohen, 'The Red Mole: Workers' Councils as a means of revolutionary transformation' in Immanual Ness and Dario Azzelini (eds) *Ours to Master and to Own: Workers' Control from the Commune to the Present*, Chicago: Haymarket, 2011.
8 Lovell, *Morning Star*, 18 November 1968, p. 2.
9 'Ford Men go back – no delays', *Daily Worker* 18 March 1946, p. 1.
10 Lovell *Morning Star*, 18 November 1968, p. 2.
11 Colin Pond, 'The Growth of Trade Unions at Fords', Thesis for Diploma in Industrial Relations and Trade Union Studies, Middlesex Polytechnic, 1978, p. 24.
12 Pond, 'Growth of …', p. 24.
13 This could, of course, have worked to the advantage of shopfloor democracy.
14 Pond 'Growth of…', p. 29.
15 As shown below, by 1962 Briggs had been 'absorbed' into the main Ford company at Dagenham.
16 Henry Friedman and Sander Meredeen, *The Dynamics of Industrial Conflict: Lessons from Ford*, London: Croom Helm, 1980, p. 127.
17 Friedman and Meredeen *Dynamics*, p. 56.
18 Friedman and Meredeen *Dynamics*, p. 57.

19 J.F.B. Goodman and T.G. Whittingham, *Shop Stewards*, London: Pan, 1969, p. 134.
20 *Dagenham Post* 20 March 1947.
21 Friedman and Meredeen, *Dynamics*, p. 57.
22 *Red Notes* 'Workers' Struggles and the Development of Ford in Britain', 1976, p. 23.
23 Huw Beynon, *Working For Ford*, London: Penguin,1973, p. 48.
24 Quoted in David Kynaston, *Austerity Britain 1945-51*, London: Bloomsbury, 2007, pp. 407-8.
25 Kynaston *Austerity*, p. 488.
26 At this point the 'main plant' was usually referred to as the Chassis Plant, but became known as the Engine Plant after the Paint, Trim and Assembly plant was built in 1959.
27 Graham Turner, *The Car Makers*, Harmondsworth: Penguin, 1964, p. 35.
28 Dennis Butt, 'Men and Motors', *New Left Review* No. 3, May-June 1960, p. 11.
29 Pond, 'Growth of…', p. 32.
30 Beynon *Working*, pp. 46-7
31 Goodman and Whittingham, *Stewards*, pp. 203-4.
32 Mike Freeman, *Taking Control*, London: Junius, 1984, p. 68.
33 Friedman and Meredeen *Dynamics*, p. 58.
34 Friedman and Meredeen *Dynamics*, p. 58.
35 Cameron (Lord) *Report of a Court of inquiry* Cmnd 131, HMSO 1957, p. 21.
36 Pond 'Growth Of…' p. 29.
37 Friedman and Meredeen *Dynamics*, p. 57.
38 Pond 'Growth Of…', p. 29.
39 Pond 'Growth Of', p. 31.
40 *Red Notes* 'Workers' Struggles' 1976, p. 23.
41 Friedman and Meredeen *Dynamics*, p. 57.
42 David Burgess-Wise, *Ford at Dagenham: The Rise and Fall of Detroit in Europe*, Derby: Breedon Books 2007, pp. 127, 131-2.
43 Mira Wilkins and Frank Ernest Hill, *American Business Abroad: Ford on Six Continents*, New York: Cambridge University Press, 2011, p. 387.
44 Turner, *Car Makers*, p. 34.
45 Language as in original minutes kindly supplied by John Davies, TGWU Ford Engine Plant deputy convenor 1976-82 and convenor 1982-99.
46 The Joint Shop Stewards' Committee (JSSC), made up of all stewards in a plant, elects a second tier of trade union representation in the plant, the Joint Works Committee, and also the convenor.
47 Len Jackson, 'Pay Rises at Fords set them talking', and 'His Smile wins Peter Job for Life', *Daily Mirror* 8 December 1953, p. 16.
48 Butt *Men and Motors*, p. 11, italics in original.
49 John Mathews, *Ford Strike – The Workers' Story*, Panther1972, p. 44.
50 Colin Pond, 'The Growth of White-Collar Unions at Ford Motor Company', Middlesex Polytechnic, BA Business Studies Final Year Project, Manpower Studies, 1982-3, p. 24.
51 Burgess-Wise, *Ford at Dagenham*, p. 134.

52 Burgess-Wise, *Ford at Dagenham*, p. 142.
53 Mathews, *Ford Strike*, p. 44.
54 H.A. Turner, Garfield Clack and Geoffrey Roberts, *Labour Relations in the Motor Industry*, Allen and Unwin 1967, p. 220.
55 Pond 'Growth Of ...', p. 36.
56 Pond 'Growth Of ...', p. 37; the comment suggests that their loss of jobs was not of much concern to other workers.
57 *Dagenham Post*, 9 January 1957, p. 2.
58 *Dagenham Post* 16-23 January 1957, p. 1.
59 Description taken from the Cameron Report – see below.
60 Pond 'Growth Of ...', p. 38.
61 Pond 'Growth Of ...', p. 38.
62 As far as is known, no relative.
63 Allen Hutt, *British Trade Unionism, A Short History 1800-1961*, Lawrence and Wishart 1962, p. 202.
64 Cameron *Report*, HMSO 1957, p. 21.
65 Cameron *Report* pp. 17-19, 22.
66 Turner, *Car Makers*, p. 80.
67 *Red Notes* 'Workers' Struggles', p. 25.
68 Mathews, *Ford Strike*, p. 44.
69 In fact this film seriously misrepresents the Bellringer dispute, presenting it as sinister mass ostracism of a 'scab'.
70 Beynon, *Working For Ford*, p. 50.
71 Kevin Halpin, *Memoirs of a Militant* Glasgow: Praxis Press 2012, p. 55.
72 Mathews, *Ford Strike*, p. 44.
73 Steven Tolliday and Jonathan Zeitlin, *Industrial Relations in the Age of Fordism*, Oxford: Berg Publishers, 1992, p. 104.

Chapter Three

THE SIXTIES: FROM DEFEAT TO VICTORY – AND THE 'UPSURGE'

By the early 1960s workers at the main Ford plant were catching up with ex-Briggs Bodies activists in terms of successful shopfloor organisation. Shop stewards in both plants had slowly rebuilt union organisation over the years since the 1957 'Bellringer' disaster, eventually combining after the merger between Briggs and Fords into the Fords Joint Shop Stewards' Committee. By 1960 the FJSSC was selling 50,000 copies a week of its bulletin, *Voice of Ford Workers*, and the organisation itself could be described as 'the most powerful unofficial body in the country'.[1]

The rise in shopfloor strength could be charted by the number of – mostly unofficial – stoppages.[2] In 1960, there were seventy-nine walkouts at Dagenham, with 100,000 'man-hours' lost; by 1961 the number had risen to 184,000, with 'only three days free from a stoppage of one sort or another'.[3] That year almost saw the first-ever official strike across the whole company – a threat only averted by last-minute concessions – while in 1962, before the crisis in October (described below), 415,000 working hours were lost at Dagenham.[4] And the newly-built Paint, Trim and Assembly plant – almost totally organised by TGWU 1107 – was at the centre of these conflicts. In 1960, an average of 78 'man-hours' per worker were lost through strikes and overtime bans in the newly-built plant – compared to 15 in the rest of Dagenham.

As Ford convenor Friedman writes: 'The Paint, Trim and Assembly Plant became operational in 1959 and from then on the intensity of conflict increased. It was a battle about control of the assembly line ... the PTA Shop Stewards' Committee operated an "anti-speed-up" plant policy which meant resistance to new lay-outs and the implementation of stop-watch timings .... The intensity of conflict which this issue generated in 1962 can be gauged from the following figures: Output lost through strikes in company plants outside Dagenham was a half-hour per man; at Dagenham (excluding the PTA), 15 hours per man; in the PTA plant 78 hours per man'.[5]

The PTA was in one sense bound to be the centre of conflict, given the massive pressures on assembly-line workers in particular. Of 32 disputes between late May and mid July 1962, 23 were sparked by speed-up, overtime and transfers of labour, with only nine on wages questions.[6] As one pamphlet put it at the time, 'Whether it is on wages, speed of work, tea breaks or conditions in general – daily, hourly, every minute, contests of strength take place between the Ford Motor Co. and the organised workers'.[7]

The much-intensified work pressure came from pressure on management in its turn, much of it from across the Atlantic. In 1960, Ford US bought a controlling portion of shares in the 'British' company, and the effects were immediately obvious: 'The pace of production increased, and the old factory "code" was systematically destroyed. The new American administration refused to honour old agreements, and constantly broke the established pattern of procedure.' The changes affected the production process at a basic level: 'Detroit was demanding more and more cars, and the production lines had to be speeded up to supply them. Disputes became more and more frequent – anyone who objected to the increased workload was told to get out.' Yet full-time union officials put up no defence: 'The FNJNC merely rubber-stamped each new provocation from management'.[8]

'The 1107 would be there ...'

TGWU 1/1107 was a major player in these early conflicts. Veteran 1107-er John Davies, who became deputy convenor of the Engine Plant in the 1960s, recalls that

> In the Engine Plant the majority union was the TGWU, followed by the AUEW, then the EEPTU and GMB[9]...1107 was the biggest branch in Fords Dagenham .... Whenever we talked to new workers in the factory they joined the union straight away and ... over 80% of them joined the T&G.
>
> In those days 1107 was starting very much as a new branch – [but] that branch played an active role in all the disputes at Fords because we had the most members. If there was a dispute in Fords the 1107 would be there, with a majority of shop stewards .... We had 69 shop stewards in the Engine Plant and out of that ... 58 or 55 would be 1107. The branch was a very active branch, all T&G workers, from the Engine Plant, truck fleet, traffic assembly, the fire brigade which was on the estate, the security people, they all belonged to 1107.

Another major 1107 activist, Ted Amos, began work at the Ford Engine Plant in 1960. He describes the period as 'a hectic time all the time – meetings, strikes…There was a pretty strong base for the union there. I joined the T&G after a couple of weeks – 1107.' Yet Amos recalls problems with Davies and some of his supporters in the plant: 'We were at war with the [Engine Plant shop stewards'] Joint Works Committee and the convenor, Johnny Davies – for me as steward he was a bigger enemy than management. Every time he could go against us, knock us down over time study etc, he would. We had closed doors in our area – then management got in and opened the doors, backed by Davies. They had a field day'.[10]

As this suggests, conflicts were already emerging inside the branch. Frankie Bland, who started work in the Engine Plant in 1959 and became a strong 1107 activist, reports that 'There was always a difference of vision certainly between the Engine Plant [1107] and [PTA-based] 1107 …. They divided into 1107A and 1107B.' As Ted Amos confirmed, 'There were so many differences between the Assembly Plant and the Engine Plant – they had more stoppages up the top of the road [the PTA] than they did down the Engine Plant. In Davies' area they had some problems, but Johnny Davies' philosophy was "[Workers] don't come here to keep going out and losing money, they come here for work, so we'll try and find ways to sort it out" .'

In fact Davies' 'moderate' approach was an exception to the rule at Dagenham, where day-to-day worker resistance continued, driven by aggressive management practices. One typical example of direct action was seen in October 1961, after union leaders negotiated a 40-hour week. Though welcome, the shorter hours were granted on the basis of cutting out the afternoon tea-break; in protest, workers simply continued to take the old tea-break, creating organised chaos for ten minutes every afternoon as cars went down the line uncompleted. Not surprisingly, the action was highly effective. In March 1962, 'although management vainly tried to implement the agreement … they eventually conceded defeat'[11] after workers had obstinately sustained the action for five months.

As Graham Turner shows in his 1964 book *The Car Makers*, the automated line speed at Fords caused endless conflicts in the plant: ' "The speed is set before the hooter blows," said one worker bitterly. "It would start if no men reported for duty that day." It was this sort of atmosphere which … caused men to down tools on the smallest pretext…'.[12]

The comment also makes clear that shop steward and workplace organisation at Dagenham was now once again posing a fundamental threat to management's 'right to manage'. One activist summed up the 'dual power'-style character of workplace unionism at the time, particularly in the PTA: 'The stewards ran the Assembly Plant at Dagenham. Instead of the stewards making appointments to see the supervisors, the supervisors had to come to the stewards. The supervisors used to hand over their production schedules, and the stewards would go over them, cross them out, and hand them back .... The stewards had so much control at that time that they *had* to be broken'.[13]

Yet full-time union officials were still at odds with the shop stewards and their members. In July 1962, 179 garage workers walked out after forty-five were suddenly taken off the line, resulting in massively increased work speeds. Management refused to negotiate, and after a week the trade union officials persuaded the workers to return 'to allow negotiations to continue'. The workers lost their case, and in response to this 'very real defeat ... speed-up was increased throughout the plant'.[14]

An October Revolution?

This episode was an ominous sign of management's increasing tendency to play dirty in the battle with shopfloor militancy. Many writers argue that the crippling blow to workplace organisation sparked by the October 1962 strike and subsequent sacking of 'the 17' was a planned management intervention; one industry analysis even compared it (on a rather different class basis) to the October 1917 revolution in Russia: 'The "endemic conflict" situation in certain Ford plants ... ended only with the "October Revolution" at Dagenham in 1962'.[15]

This drama began in September 1962, when Dagenham management announced that they would refuse to negotiate that year's wage claim unless steps were taken to improve the workings of the agreed management-union Procedure for resolving disputes.[16] Ford's trade union officials seemed to feel the same way; during negotiations over the 1962-3 wage claim, FNJNC union Chair W.B. Beard[17] reported that management 'were not prepared to consider any wage improvement until they had a firm assurance that ... unofficial walkouts were discontinued and the procedure observed .... [T]here had been no attempt on the part of a relatively small number of individuals to operate the agreement at all. Indeed, they just walked out on the job and as a result not only was production stopped, but many were laid off .... It was clear that we as a NJNC could not justify [these] walkouts and it was equally clear that unless the firm received assurances that this body had some control of their members, no progress was possible.'

Presumably to gain such 'control', the trade union leaders signed an agreement on 12 October 1962 which gave Ford management carte blanche to attack militant workers and their stewards with clauses like 'The Trade

Unions recognise the right of the Company to exercise measures against employees who fail to comply with the conditions of their employment by taking unconstitutional action'. And sure enough, five days later, the Chair of the PTA Shop Stewards' Committee, Bill Francis, was sacked after holding a so-called 'unconstitutional' shopfloor meeting – even though such lunch-hour meetings 'had been going on at Fords for years'.[18] In response, a massive strike exploded at the PTA.

Support for Francis was immediate and overwhelming, with workers walking out spontaneously as soon as they heard about the sacking. The following day, 18 October, 3,000 workers in the PTA and the Body Plant voted unanimously to stay out until Francis was reinstated; the Engine Plant was also prepared to take action.[19] On the nineteenth, a mass meeting of the PTA voted 5,317 to 6 to stay on strike.[20] But the cause was not helped by the FNJNC trade unions. On 25 October, the TGWU's Les Kealey and another official spoke to Ford Director of Labour Relations Leslie Blakeman, who offered them a phased resumption of work, with all strikers taken back within a week without reprisals; on this basis the FNJNC officials voted 10 to 5 to recommend a return to work. At a 'stormy' shop stewards' meeting the next day, the recommendation was narrowly accepted by 32 to 28, and at a mass meeting the strikers voted to go back – but only after they had received 'the clearest possible statement from [the] officials that there would be no victimisation'.[21] The officials claimed they had received just that assurance from Blakeman. Yet the same afternoon the press reported a statement by the Ford Motor Company that the FNJNC must have 'misunderstood' the agreement; there would be a phased return to work and 'some redundancy'.

By the following Monday, 600 strikers opting to resume work had received letters informing them that they would have to 'co-operate' with the company by 'abandoning all restrictive practices' once back at work. Many returning workers were sent to new departments where they had no idea of work speeds or local agreements. Meanwhile, for the remaining strikers, what was rapidly becoming a farce dragged on. At the end of October, union officials met again and decided – again – to put off any decision until certain points were 'clarified'; on 5 November, action was once more deferred after the company agreed to consider the sacked men as 'suspended' and that they would receive a payment of £7.50 a week while negotiations continued; on 19 November, the payment was increased to £11.

In the meantime the Ford Shop Stewards' Committee were still assuring members that 'Our National Officials are insisting that everyone shall be taken back and that no one shall be victimised'.[22] Yet the next day saw a statement from Ford management which announced yet more sanctions against unofficial strikes and claimed that 'These measures' – i.e., their effective lockout of the strikers – were 'designed to restore the joint authority of the unions and the company, and to combat the activities of those employees who have no loyalty to either.'

After two more weeks, 4,000 workers had returned, and those still out were sent a letter saying they would be 'sent for' if required; these workers now had no idea if they were out on strike or being made redundant. Weeks went by in this limbo, during which the FNJNC voted for official strike action five times – and, each time, deferred the strike date. On 13 February 1963, TGWU official Kealey issued a document arguing that 'It will be necessary to get down to the root of our troubles at Dagenham, and whilst we have many complaints about management antics the more important job is to put our own house in order .... Unfortunately, a number of stewards have got into the habit of trying to solve their own problems .... Their action makes it impossible to build up the sort of relationship with the Ford Motor Company which will enable the unions to obtain ... the best wages and conditions.'

Only days later, Kealey issued a further statement promising that 'Should we not arrive at a just settlement with the Company prior to 18th February, then without doubt the whole of the TGWU membership at Dagenham will withdraw its labour.' With friends like these, it was difficult for the workers to identify their enemies. Yet trust and hope still ran high, not to mention wider class solidarity; as 18 February approached, the TGWU-dominated Central Bus Committee of London Transport unions voted that no buses should be run along the mile-long approach to the works, a resolution endorsed by mass meetings of all the garages affected.[23]

'We're Not Having Them Back'

AEU activist Kevin Halpin, by now PTA convenor, was to become one of the strike's seventeen victims. His account of the strike roots it in a directly democratic method used by PTA shop stewards to unite the membership across different production lines.

> We had shop meetings across the lines. There were three lines, three different models of cars, and we had three [stewards] across three lines ... and management wanted to change that so that when a model was going out they could put pressure on that line to get new conditions of work – and if that line stopped the other two lines were still working, producing cars ... So we always took three lines together. And that was what Bill Francis was done for – having a shop meeting across the three lines.

Yet, as Halpin recalled,

> We pulled the PTA, we couldn't pull the other factories. The PTA was out with a 6000 to 4 vote ... [But] other plants didn't come out. In hindsight, if we'd have kept the PTA out on its own, we'd have won. The other factories ... didn't back us. They did at the start – they just didn't in the long run .... Management observed a redundancy of 700 [PTA workers] and then after two or three weeks of negotiations they reduced it to 350 .... Then to about 110. This went on over months .... Then it got down to 17 and they said "These are the 17. We're not having them back".

Engine Plant activist Ted Amos sheds light on some factors which may have prevented more fully-fledged support: 'There was a huge difference within the membership regarding Francis. Obviously he's sacked ... and you move for support – but there weren't wholehearted support – he got sacked in the end didn't he. They didn't stop work over that. A few. Not plant-wide ... Politics had a lot to do with that'; Francis was 'a Party member and all that.' But it was Francis' lack of consultation with his fellow-activists that was the major problem: 'He acted stupid didn't he? He didn't converse with the stewards in the plant – the PTA – before [he called the meeting]. That's it – done – and of course there was quite a few saying "Well hang on – that's not the way to bloody go about it." That's why the company took the action. They would never have taken the action if they thought there was going to be a throwback from the members. The company weren't stupid. He never should have gone down that road. Or if he'd started he should have cut it short and got off it quick.'

In spite of his own undoubted commitment to workplace union democracy, Amos seemed unaware of the key strategy of holding meetings across lines: 'The way he was acting – it wasn't a major thing, just some silly thing. It had to be really important for a strike – workers would have seen that and they would have supported it. People always say workers are stupid but they wouldn't support something daft.' This lack of full awareness may have played into management's hands, along with distance from the extremes of work pressure experienced most intensely in the PTA. As Halpin argued, the greater militancy of PTA workers was rooted in their direct exposure to assembly-line speed-up: 'When speedup occurred it was the PTA that had the pressure. The PTA plant is where the cars came out of. You can speed up a mechanical process like drilling car engines by [mechanising] and the blokes don't have to work any harder, but in the assembly plant of course you had personally to work harder to get the work out. The PTA was the most militant because of that.'

Speedup was also used to turn the screw on 'disobedient' PTA workers in the wake of the defeated strike. One ex-striker recalled that 'As we entered the PTA after the sacking of Francis we had to hand in the signed forms which declared our intention to be good boys. When the starting hooter sounded we found that the lines were set at a speed that didn't conform to the labour strength. As the numbers of men [returning to work] increased ... the speed of the line was increased likewise .... Very quickly the tasks became intolerable. The men were forced to a running pace'.[24]

The intense pressure was part of a deliberate management strategy in which Francis' sacking was the first move. As Graham Turner reports, 'H. H. Jeffries, Ford Director of Industrial Relations, commented, "We decided how the shop would start again, when it would start and who would start it ... no longer at the end of a wildcat strike would the men automatically come back to their jobs" '.[25] According to plan, militancy at the PTA slumped: 'The factory became a place of desperation .... Men were more or less afraid to talk to each other on the job'.[26] Hours lost in disputes dropped from 184,000 in 1961 and 415,000 in 1962 to 3,400 in 1963.[27] With the best militants 'creamed off' in the sackings, the workforce had now been greatly weakened. Management moved to undermine the direct democracy of workplace union relations; stewards were now to be elected by ballot rather than show of hands, undermining the immediate contact between workers and their representatives, and departmental meetings were 'discouraged'. As Mathews puts it, 'From a source of strength, the shop floor had become a graveyard'.[28]

TGWU/Unite official Steve Hart[29] agreed: 'That's how Ford dealt with shop stewards in those days .... The assembly plant ... suffered overwhelmingly the most from the '62 dispute ... [It] didn't have the discipline and tightness of the Body Plant, the Foundry and the Engine Plant.' Yet the strike defeat also affected other areas, for example the assembly line in the Engine Plant, where, as Ted Amos recalls, 'The unions agreed to mobility of labour, which was a new thing .... It was a big problem ... you were pulled from here to there – it wasn't a stable job.'

While Hart argues that at the time 'There was a great solidarity constructed in the Shop Stewards' Committee that was very very powerful, that spoke to the members',[30] Huw Beynon suggests that the lack of effective workplace leadership both during the strike and after its defeat could be laid at the door of that very organisation: 'The shop stewards' committee was incapable of leading the 22,000 workers into a strike .... They'd become mangled by compromise – by wheeling and dealing.' This weakness was seen as rooted in the ever-changing 'line' of the then-influential Communist Party, which dominated the shop steward leadership – something not unusual at the time. Adherence to the 'Party line' rather than to the immediate needs of workers led to 'a feeling within the plant that the stewards' committee no longer *represented* the lads …'.[31]

In fact, Graham Turner reports that the post-1962 strike period saw 'a number of times when the leading Communists … urged the men to stay at work rather than come out on small issues. Several times I was told…that right-wing Labour Party and even Tory stewards had…been more strongly in favour of stoppages than members of the Communist Party.' Later he adds that the rise of a more 'moderate' steward leadership took place 'largely as a reaction on the part of the workers against left-wing stewards who couldn't lick the management when it came to a show-down'.[32]

Yet interest in socialist politics in the plant went beyond the Communist Party. Writing in 1963-4, Graham Turner remarked that 'all the years of struggle and … grievances have produced an extraordinary amount of political and ideological militancy at Ford. The very air reeks with the language, and the bookshelves are full of the literature of class war. Men who are far from being members of the Communist Party will produce a tattered Karl Marx from glass-fronted cabinets'.[33]

'Men Will Start to Kick Again …'

Yet by early 1964 the militant PTA union leadership had been transformed, with 'a group of moderate socialists – the militants call them "right-wingers" hold[ing] the top jobs'.[34] The new leadership – known collectively by workers as 'the mods' – included Body Plant convenor, Jock Macrae, described as 'a left-wing Labour man', with Freddie Brown as PTA convenor and Bert Bassett – a Catholic and a convinced anti-Communist – as his deputy. Joe Bedford, much respected by Johnny Davies, was convenor in the Engine Plant; these last three were all, of course, 1107 members.

In fact, the numerical dominance of semi-skilled workers and therefore – mostly – 1107 members was beginning to change the balance of power in the plant. As Turner notes, 'All the new men … are members of the Transport and General' by contrast to 'the old, militant regime, [when] it was AEU men who held most of the top steward jobs.' Eventually the tables were turned, with the T&Gers becoming the militants; but the rebirth of effective organisation took a few years.

In the meantime, the reign of 'the mods' saw the end of some effective methods of activist communication. Graham Turner notes that 'the network of subterranean communication which used to link steward committees in each of the plants' disappeared during this period.³⁵ This point was endorsed by *Solidarity* activist Ken Weller, who started at Dagenham's 'Body in White' shop in 1959:

> Our steward one day went along to see his opposite number in the PTA – and the way you got into the PTA [from the Body Plant] was just to walk along an enclosed bridge across the road along which the track goes …. And there was an uproar in the shop stewards' committee because they were saying that he should have raised his issue at the Body in White shop stewards' committee, and they would pass it on to the Joint Shop Stewards' Committee of the whole site, which would pass it on to the PTA shop stewards' committee and if they agreed they would pass it down to the individual shop steward. That would have taken about three months!

It was a depressing example of the trend against shopfloor democracy.

In spite of this increased bureaucratisation, activists of the time were optimistic that their time would come again; organisation remained based on an impressive degree of direct contact between activists in the workplace. Weller himself described the effective method of communication between shop stewards on different shifts: 'The old shift would go off and the steward would spend a few minutes longer there, the new shift steward would come in a few minutes early – all sorts of important connections. And then you'd have the write-ups – each steward on a shift would leave a note for the other shift's steward – anything untoward would be written in.'

As one ex-Communist worker commented when asked for his thoughts about the future of the plant after the 1962 defeat, 'It'll be strike-free compared with the past … but I don't think we'll maintain the almost complete peace of the last year …. Men will start to kick again, they won't accept the 'what we say goes' attitude of the company – and whatever sort of New Deal they bring in, unless shop stewards are consulted on the speed of the line, there'll be trouble'.³⁶

Cheap Labour?

And before long, Dagenham activists would find sisters and brothers in their struggles further north. In 1963, Ford opened a major new plant at Halewood, an area of high unemployment near Liverpool. Terms and conditions in the new factory were the subject of some early battles as Ford management moved to undercut Dagenham rates. According to Kevin Halpin, then still active despite his sacking,

The plant was built by agreement with Liverpool Council and [councillors] Bessie Braddock and her husband Jack[37].... They got agreement with the AEU and the [General and] Municipal which gave those unions exclusive trade union membership. We opposed that on the grounds that there was a common agreement and it shouldn't be undercut – because part of the agreement was ... that the hours were longer and the wages were less. [Liverpool Council] wanted the plant running on the basis of a limited agreement for unions, the ones Ford thought were sweetheart unions – the AEU and the GMB. The T&G was the best – the company didn't want the T&G.

Ted Amos agrees: 'They opened up the Halewood plant because they wanted them to work for a shilling an hour less than us – that was cheap labour as far as we was concerned. We went out on strike over it because we knew that's where the work would go .... Not all the Engine Plant came out but all the assembly workers did.' Just as in the PTA, assembly-line workers in the Engine Plant, like Amos, tended to be more militant than the skilled or even semi-skilled off-line workforce.

The introduction of the new Halewood plant, by far the largest 'rival' to Dagenham, worried workers at the older plant; as Turner reports: 'Insecurity still lurks constantly in the corners of men's minds. There is talk about how much production will have to go to the new plant at Halewood ...'. Such insecurities were intensified by the company's habit of moving workers abruptly from job to job: 'At the dictates of the production machine, they can be sent from one end of the factory to the other. "You can move from the biggest castings to the smallest nuts just like that," said a steward in the TGWU, adding "it doesn't half affect the workers. You've palled up with the people around you, then you're thrown somewhere else. One great surge, and you're torn from your job and your pals."'

Another worker, described by Turner as 'the most militant anti-Communist I met' put the point in a way that would have seen Karl Marx nodding in agreement: 'In the factory, we are rootless. We are just nicknames and members.' In this period there was no seniority built into the employment contract; one 61-year-old complained, 'We are just hourly servants ... I've been at Ford twenty-three years, but if there was a redundancy I would have to go out with the rest'.[38]

By contrast with the doubly depressed mood at Dagenham in the wake of the 1962 defeat, Halewood itself quickly developed a militant reputation after the slow start to be expected on a 'greenfield site'; by the mid 1960s, in fact, the new plant was posing something of a rival to Dagenham in its record of opposition to management, as Beynon shows in his classic *Working For Ford*.

'A Few People Get a Bit Uppity ...'

1963 saw yet another Court of Inquiry, set up to look into the 1962 dispute and industrial relations at Fords Dagenham in general. The company's case at the hearings, chaired by Professor D.A. Jack, was based on activists' overstepping of 'procedure'. As Ken Weller puts it, 'The Court of Inquiry consisted of an urbane discussion between Professor Jack, the trade union officials and the management on the best way to emasculate the shop stewards'.[39] Yet TGWU officials like National Organiser Les Kealey were more forceful than in the past, commenting that 'nearly every matter ... likely to become a dispute was within the field in which shop stewards were not allowed to negotiate. They were not allowed to discuss merit pay, line speeds or labour content, work standards and movement of labour'.[40] Quite a comprehensive list. Yet, as Weller sums up his study of the 1962 strike, 'Every gain at Fords was by the unofficial action of the men alone. Every defeat was the joint work of the management, trade union bureaucrats and state.'

Like his predecessor Lord Cameron, the Professor condemned the impact of the geographical rather than union-based system of shop steward representation at Fords, commenting that 'This deprives the unions of effective control over the stewards and makes it easier for a highly organised militant element to exercise a dominant and disturbing influence.' As Turner writes, 'Mr Jack went over almost the same ground as Lord Cameron had six years before. It was like an episode in some interminable medieval disputation ...'.[41] Yet one ominous outcome of the inquiry was 'the belated recognition by the Unions that they must finally deal with the activities of the unofficial Joint Shop Stewards' Committee'.[42]

In fact the 1962 strike and its aftermath were something of a watershed in steward-management relations from a very different point of view – union-management cooperation. For River Plant convenor Bernie Passingham, the 1962 strike and sacking of the 17

> woke us up to the fact that it's a bit stupid the way we're carrying on. We wouldn't tell the company this, but we saw we were getting into weak positions through our own fault .... That's when we decided there's got to be a different system regarding negotiations etc. .... The company had to learn as well, industrial relations. Which they did. They hired people in relation to that .... It was an achievement. Instead of arguing,

there's got to be a way of coming together. We couldn't carry on the way we were without coming to some basic understanding – basically they [management] didn't bloody know what they was talking about!

Certainly, facilities were becoming available to convenors and senior stewards at Ford by the mid-1960s, some time before these spread more widely in the 1970s:

> The company decided that convenors should have an office, etc, and that facilities should be available, paperwork, typists and all this sort of stuff – and slowly and surely, that worked, because we also now started thinking that it's bloody silly keeping having these stoppages of work. A few people get a bit uppity, this and that, and the few people lay off a few thousand – which in our opinion weren't doing us any good ...'.[43]

As the next chapters show, any real 'achievement' along these lines was a long time in coming, but Passingham's comments make it clear that even at this early stage both management and some convenors were beginning to seek a more 'cooperative' approach. By the mid-to-late 1960s, in fact, the company had provided all plant convenors with offices and telephone facilities, ironically enabling the shop stewards' committee to run the famous 1968 sewing machinists' strike (see below) from inside the plant.

Graham Turner shows how unusual it then was to take this kind of joint approach: 'The new Ford management elite which had come to power in the spring of 1962 made a member of the board responsible for labour relations, a step which before the war would have been regarded as some sort of lunatic joke ...'.[44] Yet Dagenham management's conversion to labour-management talks began only two years before the election of a new Labour government determined to introduce its own 'modernisation and rationalisation' of British industry, again centred on union-management cooperation. By December 1964 the government, employers and TUC representatives had signed a joint 'Declaration of Intent on Employment and Productivity' which was to have severe implications for workers at Ford and elsewhere. By 1965 the loss of working hours in the car industry through strikes had increased to over six million, and industry employers across Britain began submitting evidence to the 1965-8 Royal Commission on Trade Unions and Employers' Associations,[45] whose findings spoke of an 'irreversible devolution of bargaining to the shop floor' during this period.

In response, the new Labour government set up the Motor Industry Joint Labour Council in October 1965, with Jack Scamp (later to become notorious in the sewing machinists' strike) in the chair. Yet another investigation of labour relations at Fords began under this body, sparked by a paint-sprayers' dispute in March that year. These workers' abnormal conditions allowance had been fixed at 2 old pence an hour (less than 1p) over 15 years before – hardly a generous 'perk'. Their rebellion prompted foundry workers to make a similar demand; both claims were referred to the FNJNC, which offered a pay increase – but only subject to union cooperation in achieving 'increased overall efficiency'. When that was turned down, the company again made a conditional offer, this time based on a reduction in 'excessive relief times'. The so-called 'relief' consisted of paid rest breaks outside the paint-spraying booths – clearly essential in so dangerous an occupation. When their demand was rejected, the company reduced the relief times unilaterally – at which the paint-sprayers walked out.

The whole plant stopped as a consequence, and, unusually, the TGWU made the strike official. Les Kealey's explanation of this support for shop floor action was: 'We have never had a victory against Ford – this is our chance to get one'.[46] The union's backing prompted Ford to resort for the third time to a Court of Inquiry, again under Jack Scamp. Here the paint sprayers' union representatives justified the current relief times as established by custom and practice, raising the crucial issue of whether the company had the right to change timings unilaterally. Yet, ignoring this issue of principle, Scamp simply 'split the difference' between the company's and workers' demands, focusing only on the arithmetical gap between them. Ford manager Meredeen argues that Scamp's 'walk[ing] away from the fundamental principle without regard for its consequences ... led indirectly to the [1968] Sewing Machinists' dispute'.[47] But before we go on to the story of that historic strike, we need to take a step back to look at the factors which lay behind a major regrading exercise commissioned by in the mid-to-late 1960s.

'Leapfrogging'?

Following on the Scamp judgement, the issue of pay rate standardisation throughout the merged company came increasingly into play. At first this was spurred by the paint sprayers' dispute; various groups of workers began arguing that their own working conditions justified a higher allowance. Foundrymen claimed an increase, and were followed in 1966 by toolmakers who threatened to withdraw their personal tool-kits unless they were also granted a special rate. Stanley Gillen, an American who had now been appointed managing director, was worried by the likelihood of more 'leapfrogging' claims. Although he conceded the toolmakers' claim with a special 'merit money' payment of 3d an hour, Gillen went on to announce a comprehensive review of the pay structure based on four proposals. Firstly, the existing four-grade structure would be replaced by five new grades; secondly, 'conditions allowances' like the paint-sprayers' would be discontinued, with all working conditions now fully covered by job evaluation; thirdly, the hated merit money would be replaced by 'service increments'; and fourthly – ironic in the extreme, given the historic conflict a year later – women's jobs were to fall into 'appropriate grades ... without sex discrimination'.[48]

To start the whole thing off, a job evaluation programme was to be carried out by management consultants Urwick, Orr and Partners.[49] The resulting new grading structure would be part of a 1967 pay agreement with strings – productivity increases built into the new pay grades as part of a 'bonfire' of thousands of custom and practice pay rates at Dagenham. The exercise was to take place under the supervision of the FNJNC, and in fact 'As soon as the gradings were known, the trade union officials were inundated with appeals ...'.[50]

Proceedings were further complicated by the Labour government's incomes policy, which set a zero norm for settlements until the end of 1967 unless they contained provisions which could define them as a 'productivity deal'. In response, the company 'reluctantly embarked on its first and only experiment with plant productivity bargaining.' This involved the scrapping of many 'traditional practices' and thereby increased flexibility of labour and additional work tasks for craftsmen, who had to accept some craft work being carried out by non-craftsmen, while production workers were subjected to increased 'efficiency' through revised manning standards, different shift patterns and a 'better overtime response'.[51]

The huge regrading exercise threatened to create more problems than it might solve, with its potential for thousands of disputes over unfair grading decisions. But the company went ahead with the complex project, which involved reviewing the pay of over 40,000 hourly-paid workers across 24 plants and classifying tasks into more than 700 job titles. During the process Fords saw itself as 'regaining control by sharing it', following the principles recommended by the Donovan Commission, by including shop stewards in the process of deciding job gradings; any appeals would go to a Review Committee with equal numbers of management representatives and company-trained stewards. Yet 'after a few months ... the stewards withdrew from the committee. They felt they were being used as a management "rubber stamp"'.[52]

As Henry Friedman recalled, 'For about six months the Company, and the Trade Unions, were totally absorbed by the task of analysing and evaluating jobs. Personnel Managers and Convenors alike remarked "Whatever did we have to talk about prior to the job evaluation scheme?"'. Significantly, Friedman adds that 'It was a classic example of how trade union representatives can become fascinated with the routines of management and absorbed by them'.[53] At the time, though, the officials' happy 'absorption' contrasted sharply with the response of the workforce, who bombarded the Review Committee with regrading claims.

Bernie Passingham, by now convenor for the River Plant sewing machinists, was open to a reform of the pay structure. As he commented later,

> We wouldn't have said the company shouldn't have done the exercise. Most of us stewards, especially the convenors, always felt there should be some system where someone could look at where you are and say "That's where you should be" – and that meant doing an exercise, because [the payment system] got out of hand. People used to have merit money, and the workers obviously used to put pressure on the foreman – get me extra merit money …. So what happened slowly over the plant was, you got all different evaluations. Everybody knew it was going to blow up. We blamed the company – they had this merit money and of course we used to play on it – just have a go and you get merit money …. What they didn't realise was you got different wage rates all over the plant – and once that leaked out to different members [they'd say] "Why can't I have the same as him?" And that question's very hard to answer.

Although the company had 'democratically' moved to involve shop stewards in the exercise, convenors like Passingham were not asked to participate. Passingham accepted this: 'I'm not going to get involved in something like that – it wouldn't be safe. You could be in a very sticky situation agreeing something where half the workers didn't want it! We stood on the side watching. But we didn't disagree with the company in doing it – though it must have cost them a heck of a lot of money, bringing in them consultants …. But if the company want to do it they get on with it, which they did in the end – and as a result of that they had the bloody sewing machinists' dispute didn't they!' As he concluded, 'Once again when you look at the company you think "How stupid can they get?" They must know that we're going to really move in on it. They know all that's going on, rates and things like that, and all the time I've got 200 sewing machinists and no one's saying a dicky bird.'

'Not least because they were all women ...'

Passingham's scorn was justified; the new grading structure, introduced in 1967, caused explosive conflict across the entire Ford workforce. The River Plant sewing machinists were far from the only work group outraged by unjustified grading decisions; the slogan 'equal pay for equal work', usually associated with the gender pay gap, was used by both male and female Ford workers at the time to fight over the grading issue. But it was the sewing machinists' dispute of 1968, then and forever mythologised as a strike 'for equal pay', which has attracted international attention ever since (including a recent film, *Made In Dagenham*[54]).

This historic conflict can be traced back to August 1967, when the sewing machinists first submitted a claim for upgrading to the company's skilled C grade. At this point the circumstances were the same as those surrounding any of the routine regrading claims, almost always made on grounds of skill, being submitted throughout Fords; the fact that it was women who had submitted the claim was a minor factor. Yet it was the long delay over the company's consideration of the claim – possibly due to the fact that, as the sewing machinists sardonically put it, they were 'just women' – that finally drove these workers out on strike.

The sewing machinists' first move was to contact Charlie Gallagher, the Assistant General Secretary of their union, the National Union of Vehicle Builders,[55] to complain that their job should have been allocated a C grading. This grade had already been awarded to the two 'prototype sewing machinists' who worked at the Ford Research and Development Centre making up seats and cushion covers for use on new car models. The sewing machinists' claim revolved around both this comparison and the fact that their own job had originally been awarded a much higher 'benchmark job profile' by the Divisional Review Committee (DRC) appointed to work out the initial grading criteria. It was 'common knowledge to the workers and the shop stewards in the trim shop that the DRC had rated the sewing machinists' job highly'. And a high rating was logical; as Trim Shop steward Rosie Boland pointed out, 'When we go into the Ford company, we have to pass a test on three machines. If we don't pass that test, then we don't get a job. So why shouldn't they recognise us as skilled workers?'[56]

Yet the company took two months to report back to the sewing machinists after their first complaint, and then waited until October 1967 to inform them that their B rating would be maintained. The sewing machinists appealed again, but again faced long delays; even as late as April 1968, when a complete review of all outstanding grievances took places, there was no mention whatsoever of the sewing machinists' grading grievance. Faced with this unacceptable lack of response, the workers voted to impose an unlimited overtime ban on 22 May, followed by a one-day strike on 29 May if their job was not upgraded to C by that date.

It was on 29 May, in fact, that manager Sander Meredeen finally managed to raise the issue at a meeting of the company's Profile Review Committee. River Plant convenor Passingham and the sewing machinists' stewards waited outside the meeting; but discussions dragged on so long that they interrupted to say that unless they got a satisfactory answer 'the girls' would strike the following day. In fact, when the convenor phoned the plant, the sewing machinists were already downing tools; and with that, as Meredeen puts it, 'Ford's sewing machinists had not merely walked out of the Dagenham River Plant: they had walked into the pages of history'.[57]

There was a lot of history going on. The same month, May 1968, saw near-revolutionary strike action by French workers, while huge political upheavals in Czechoslovakia and elsewhere were rocking the industrialised world. Yet in the less dramatic British environment the sewing machinists' strike proved quite 'revolutionary' enough for Ford management – and the Labour government. As Friedman and Meredeen put it in a joint analysis of the dispute: 'The company ... raised the problem to the level of ... Barbara Castle, Wedgewood Benn, Harold Wilson .... Only Her Majesty left out!'.... Only Her Majesty and the United Nations left out!'[58]

After the sewing machinists had voted unanimously at a mass meeting to continue the strike until their claim had been met in full, Ford executives were forced to accept that serious strike action was in prospect amongst, as Meredeen put it in the style of the times, 'a group of normally well-disciplined women workers ... whose future action nobody was prepared to predict – not least because they were all women'.[59] The workers had also decided to wait two weeks before meeting again, making sure that the conflict would be more than a series of one-day stoppages, and in fact the dispute was to escalate rapidly, with the women's Halewood counterparts soon joining in. A strike still making waves nearly half a century later had been launched – and the sewing machinists were not backing down.

'It's not just a women's job ...'

For these women workers, the strike was categorically about a grading dispute – and it was from this point of view that male Ford workers supported the women's action. Most walkouts at both Dagenham and Halewood at the time were connected in one way or another with the 'New Wages System', and men in both plants hailed the women's all-out action as signalling some hope that the hated structure could be defeated. As Bernie Passingham commented, 'I can say that, quite honestly, not once was I approached by a man [opposing the strike]. Nothing at all. Not once. It was all accepted. What else could they do? Over the years they'd had their strikes, hadn't they, and what else could they do? They couldn't go and sit on the sewing machine and do their job, could they?' On 18 June, when the strikers visited the NUVB union conference, they were given a 'heroines' welcome' by the entirely male delegation. The conference passed an emergency resolution pledging the union's support 'to our women members in their struggle to obtain the appropriate grading structure...'.[60]

Although the strikers had been quoted by the press as making the point that Ford's 'New Wage Structure' discriminated against women – which of course it did – gender equality was not the main issue for the sewing machinists. Bernie Passingham was vehement on this point: 'I got fed up hearing about a "woman's job". I said it's not just a women's job. I said we've got men doing sewing machining[61].... It's not a "women's job" – it's a job. And it's like every other job, you should be taking every action through the same system you did with the others.'

Yet, almost without the strikers' knowledge, their grievance was reworked by the (male) shop steward leadership and union officials into a claim for 'equal pay'. It was the Ford Shop Stewards' Committee that – over the women's heads and without their knowledge – sent out a letter urging support for the dispute on the basis not of the grading issue itself but the broader question of equal pay for women. This letter 'denied that the strike was over the simple issue of grading or pay; the basic cause was discrimination against women workers ....' By the time management met the joint unions for negotiations, one official at least – the engineering union's Reg Birch – had declared that for him and for the AEF, the issue was not grading, but equal pay for women: 'We declare the strike official, but purely and solely in support of the principle of Equal Pay'.[62]

The sewing machinists of course knew they were being discriminated against, and that this discrimination itself meant unequal pay. As one of their leaders commented, 'Women are discriminated against because the management employ them as cheap labour.' Yet the Trim Shop strike committee expressed 'doubts about making equal pay the main issue .... Some said, "But we have never even asked for it"'.[63] Sewing machinists' convenor Bernie Passingham dismissed the suggestion that the sewing machinists' dispute was about equal pay: 'No, no, no, no. I wouldn't say that. I wouldn't say that ... when you talk about equal pay, the women would never have gone for it, to be quite honest. They would have gone through the 'skill' route. They weren't talking about equal pay'.[64] Trim

Shop co-steward Rosie Boland, asked by a left-wing journalist whether 'the women [would] go out on strike for equal pay', answered: 'I don't think the women will go out for 100 per cent equal pay in the C grade just yet, if they could just get C grade. What we're concerned with is proving that we are skilled workers …. It's up to the girls to decide what to do, but last week they were really ready for another fight, but only for C grade – not for equal pay'.[65] Another striker, Violet Dawson, confirms this point: 'We didn't want equal pay because if we'd got that, we would have had to have done shift work and we didn't have the cover for the kids'.[66]

As this makes clear, it was the workers' focus on the specific issue of grading, and not the supposedly more 'political' demand for equal pay, that launched a devastating strike which shut down the entire Ford Motor Company for a four-week period. By late June Ford was losing £1 million of sales revenue every day, and the desperate company had appealed – successfully – for the involvement of the Labour government, telegramming the prime minister for government help to end this 'national disaster'; Barbara Castle rushed to the rescue, inviting the strikers' leaders to meet her at Downing Street. By the next day, 28 June, she was shown on TV daintily sharing a cup of tea and engaging in cosy feminine chat with the stewards and strike committee. Yet the 'all girls together' approach fell flat; when Castle suggested that they return to work while negotiations proceeded, one striker responded, 'This negotiation while we work just doesn›t work – once we get back, they›ve got us back, then negotiations can go on for ever, and we›re not having that ….'.[67] She was absolutely right; but the minister was not so easily put off.

Faced with the strikers' stubborn refusal to fall for her charms, at a further meeting that afternoon Castle 'decided to adopt a different approach and let her hair down. She kicked off her shoes and tucked her legs under her, on the settee … "She was brilliant!" raved Ramsey, the Ford managing director'.[68]

Using the 'equal pay' strategy approved by both union officials and Ford management itself,[69] Castle persuaded the machinists' representatives that, without changing the grading decision itself, the question of differentials could be addressed with a significant pay rise amounting to 92 per cent of the men's Grade B rate. She 'trusted the company and the girls must trust her. But … first, you've got to go back to work.' The 'girls' adjourned for an hour – and came back with the decision that they would recommend calling off the strike. Not surprisingly, this was toasted (literally) by the comradely Castle as a 'victory for common sense'.[70]

As well as the pay rise, Castle's main offer on the regrading issue was to set up yet another Government Inquiry under the usual suspect, Sir Jack

Scamp. On this basis the Dagenham strikers voted to return to work, though the Halewood workers, scenting a sell-out, stayed out a few days longer. The Scamp inquiry, published in August 1968, identified 'discrimination against the machinists' as 'symptomatic of the Company's more general discrimination against women';[71] its 'findings' eventually led to the Equal Pay Act of 1970, which established the right to equal pay for 'like work or work rated as equivalent'. This fell short of the principle of 'equal pay for work of equal value' which had been demanded by women trade unionists and the women's liberation movement. However, it was a significant victory which demonstrated once again that some of the major political developments of the period could be rooted in the resistance of shopfloor workers.

'Fords Are Making a Big Profit out of [all of] Them …'

The problem was that in winning the supposed war for 'equal pay', the strikers had lost the battle for their actual demand – upgrading. As Beynon concludes, it was 'ironic but … true that the diversion of the claim to one of Equal Pay got the … company off the hook' – although the women's jobs were obviously eligible for the skilled workers' C grade, 'If the women got grade 'C', the assembly line would have stopped',[72] with semi-skilled workers across Fords demanding the same grade. Steward Rosie Boycott confirmed this point: 'Let's face it, if the women had got C grade … it would have broken Ford's wages structure. There are so many men fighting for upgrading that if Ford's gave it to us, they would have to give it right through the firm. And the men know that if Ford's turn round to us and say "Right, you've got C grade", well they're going to have a better chance to fight'.[73] The majority of (male) production workers were on grade 'B'. If union officials had supported the sewing machinists' upgrading claim and convinced other workers of its justice – and there was clear potential for that – this could have struck a much greater blow for women's equality with male workers than the Equal Pay Act itself.

The sewing machinists themselves saw their fight not as some kind of moral or political crusade for 'equality', but fundamentally as a fight against exploitation. One of the best arguments for equal pay during the dispute – if not ever – was put by shop steward Lil O'Callaghan: 'As regards equal pay, some women even today think they shouldn't earn as much or more than their husbands, but they should realise they are working for what they can get, and Fords are making a big profit out of them … they are not working for their husbands, they are working for Fords, and the car is the same price whether it is men or women doing the job'.[74] Here, this committed workplace fighter – now sadly dead – defines equal pay not as a high-level 'political' demand or an idealistic call for 'justice', but simply as what it is; the recognition that workers provide the maximum amount of (gender-neutral) labour required by the employer's demand for profitability, and that in return they need the most they can get out of the company to live on: 'They are working for what they can get'.

As Henry Friedman concludes his account of this historic strike, the sewing machinists' impressive stand was rooted in decades-long traditions of militant resistance at Fords Dagenham: 'Most importantly ... the Company failed to take sufficient account of the historical experience of the [strike] leadership ... Ford workers had been in the forefront of the industrial struggle since the war...Due to this environment and background, the rank and file leaders at Dagenham were not merely "good" industrial militants, but had also mastered the art of strategy and tactics and built up a rank and file organisation with a level of political consciousness which, at that time, was second to none .... The Sewing Machinists had three vital elements at their command: organisation; leadership; and news value, without which ... they could not have succeeded'.[75] It is a fitting tribute – and also an epitaph – to a struggle which, for all its courage and defiance was betrayed by a deceitful government and a trade union leadership more concerned with 'image' than with the real concerns of rank and file workers and activists.

'Quids In'? Productivity, Penalties and Parity

In the wake of the sewing machinists' strike, levels of resistance grew at Dagenham in line with the general 'upsurge' of the late 1960s, when strike levels soared and 92 per cent were classed as unofficial.[76] Ford stewards were affected by the radical atmosphere; on 9 November 1968, some attended a car-worker conference put on by the 'All Trade Union Alliance', a revolutionary umbrella group;[77] the (then) industrially-oriented International Socialists (IS) began building a group at Dagenham which grew over the next few years into a 'factory branch'.[78] Solidarity, the organisation which had put out the pamphlet *What Happened At Fords* in the wake of the 1962 sackings, had very few members on the plant, but as co-author Ken Weller[79] put it 'We were part of a movement – our pamphlets and leaflets were influential .... We worked with IS, with stewards who were ex-IS members.' In this way, although most workers' concerns were related to workplace conflict rather than to broader revolutionary politics, there were strong links between the two.

One growing source of shopfloor conflict was constant layoffs without warning and without pay, and by late 1968 anger over this was rising to boiling point. On 28 November, a thousand PTA assembly-line workers – always the first to be laid off – took direct action; they stormed into the Dagenham administration block and sat down in protest at yet another layoff, this time caused by a strike at Girling brake manufacturers in Cheshire. The offices were paralysed, with workers blocking all entrances to the building and threatening to break up the machinery unless their demands were met. Displaying their own version of 'militancy', management held out without conceding, and the workers dispersed after an hour. But the action forced Fords to concede at least the principle of guaranteed weekly payments for loss of work caused by strikes. The amount offered was pitiful, sparking a 10-week overtime ban which eventually led to an increase, though full payment during layoffs was a very long time in coming.

But it was a battle on three fronts – productivity deals, 'penalty clauses' and parity – which dominated workplace action at Fords at the end of the decade. On Friday 13 December 1968, Barbara Castle recorded in her diaries an 'interesting lunch with the three Ford directors – Batty, Leslie Blakeman and Gillan – about their new productivity deal, including a novel financial sanction for unofficial action …. Under this the unions would agree that those who engaged in unofficial action would forfeit certain financial advantages, such as holiday premia. The saving to the firm … would be considerable …'.[80]

Although Ford workers had not been invited to the 'interesting lunch', its after-effects were felt when FNJNC union officials began negotiations on the 1968-9 pay claim for an extra shilling (5p) an hour, bringing workers somewhere near rates at piecework plants like Vauxhall and BLMC (British Leyland Motor Company). The company responded reasonably well to the unions' pay demands, offering 10.5d (about 4p) for some grades and 9d (3p) for others. But negotiations were sidetracked by a clause in the offer which based the pay rise and other concessions on 'good industrial behaviour'.

This rather vague category was made clearer in January 1969, when all Ford workers were sent a company pamphlet coyly entitled 'Pay Security and You'. This presented the company's 'Income Security Plan' for 1969, which included the clause 'There must be an assurance of uninterrupted production … in the event of your taking part in any form of unconstitutional action, you would disqualify yourself from benefits for six months'. Although Ford stewards arranged a meeting with trade union officials to discuss this bizarre proposal, only eleven of the 22 union reps on the FNJNC turned up. Even of those who attended, 'Not one official on the platform spoke against these harsh measures. I would not have believed it' in the words of one veteran steward. Yet activists' outrage was clear: 'Steward after steward at the meeting got up to ask whether rights won after decades of struggle were to be given away for this paltry rise'.[81]

There was more – in February 1969, Ford 'enhanced' its pay package to include a clause on 21 days' notice for industrial action. By now, as one sympathetic writer puts it, 'It was no longer clear whether Ford workers were being asked to accept a wage increase or the full gamut of Barbara Castle's anti-strike measures!'.[82] The following week, on 8 February, Ford shop stewards and convenors at Dagenham voted overwhelmingly for a total stoppage if the 'penalty clauses', as they were now being called, were not removed. Yet on 11 February fifteen of the twenty-two FNJNC union reps voted to accept the pay offer, penalty clauses and all. There was uproar as the news reached the shop floor.

The workers were not only fighting Ford management and their officials. The Labour government was increasingly seeing the need to take action over the kind of 'industrial relations problems' symbolised by worker resistance at Fords. As Beynon notes, 'The Company's insistence on "penalty clauses"... took place against a backcloth of a Royal Commission and a White Paper from the Labour Government advocating control of the activities of shop stewards'.[83] That White Paper, entitled 'In Place Of Strife' (soon shortened to IPOS) seemed to have been tailored directly to the concerns of companies like Fords; as John Mathews writes in *Ford Strike*, 'the State was here working in close cooperation with Ford management ... the idea being that modern capitalism had to secure itself against the actions of small groups of strikers by isolating them from the non-striking majority'.[84] In other words, Ford workers pursuing a standard pay claim, and involved over the past few years in a number of everyday skirmishes over issues like speedup and mobility of labour, were the focus of government policy at the highest level.

Action on all these issues was now inevitable, and on 24 February 1969, stewards from across the company voted to back the convenors' call for strike action. By 1 March 1969, the whole Dagenham works was at a standstill. The strike was impressively solid, reinvigorating the union on the shop floor: 'Previously moribund shop stewards' committees were being brought to life .... Mass meetings voted enthusiastically to continue the strike'.[85] Dagenham workers received widespread support in the area. In a speech to the newly-founded Institute of Workers' Control, Convenor Sid Harroway described 'heartening' solidarity from other groups of workers: 'I phoned up one T&G lad ... who got up at four in the morning to drive around all the local bus garages and make sure that no bus would move over Ford territory .... There were expressions of solidarity from the dockers and the broad labour movement.'

Infuriated by its powerlessness against this solid wall of action, Fords turned to the law; in early March, management took out a court injunction against the two majority unions on the FNJNC, the Amalgamated Engineering Federation (AEF) and the TGWU. This was based on the fact that although the FNJNC unions as a whole had agreed to the penalty-clause deal, the AEF had voted against and the TGWU abstained. The lawsuit was a failure, making the company something of a laughing-stock in official circles; Harroway comments that the judge's summing-up 'was like [reading] recommended material for shop stewards.'

Admitting defeat, Ford's Director of Labour Relations met national union representatives from the TGWU, AEU and ETU (electricians' union) on the weekend of 15 and 16 March; finally, on 18 March, the union side agreed to a formula which withdrew the requirement for 21 days' notice of strike action, guaranteed no victimisation of strikers, and suspended the original penalty clauses in favour of an 'Income Security Plan' which generally reduced their impact; meanwhile, the original pay offer was retained. Yet in some ways the strike had failed in its demand for total elimination of the penalty clauses; as Barbara Castle recorded in her diaries, 'Hugh [Scanlon] stated with one of his disarming outbursts of frankness, "We were out to abolish the penal clauses and we haven't achieved that"'.[86]

Yet the outcome of the strike could be seen as a massive blow to the government's strategy. Penalty clauses of one kind or another were a standard feature in the series of productivity deals negotiated from the mid-'60s onwards. In a book written at the time, Tony Cliff[87] noted that 'All Productivity Deals tighten labour discipline. Hence many of them include penalty clauses'. He went on to give examples in municipal buses and the chemicals industry, the building industry, Swan Hunter shipyards, and a 1967 construction electricians' agreement which went 'furthest of all' in threatening to suspend, fine and withdraw all benefits from workers taking part in unofficial action. Yet the 'most famous' example of penalty clauses was at Ford, where 'as a result of a very militant and massive strike [they] were smashed to pieces'.[88]

Cliff was perhaps over-optimistic; when workers were finally, reluctantly, forced back on 20 March by their officials, acceptance of the deal was as much a matter of strike weariness and fatalism over the union leaders' takeover of the dispute as any real satisfaction with the outcome. According to *Socialist Worker*, 'The men heard promises of workers' consultation, a new spirit of trade unionism and talks on equal rates with the Midlands as soon as they resumed work …. What hopes they had then. What despair they are feeling now ….'.[89] Although the union's decision to declare the strike official had been welcome, it had also limited the freedom of the stewards to run the strike in their own way. Perhaps for that reason, the strike settlement itself was something of a let-down. First of all, the original wage offer – incredibly – had still not been increased, meaning no resolution of the ongoing parity issue. Secondly, the penalty clauses still stood, although the 'Income Security Plan' presented a much weaker version; as Beynon puts it, 'the stick it wielded was not a particularly hefty one'.[90]

Under this 'plan', management had also agreed to set up a fund for lay-off pay – with its own built-in penalty; in any plant where 'unconstitutional' action took place, management would withhold its contribution into the lay-off pay fund for one week. A holiday bonus fund was also started to which the same penalty conditions would apply. Worse, any hopes for parity in 1969 were snuffed out; to end the strike, Ford had supposedly accepted 'an "open-ended" [pay] agreement ... but once the men were back at work they inserted a clause that there should be no more pay demands until July 1970'.[91]

A further 'Enabling Agreement' operative from 25 July included a new Disciplinary Code giving supervisors the right to arbitrate on disciplinary grievances, with the worker's shop steward present at the meeting. This was criticised as nothing more than a rehash of the agreement already thrown out by the workers during the strike; although shop stewards were allowed to attend such meetings, they would not be able to speak on members' behalf. In general, there was seen to be no redress for workers on disciplinary decisions by Ford's 'court'.

More promising was the proposal to admit two convenors on to the FNJNC, although haggling over these seats was to go on for many months. One convenor who rose to the occasion was 1107's John Davies: 'As steward I got on to the Joint Works Committee in the Engine Plant, representing the T&G. I then got on to the FNJNC ... as convenor'. But even once appointed, the convenors were not expected to have much influence and would possibly not even speak; Jim Conway of the AEF insisted that 'They are just convenors and have no negotiating rights.' The controversy over this issue prompted Sid Harroway to call for the 'application ... of workers' demands and workers' control to the trade union machine itself .... We think [bringing convenors on to the FNJNC] is a great break-through and opens up possibilities for much greater participation by all workers. By accident we find ourselves in the vanguard of this important movement.' Since Harroway was speaking at a conference of the recently-founded (in 1968) Institute for Workers' Control, he may have felt moved to emphasise these issues – and in fact, in applying the IWC's sometimes confusing calls

No Wage Drift at Fords ...

But FNJNC representation and even 'penalty clauses' were not workers' only concern. Another basic issue in the strike, which resurfaced in 1970, 1971 and even 1978, was parity – equality of earnings with other car workers. As shown above and in the previous chapter, the demand for parity had 'been in the air for years ...' and by the late 1960s, 'in terms of average gross wages Ford workers had drifted significantly behind, despite their long hours of "voluntary" overtime'.[92]

The main factor keeping pay at Fords behind the Midlands was that Ford workers were paid on time rate rather than piecework. This argument was backed by a confidential report put out by Coventry engineering employers in 1968 which had specifically attributed low Ford wages to this method of deciding pay. Across the car industry, the piecework payment system then prevailing in almost all car factories was used by stewards as a basis for enhancing earnings through collective setting of production 'norms' by each workgroup. Backed by small sectional walkouts over the timing of jobs, etc, this led to the 'wage drift' of earnings away from national agreements. Another important effect of Ford's insistence on time rates was the company's obsessive control of productivity: 'Ford ... regard[ed] workloads as exclusively a matter for managerial determination'.[93] Another, of course, was that the pay in these other car companies, particularly in the labour shortage-affected Midlands, tended to be much higher.

But by autumn 1969, the still unsettled issue of parity with piecework plants was again fuelling militancy at Fords. Continued shop floor pressure had pressured the FNJNC union leaders to demand a 38 per cent pay increase – just over £8 a week – to bring Ford workers closer to other car companies in the 1969-70 pay round. Yet there was little progress on the joint pay talks, though not for lack of ability to pay; as Dagenham shop steward Dennis O'Flynn reported in October, Ford's profits for 1968 were £75.1m, compared to £33m in 1967 and £32.7 in 1965. By now, union figures showed Rootes workers at Ryton, Coventry on 17s 5d an hour, and 16s 11d at Stoke, while most Ford production workers' hourly rate was only 10s 6.5d (52-53p).

Yet Ford Industrial Relations Director Bob Ramsey simply ignored the claims for parity and abolition of the penalty clauses presented at the December FNJNC meeting; and the FNJNC unions deferred the issue, agreeing to meet again in the new year. But the rank and file were not giving up; stewards' meetings at Dagenham and Halewood passed resolutions emphasising workers' solidarity and their determination to win on this issue.

The last weeks of 1969 also saw Ford convenors set sail for a meeting in Ostend called by the Belgian Metalworkers' Union; this was the first international conference of Ford reps and could be seen as the first stage in setting up a permanent European Ford Combine Committee. At this historic meeting, Belgian and German convenors pledged to block any attempt to weaken strikes in Britain by allowing increased production or the transfer of machinery in Europe; the British stewards made the same promise. But, returning to earth, as a new year – and new decade – came in it was clear that the battle for parity at Ford UK was still very much on the cards.

NOTES

1   Huw Beynon, *Working For Ford*, Harmondsworth: Penguin, 1973, p. 51.
2   By this time, unofficial strikes were beginning to rise across the country as part of the eventual 1968-74 'upsurge'.
3   Graham Turner, *The Car Makers*, Harmondsworth: Penguin, 1964, p. 80. As a highly detailed portrait of car companies during a short period in the early 1960s, Turner's book is much quoted in this chapter.
4   Ken Weller and Ernie Stanton, *What Happened at Fords*, London: Solidarity, 1967, p. 3.
5   Henry Friedman and Sander Meredeen, *The Dynamics of Industrial Conflict: Lessons from Ford* London: Croom Helm 1980, p. 62.
6   Weller and Stanton, *What Happened*, p. 4.
7   Ford Dagenham Communist Party Branch, *Fords – Whose Hands on the Wheel?* 1960, p. 2.
8   John Mathews, *Ford Strike: The Workers' Story* London: Panther, 1972, p. 45.
9   The GMB is also mentioned here in its 1960s guise as the National Union of Municipal and General Workers, whose 'main strength' within the car industry was then 'at Ford, where it has perhaps 4,000 members ...'. The much older National Union of Vehicle Builders also staunchly held its own, with general secretary Alf Roberts declaring, 'We want to be *the* union'; Roberts claimed that 'We would certainly take a very dim view ... of the AEU and T & G negotiating for us at Ford' (Turner *The Car Makers*, p. 83). Interestingly, the GMB rivals UNITE at today's Dagenham plants (see Conclusion).
10 Interview with Ted Amos.
11 Weller and Stanton, *What Happened*, p. 4
12 Graham Turner, *The Car Makers*, pp. 136-7.
13 Quoted in Mathews: *Ford Strike*, p. 45 (author's italics).
14 Mathews *Ford Strike*, p. 46.
15 H.A. Turner, Garfield Clack and Geoffrey Roberts, *Labour Relations in the*

    Motor Industry, London: Allen and Unwin, 1967, p. 216.
16. After 1955, these procedural rules were contained in a small booklet known as the Ford 'Blue Book'. Its size contrasts significantly with the weighty volumes used to document such rules in the US plants of Ford and other large companies.
17. The fact that Beard had the letters OBE after his name gives some idea of the lofty self-image of these national union leaders.
18. Weller and Stanton, *What Happened*, p. 6.
19. Mathews, *Ford Strike*, p. 47.
20. Weller and Stanton, *What Happened*, p. 6.
21. Weller and Stanton, *What Happened*, p. 7.
22. Ford Shop Stewards' Committee leaflet, 'What This Fight Is All About', November 1962.
23. Weller and Stanton, *What Happened*, p. 9.
24. 'Murder at Fords', *Solidarity* Vol 4, No. 4, November 1966, p. 15.
25. Turner, *Car Makers*, p. 93.
26. Workers quoted in 'After the Ford Defeat', *Solidarity* Vol 4 No 2, June 1966, p. 9.
27. Weller and Stanton, *What Happened*, p. 6.
28. Mathews, *Ford Strike*, p. 49.
29. Hart worked at Dagenham in the early-mid 1970s and was appointed as a District Official in 1976; the comments are from interviews carried out in 2011-2 (see Biblography).
30. Interview with Hart, 2011.
31. Beynon, *Working For Ford*, p. 61 (author's italics).
32. Turner *Car Makers*, pp. 138, 145.
33. Turner, *Car Makers*, p. 137. This reflects my own experience when interviewing Ford activists of this generation.
34. Turner, *Car Makers*, p. 145.
35. Turner, *Car Makers*, pp. 145-7.
36. Turner, *Car Makers*, p. 154.
37. At the time the Braddocks were notorious for, as Halpin put it, 'running Liverpool'.
38. Turner, *Car Makers*, pp. 133-4.
39. Weller and Stanton, *What Happened*, p. 10.
40. J.F.B. Goodman and T.G. Whittingham, *Shop Stewards* London: Pan Books, 1973, p. 145.
41. Turner, *Car Makers*, p. 13.
42. Friedman and Meredeen, *Dynamics*,1980, p. 35.
43. Quoted from interviews carried out in 2011 (see Bibliography).
44. Turner, *Car Makers*, p. 80.
45. This Commission met between 1965 and 1968 and produced what is usually referred to as the 'Donovan Report', which recommended more rights and facilities for shop stewards in the workplace.
46. Dave Lyddon, 'The car industry, 1945-79: shop stewards and workplace unionism' in Chris Wrigley ed. *A History of British Industrial Relations 1939-*

1979, Cheltenham: Edward Elger, 1996, p. 195.
47 Friedman and Meredeen, *Dynamics*, p. 43.
48 This apparently 'progressive' attitude to women was undermined not only in the ensuing sewing machinists' strike but by a 1960s Ford pamphlet on 'Effective Letter Writing' which commented coyly, 'A good letter should be like a woman's skirt: short enough to be interesting but lucky enough to cover the subject' (Industrial Relations Staff, Ford of Britain, April 1965: supplied by Roger Dillon).
49 The consultancy which, as Friedman points out in *Dynamics*, p. 66, was set up in the US 'at the time of Frederick Taylor, shortly after Henry Ford had begun to base his production methods on "Taylorism".'
50 Sabby Sagall, 'Fords wait for vital pay talks', *Socialist Worker* 15.1.69, p. 4.
51 Friedman and Meredeen, *Dynamics*, pp. 46-7.
52 Sagall, 'Fords wait…', *Socialist Worker* 15.1.1969, p. 4.
53 Friedman and Meredeen *Dynamics*, p. 67.
54 The popular 2011 film *Made In Dagenham* incorrectly portrays the strikers as demanding to be upgraded from an *un*skilled *to* semi-skilled grading. The logic of this seems to be, once again, to turn the strike into a crusade for 'equal pay'. The film is inaccurate in a number of other respects, ignoring for example the major role of the Trim Shop stewards, and 'canonising' Barbara Castle.
55 They were members of the National Union of Vehicle Builders, though staunchly supported by their TGWU convenor Passingham.
56 Friedman and Meredeen, *Dynamics* p. 129.
57 Friedman and Meredeen, *Dynamics* p. 80.
58 Friedman and Meredeen, *Dynamics*, p. 213.
59 Friedman and Meredeen, *Dynamics*, pp. 84-5.
60 Friedman and Meredeen, *Dynamics*, p. 161.
61 Male sewing machinists, often recent immigrants, worked on the night shift; until the 1980s and '90s, Ford was unable to get around regulations preventing women from working nights.
62 Friedman and Meredeen, *Dynamics*, p. 143.
63 Friedman and Meredeen, *Dynamics*, p. 140.
64 2011 interview (see Bibliography).
65 Sabby Sagall, *Socialist Worker* 21 September 1968, pp. 2-3.
66 Yvonne Roberts, *Mad About Women: Can There Ever Be Fair Play Between the Sexes?* London: Virago Press, 1992, p. 215.
67 Newsreel shown in *The People's Flag*, director Chris Searle, Film Four, Platform Films, London, 1987.
68 Friedman and Meredeen, *Dynamics*, p. 108.
69 According to one report, Ford's Labour Relations Director went along with the 'equal pay' scenario as a means of resolving the dispute: 'Blakeman … visited the AEF conference and…discovered there that a move towards equal pay as a means of giving an immediate increase might be acceptable. A figure of 92 % of the men's rate was talked about' Ronald Kershaw, 'How the Ford machinists won a 7 per cent rise', *The Times*, 8 July 1968, p. 25.
70 Friedman and Meredeen, *Dynamics*, p. 109.

71 Report of the Court of Inquiry, August 1968.
72 Beynon, *Working For Ford*, p. 168.
73 Sagall, 'I don't know what Wilson's trying to do, but I'd like to shake the living daylights out of him …', *Socialist Worker* 21.9.1968, p. 2.
74 Friedman and Meredeen, *Dynamics*, pp. 179-80.
75 Friedman and Meredeen, *Dynamics* p. 185.
76 Sheila Cohen, *Ramparts of Resistance: Why Workers Lost Their Power, and How to Get It Back*, London: Pluto, 2006, Chapter One, pp. 9-29.
77 Alan Thornett, *From Militancy to Marxism*, London: Left View Books 1987, p. 118. Needless to say, this promising 'alliance' soon turned into a front for the 'revolutionary' group concerned.
78 Ian Birchall, *Tony Cliff: A Marxist for his Time*, London: Bookmarks, 2011, pp. 283, 340.
79 Interviewed in 2010 and 2012 (see Bibliography).
80 Barbara Castle, *The Castle Diaries*, London: Weidenfield and Nicolson 1984, p. 570.
81 *Socialist Worker* 25 January 1969 p. 4.
82 Mathews, *Ford Strike*, p. 59.
83 Beynon, *Working For Ford*, p. 243.
84 Mathews, *Ford Strike*, p. 57.
85 Mathews, *Ford Strike*, pp. 61-2.
86 Castle, *The Castle Diaries*, p. 622.
87 Leader of the International Socialists, which became the Socialist Workers' Party in 1977.
88 Tony Cliff, *The Employers' Offensive: Productivity Deals and How to Fight Them*, London: Pluto Press, 1970, pp. 79f and 82-3.
89 'Fight Against Penalty Clauses Must Go On,' *Socialist Worker* 14 March 1969, p. 1.
90 Beynon, *Working For Ford*, p. 284.
91 'Fight Against Penalty Clauses …', *Socialist Worker*, 14 March 1969, p. 1.
92 Mathews, *Ford Strike*, p. 71.
93 Turner Clack and Roberts, *Labour Relations in the Motor Industry*, p. 215.

Chapter Four

THE SEVENTIES: HIGH NOON AT DAGENHAM

The 1970s were a militant period for British workers in general, and for workplace trade union activists at Dagenham in particular. But at first this militancy was less apparent. Although early in the new year union leaders declared their willingness to continue with the fight on parity, their members held back, disillusioned by the disappointing outcome of the 1969 strike. When Ford finally offered £4 a week, stewards arguing to strike for more were met with chants of 'no-strike-no-strike-no-strike', while 'the mike was pelted with snowballs'.[1] The anti-militant mood was partly explained by the fact that the £4 was, at the time, one of the largest offers ever made in any section of the industry.

For the moment at least, the parity issue was deferred. Yet typical workplace militancy continued at Dagenham, and before long this indicated ongoing resentment over pay. Early in the year, checkers in the Knock-Down department began a five-week strike over grading grievances, and in March 1970 twenty-two production workers at Dagenham sent a letter to the *Daily Mirror* attacking the previous day's front-page headline, which had warned of 'chaos and anarchy in the motor industry'. The workers' statement displayed simmering resentment over pay:

'We have years of long service in the Ford factories and let us assure you that "chaos and anarchy" are brought about by management's refusal to cut the profit cake fairly...Management believes in its divine right to manage and to make arbitrary decisions which affect wages [and] conditions ... of workers .... Differences in payment to workers inside one organisation alone – apart from terrific differences up and down the country and between one motor car manufacturer and another – make nonsense of the average earnings advertised in the press.' The workers enclosed pay slips to illustrate their letter (which the *Mirror* refused to publish). It heartfelt contents showed that the parity issue was still high on activists' agenda, in spite of the demoralisation shown earlier.

Meanwhile, Ford management seemed determined to maintain the failed 'penalty clause' policy of the previous year. In late July, pattern-makers walked out over a grading claim, leading to a ten shillings (50p) pay cut imposed on all 4,500 foundry workers; hundreds stopped work in protest. But by now much bigger issues were in the air. In June that year the Conservatives had beaten Labour, producing an anti-strike Industrial Relations Bill as part of their offering to the electorate. Ford activists were clear that the struggle on parity was linked to the wider policies of the new government, and at a meeting the next month they issued a call for joint industrial and political action against the Industrial Relations Bill. Sid Harroway, Chair of the Body Plant Shop Stewards' Committee, argued 'There is no future for parity unless we defeat the Tory proposals', and Dagenham Body Plant convenor Jock McCrae moved a successful resolution to link the demand for parity with support for a TUC strike against the Bill on 12 December.

The stewards' political analysis was accurate. Before long, the battle lines on parity and other pay issues were being drawn up far beyond the workplace. In January 1971, the Tory government ordered Fords to stand firm on its current pay offer; employers' leaders in the Confederation of British Industry also demanded of top Ford management that the company refuse to yield on parity, arguing that it would create inflation.

Yet inflation affects workers as much as (or more than) employers, and rising prices made the demand for parity even more urgent as Ford workers fell further behind those at other car companies. The stewards had calculated that to catch up with pay rates at Morris Motors, for example, Ford workers would need a pay increase of £17 a week, while to match Chrysler they would have to earn almost double; £19 shillings and 1.5 1/2 pence (almost a pound) compared to 11 shillings and 6 1/2 pence (about 51p). In this context, Ford workers' earnings had slipped to only 60 per cent of top rates in the industry – in spite of their long hours of overtime. Faced with the continued reality of this gap in earnings, by 1971 Ford workers had begun to move away from the disillusionment they had shown the previous year.

As preliminary discussions on the new pay offer began on 29 January 1971 at Ford's Regent Street headquarters, activists with placards and banners gathered outside to picket the FNJNC meeting. The Dagenham convenors now on the committee, Jock McCrae from the Body Plant and the Foundry's Seamus O'Sullivan, were as determined as their counterparts at Halewood to push forward on parity.

Yet Bob Ramsey, Ford's Director of Labour Relations, rejected almost every demand put by the union side. The convenors' repeated demand for the abolition of penalty clauses was met with an unqualified 'no', while the demand for parity, expressed as a joint union claim for a £16 a week increase, was dismissed it as having 'absolutely no case'. Instead, Ramsey offered two pounds a week, claiming that Ford workers' weekly earnings averaged £35 – a 'calculation' which included white-collar and management rates. In reality, weekly wages for Dagenham shopfloor workers averaged £18 on days and £22 on nights.

But Ford was not to triumph this time. As soon as the activists outside the meeting heard of the £2 response to their demand for parity, they unanimously called for strike action the following Monday. Shop stewards conveyed the news of the company's 'offer' to Ford workers across the country, and spontaneous strikes took place on the night shift at the Dagenham Body Plant, Foundry and PTA. These Friday walkouts 'set the precedent and made it that much easier to rouse the sleeping giant of Dagenham on Monday morning'.[2]

Parity Not Charity ...

In fact, by Monday the 'sleeping giant' had already joined the fray. On Sunday night half the factory had shut down, and on Monday morning all but 1500 Dagenham workers surged into Leys Baths for a mass meeting; 'to the platform's challenge "Will you accept the £2?" the cry came thundering back: "NO"'.[3] By that night, 20,000 out of Dagenham's total labour force of 23,000 had stopped work.

The initial strike action was unofficial, meaning it would be illegal under the forthcoming Industrial Relations Act, with its leaders open to prosecution. As it happened, trade union leaders soon backed the dispute. But, as Dagenham JWC member Tommy Osman put it, 'Whether the union officials had moved in and put their seal on this dispute or not, I am convinced that all Ford workers would still be out ... Officials and men have responded better this time than ever before. To my mind this makes us unbeatable.' This time round, unlike the previous year, the workforce was clearly determined to fight all out for a decent deal in relation to other car workers. And on 1 February 1971, Dagenham workers were among the 40,000 who began their battle for justice with the slogan 'No more cars till we get parity' – or, more snappily, 'Parity not Charity'.

Later the same week, TGWU convenors from all Ford's British and European plants met in Belgium to discuss wider action to strengthen the strike; one immediate result was an overtime ban at Genk and Cologne. Messages of support came from all over the Ford 'empire', including a telex message from US Ford workers pledging solidarity and affirming that 'Your wage claims against the multi-national giant are fair and just. Parity in

Britain is an essential part of the continuing search for justice and equality'.[4]

At home, Ford management piled on the pressure with misleading press advertisements proclaiming the 'fairness' of the pay deal; the adverts boasted, absurdly, that the company paid 'the same rate for the same job whether it is being done in Swansea, Southampton, Liverpool, Langley, Dagenham or anywhere' – hardly the point. On 8th February Dagenham workers protested outside the offices of the *Daily Mirror* and *Evening News*, which had run the advert, pointing out on a specially-produced poster, 'Of course all Ford workers in Britain are paid the same. That's why they are all the lowest paid.' Ford's argument that 'the company intends to protect your job security – you know that can't be done by paying ruinous rates' was countered by quoting Ford's profits – the highest of all the car companies. To Ford's claim that the average pay for manual workers at Ford plants was £35 and 6 shillings, workers retorted that the company's figures included shift allowances and 4.5 hours' overtime a week.

After three weeks, the strike was still totally solid, and management's nerve was beginning to crack; on the twelfth, Ramsey wrote to the AEU's Reg Birch, Secretary of the union side of the FNJNC, requesting an early meeting to 'undertake any necessary clarification of the company's position.' A meeting was arranged for the following week, but management succeeded only in embarrassing itself by 'offering' a service-related increment which had already been presented at the initial pay talks as 'entirely optional and ... a separate item to the wage offer.' As Reg Birch put it, 'What was embarrassing for Ramsey was that he had originally put his two lump sums on the table and made a rather clumsy effort to convince us that they were separate .... To us on the NJNC it was obvious that the man was acutely embarrassed to have to reveal his hand so openly.' Birch rejected the offer on the basis that 'it would be greeted with ribaldry'.[5]

'They didn't need calling out'

If anything, the strike was now increasing in strength. In mid-February workers in the Engine and Foundry plants at Dagenham voted unanimously to stay out without meeting again for two weeks; meanwhile, Ford's propaganda became increasingly shaky. The company claimed that convenors had taken the law into their own hands by calling for a total strike, which had forced the unions to break off negotiations, but according to PTA steward and 1107-er Colin Beadle, 'The truth is much simpler. At Dagenham, Halewood and Swansea – the three main plants – all the workers walked out when they heard the offer. They didn't need calling out'[6]. Sid Harroway, Chair of the Dagenham Body Plant Shop Stewards' Committee, described the Ford workers' response as of a 'magnitude that had never been seen since pre-war days ... It was a unique experience to see meetings of thousands of workers at Dagenham solid .... The company completely misunderstood the mood of the workers.'

In fact, Dagenham workers were moving at a pace ahead even of the stewards and convenors, who recognised that with their 'spontaneous militant action ... the men have been educating us.' Commenting on the 'illegality' of the action under the Tories' Industrial Relations Bill, steward Charlie James said, 'Were the Bill law now it would not have made the slightest bit of difference. How would [Employment Secretary] Carr have dealt with 50,000 militant men who are actually telling the shop stewards what to do?'. By this time, the strike was influencing other car workers. Vauxhall workers also put in a parity-based pay claim, comparing their rates with car workers in the Midlands. Ford production was increasingly affected in Europe; by the end of the third week, the company had imposed short-time working in its Saarlouis plant due to a serious shortage of parts. British component suppliers like Wilmot Breeden and Girling were forced to put their workers on short time, and the major car-hire firm Godfrey Davis announced that if the strike was not over by 1 March they would cancel their £1m order for new Cortinas.

By the fourth week of the strike Ford's loss of production amounted to about 60,000 cars, equivalent to £36m in profits. Ramsey was forced to swallow his pride and write to Birch asking for another FNJNC meeting on 2 March. This meeting lasted almost twenty hours, with the offer edged up by a further two pence (old money) an hour, to be rounded up to 2p under decimalisation. When the NJNC rejected it, Ramsey 'worked himself up into a rage ... He fumed: "This is the parting of the ways ... this is as high as we can possibly go – our employees have got to know this is it"'. Reg Birch saw the outcome a little differently: 'They made so meagre an offer that it's enough to try anyone's patience'.[7]

Workers clearly agreed; a mass meeting on 14 March saw militant support for sustained action on pay, with the 10,000 Dagenham workers voting overwhelmingly against a motion of confidence in the national negotiators. As one steward wrote, 'The only shouts were for "parity". The only jeers were for the handful who wanted to go back to work.' Ford's efforts at propaganda were unsuccessful; letters sent out to the workforce proclaiming that its offer was 'final' were in many cases 'promptly returned ... with suitable comments added'.[8]

The success of the dispute inspired Ford activists to discuss broadening their organisation, with proposals to form a Combine Committee across the motor industry which would allow workplace representatives from all the car companies to liaise and coordinate strategy. Such a committee – an increasingly common form of organisation in the 1970s – would be particularly timely now that employers at British Leyland and other car companies were trying to get rid of piecework and bring in MDW (Measured Day Work). As onetime Dagenham steward and 1107 member Mick Murphy argued, 'There is a real need in the car industry for an organisation of shop stewards and convenors to ensure that we will be informed enough to deal with the many common problems we have to face.' Murphy claimed that as a result of the Ford workers' stand, 'other workers are using the [parity] word up and down the country and our struggle is relevant to their success in their battle for higher wages'.[9]

Terrible Twins?

Meanwhile, bigger political and industrial issues were at stake. The Ford strike had coincided with a courageous (though eventually unsuccessful) seven-week action by low-paid postal workers; Ford workers donated £1000 out of their strike pay to the postmen, who sent their own donation to the car workers in a heartening example of cross-class solidarity. But such idealism was not to be found in the upper echelons of the trade union movement, where the so-called 'Terrible Twins',[10] Jack Jones and Hugh Scanlon (TGWU and AEU respectively), were now, quite unknown to their members at Fords, working up to a deal to end the strike.

Discussions on this had begun as far back as 23 March, when Leonard Woodcock, President of the US United Auto Workers, had visited Britain for the annual conference of the International Metalworkers' Federation. Rather than discussing issues affecting metalworkers, Woodcock spent most of his time in talks with Tory Prime Minister Heath and Employment Minister Robert Carr – talks which, inevitably, turned on the now notorious Ford strike. These discussions were also attended by Scanlon and Jones. Carr was reported to be 'very interested in Woodcock's exposition of US-style 3-year labour contracts'[11] – something which also, apparently, made a strong impression on the supposedly left-wing leaders of the AEU and TGWU.

Though a photo from the period shows Ford Dagenham workers shouldering TGWU official Moss Evans, with a placard declaring 'Our Officials Line Suits Us Fine!!',[12] a very different 'line' was all too soon to be revealed. On 25 March the chairman of Ford Europe, Stanley Gillen, phoned Robert Carr and asked him to arrange a meeting with Scanlon and Jones. Carr suggested Gillen contact TUC General Secretary Vic Feather, who was 'only too pleased to oblige', and a meeting was arranged for 29 March.

FNJNC delegates had already read newspaper reports about trade union leadership intervention in the dispute; when some Ford stewards bumped into Jack Jones at Euston Station on 25 March, they questioned him on the press speculation. Jones dismissed it as unfounded, commenting, 'I'm not involved. It's up to you lads – you're running the strike.' Yet the very next day Jones agreed to meet Gillen for a top secret 'summit conference', and by the Tuesday of that week – 30 March – he and Scanlon had negotiated the settlement that was to end the strike.[13]

The roots of that deal were highly political negotiations between employers, union leaders, and the government. One analysis suggests that the defeat of the postal workers' seven-week strike, also in 1971, was the result of a deal between the TUC and the government in which the TUC would tone down union militancy in return for keeping the legal right to the closed shop in the current industrial Relations Bill.[14]

This 'logic' is argued to lie behind Scanlon and Jones' behind-the-scenes settlement of the Ford strike.[15] A closed shop at Fords for any one union was not a possibility, but an 'agency shop' as defined in the government's Industrial Relations Bill – a voluntary agreement limiting the number of unions who could represent employees in any one workplace – would have been a tempting prospect to the 'terrible twins'. Whatever their motive, the resulting deal fell well short of Ford workers' hopes for achieving anything like parity. The offer included an immediate increase of 9p an hour (the NJNC had rejected 8p an hour almost a month previously) with further increases of 5p on 1 December 1971 and 1 August 1972. This offer – which also conceded a standstill on upgrading claims – would still leave Ford workers on the lowest pay in the industry, defeating the whole purpose of the 9-week strike. It was also – a first in the UK – a two-year agreement.

Any paltry improvements offered, such as 'equal pay' for women (in fact Ford sewing machinists would not reach anything like real pay equality until the mid-1980s) were made conditional on an agreed procedure which guaranteed no strikes 'or other action on economic claims' before the current agreement expired – a provision which was, like the two-year deal, common in the US. And finally, to add insult to injury, Scanlon and Jones agreed – on Gillen's insistence – to put the proposals to a secret ballot rather than the traditional show of hands vote.

The week after this bureaucratic stitch-up, the FNJNC unions were summoned at short notice, with delegates unaware of what was to happen; the meeting was – unexpectedly – attended by Scanlon and Jones.

The TGWU general secretary told his audience that the two leaders had negotiated the 'best possible deal', and if the NJNC chose to oppose it he would simply ignore the decision. This, of course, left the union delegates with an impossible choice: allowing Scanlon and Jones to recommend the settlement over their heads, or themselves endorsing an agreement very few could accept. In the end, four out of the five convenors on the FNJNC voted against, among them Dagenham Engine Plant convenor and 1107er Joe Bedford; but the full-time officials secured a majority for acceptance.

The bad news travelled fast; next day at Dagenham an emergency meeting of the Joint Shop Stewards' Committee was packed out, with at least 100 stewards and militant activists crowding into the JSSC office to voice their fury at the settlement. The ballot was to be held at the Leys Baths, Dagenham workers' usual meeting place, and as early as 8.30 am the next day a mass meeting was held which voted three to one to oppose the offer.

But the activists were unprepared for the effects of secret balloting, then a very unusual procedure. As the Tories under Thatcher were well aware when they introduced compulsory secret ballots in the 1984 Trade Union Act, their effect is to sow confusion and undermine unity amongst rank and file members. Tom Langan, a Dagenham Body Plant steward, commented: 'The ballot was a company ballot – they had control over everything … Who printed the forms? Who composed the wording? "Do you want to accept this generous offer, or do you want to carry on with this strike which is starving you and your family? …" That's what it means to have a company ballot …'

Ford workers were disoriented not only by the secret ballot but by the sudden, unexplained offer, a general absence of information and the sudden ending of strike benefit. No discussion was allowed, and no proper explanation of the offer provided to stewards. Even Sid Harroway, who had reluctantly approved the offer, commented (prophetically), 'Many feel, as I do, that acceptance of this ballot could have the effect of weakening the fight of the unions against Tory efforts to impose secret ballots as a general rule'.[16]

Occupy!

Yet the defeat – if not betrayal – of the 1971 dispute had little impact on levels of resistance at Dagenham. As 1107 activist and Paint Shop steward Berlyne Hamilton[17] recalled, 'At that time within Fords we had on a more or less daily basis what they choose to call wildcat strikes – and from that period of time up to the '80s that never really stopped.' This militancy was almost entirely caused by the injustice of constant unpaid layoffs: 'The first six weeks working in Fords I never got a week's wages – it was "Clock in and go home" – two hours' pay. You never got a whole week's wages .... You ask "What am I being laid off for?" – they can't give you an answer.'

In the wake of the strike defeat, a still more militant response – occupying to fight for shop-floor demands – soon developed. In May, 25 workers from the KD (Knock-Down) plant were asked to work in the PTA at a moment's notice; they refused and were suspended, at which they moved into the canteen and occupied it. The company made the same demand of a further 25 workers, who also refused, were suspended, and joined the occupation. This continued for two days until there were several hundred workers occupying the canteen; by now they were spilling out into the plant and refusing to move. Management gave them a 24-hour ultimatum – work or be sacked – but not one worker responded, and the company was forced to back down and agree to talks. Eventually the original 25 who had refused to move were allowed to stay in their section. As one writer pointed out in *Solidarity*, this action was entirely worker-led: 'There was no tightly-knit group of militants taking charge of events ... The episode[s] ... remained at all times directly under the control of the men'.[18]

The high level of militancy continued. In October 1972, eight women in the KD department had their wages stopped because they were late for work – though only because of a traffic jam inside the Ford works itself. A hundred and twenty of their fellow-workers stopped work in support; by the next day 300 workers had stopped, and, as *Solidarity* put it, 'the girls got their money'.[19] A further sit-down followed in late November that year as 40 workers on the Cortina line protested against a particularly vicious supervisor.

Yet by early 1973, activists at Fords Dagenham were depressed and angry at what was seen as a retreat. In February, electricians' shop steward John Aitken reported that 'workers feel ... frustrated and angry. There have been virtually no disputes for 12 months, an economic freeze for two years, a massive increase in productivity and fantastic profits. You can't just tolerate a situation when someone then comes along and says: "Sorry lads there's nothing in return, the country's in dead trouble." People are starting to think about the whole thing, this whole desperate system of society.'

PTA steward and 1107-er Colin Beadle agreed: 'With this freeze, thousands of other workers are watching us, looking for a lead .... With the state inevitably ranged against us in all or battles, and with almost every plant in the industry on MDW [Measured Day Work], we need to develop a national shop stewards' movement in the industry ....'

This argument was backed up by the example of a recent Dagenham walkout over speedup in which 'the trade union did not back us. After 10 days we came back and then operated a go-slow for six weeks. We were 100 per cent successful.' The writer put the lack of official trade union support down to the ongoing problems of 'procedure' in which if stewards tried to hold workplace meetings they would still probably be sacked, as had 'the 17' less than 10 years ago. Action and organisation from committed trade union representatives across the movement would be the only force to successfully fight this threat.[20]

Yet workplace militancy was still at peak level as part of the ongoing rank and file 'upsurge'.[21] In February 1973. PTA workers staged a series of sit-ins over a two-week period in order to get all Dagenham workers to stick to an agreed overtime ban until Ford boosted its 1973 wage offer. The amount on the table was only £2.40 pw, the excuse being the Tory-imposed pay freeze. In April, a mass meeting of 20,000 workers at Dagenham once again rejected the offer, but the fight was not taken up by the trade union officials, and workers were forced into other methods. These included short sectional walk-outs in the body plant, an overtime ban in the PTA and a work to rule in the press shop, all of which caused lay-offs in other sections and created potential disunity among a resentful and harassed workforce.

The left-wing magazine *Solidarity* reported on the 'fiasco' that a majority of workers had refused to support the unlimited strike called by the National Ford Convenors' Committee.

Partly, the writer argues, this was due to 'the lack of confidence … shown by Ford workers for the Ford shop steward apparatus …. Most workers and [even] stewards … have been for years completely pissed off with the way shop stewards' committees operate …. The Shop Stewards organisation at Ford is much more institutionalised than at most other car firms'.[22] As River Plant convenor Bernie Passingham had pointed out (see previous chapter), the company had already provided convenors with their own offices, leading to the physical and organisational isolation of senior workplace reps from the 'shop floor'.

Sent to Prison?

Yet in fact, at workplace level, a high level of conflict continued. This was hardly surprising; Fords in the early 1970s was a very grim place. Alf Richards, an immigrant from the West Indies who later became a staunch supporter of the 'new' 1107 (see next chapter) started work at the Engine Plant in 1973. He described the experience as 'Frightful. There were 5,500 people in the Engine Plant – I'd never worked anywhere where there were so many people. The building was one of the largest factories in Europe.

The workforce was 60% immigrant – a very high proportion. The work was very mundane.'

Like so many others, Alf found refuge in the union: 'When you first arrived you had various people come and meet you, including the shop stewards. I chose the T&G because they were well known for their activity .... The production people were for the T&G, so 80% were in the T&G, and a high percentage in 1107 .... When I became a steward in '76 and started to attend branch meetings, all the new recruits were 1107. The deputy convenor at that time, Johnny Davies, was in 1107.' Alf worked 'only briefly in assembly – I was mostly in the machine area', yet 'that brief spell was like I'd done something wrong and got sent to prison. Terrible'.[23]

But assembly workers were fighting back against their 'imprisonment'. On 29 August, a combination of unpaid layoffs and speedup infuriated Body Plant workers, who stormed the personnel manager's office and locked him in; and in September a major struggle broke out over layoffs following a strike by 170 Body Plant workers after West Indian worker Winston Williams was threatened with the sack. According to management, Williams had tried to attack his foreman with an iron bar; he had then worked at Ford for 11 years and, as the company was forced to admit, had an 'exemplary' record. But in the frame shop where he worked there had recently been huge demands for increased productivity, with work quotas raised by 75 per cent; Williams' foreman, Fuller, was in the forefront of these demands.

Ron Todd, then full-time TGWU official for Dagenham, commented in Williams' defence that 'The company had raised the number of completed units required to 700 a day. The men were attempting to achieve this target by a gradual buildup. The week previous to the incident Mr Williams had reached 480 .... By the Tuesday night, he had reached 620 .... On his next [Wednesday] shift, the foreman harassed Mr Williams on five separate occasions, even following him to the toilet to ask how many he had done. Mr Williams was demoralised, emotionally broken. Witnesses saw him fall to the floor, crying. He had to be supported by two men. A nurse confirmed his nerves had completely cracked up and that he was taken to a sick bay. It is certain the foreman was never struck ....'

Yet the response of Dagenham management was to allege an assault on Fuller and give Williams the sack, provoking an immediate strike by 180 workers on Winston's shift. At this management immediately laid off 3,000 other body and assembly plant workers without pay. Demanding 'Work or full pay', the affected workers decided to occupy. Nor was theirs a peaceful protest: 'Such was the rage and frustration when their demands were refused that windows were smashed, cars damaged and offices besieged'.[24]

Ford management hushed this up, though they publicised the Winston Williams episode, assuming their action would be seen as justified. But by this time all 8,000 workers in the Dagenham Body Plant were out on strike in Winston's support, and the TGWU had produced unshakeable evidence to show that he was being victimised. John Knight and Ted Allan, two workers lobbying the FNJNC in his support, spoke to a *Morning Star* reporter about 'the appalling strain and crushing boredom of production line work … a man might have to cope with 84 jobs an hour passing relentlessly along the production line. "That is about 42 seconds per job. Christ Almighty, you blink twice, and the car's gone by you"'.[25] Williams was reinstated, though in a different department. But the other issue raised by the strike over his sacking, that of winning lay-off pay in 'internal' disputes, remained unresolved for some years to come.

Alan Deyna-Jones, a newly-employed worker who was later to become a steward and staunch 1107 activist, remembers the Winston Williams episode from when he had just started at Fords. He was just about to get married, but was laid off because of the dispute, a stressful experience then for a young worker anxious to finance his wedding plans. The same year, he recalled, 'There was a strike over cheese rolls – not enough cheese in the roll. We started to walk out and the stewards were saying Go back, Go back – "No, I'm going out"'[26] It was symptomatic of an everyday militancy – in many cases defying workers' own shopfloor representatives – that seems almost other-worldly as this history is being written, over forty years later.

Joining with Management?

In this context, Industrial Relations Director Bob Ramsey's target of keeping strike losses below 5 per cent by 1973 was unrealistic, to say the least. In fact they were almost four times that, with 'a marked increase in disputes over work standards, manning levels … and working conditions'. To address this situation, management turned to the last resort of industrialists and politicians – worker co-option. In September 1973, Ramsey announced his intention 'to invite the Unions and Shop Stewards to join with management in a careful investigation into the fundamental causes of disputes … as the first step towards working out jointly agreed solutions.' This was to be attempted through setting up joint management-union 'Briefing Groups'.[27]

Yet conflict continued. In February 1974 the Ford joint unions rejected a £2.60 pay offer, demanding instead a 'substantial' wage increase, along with four weeks' annual holiday and the abolition of the lowest production grade. Despite their ongoing militancy, Ford workers were still the lowest paid in the industry, and the battle for parity now seemed far in the past.

Many plants (though not Dagenham) were on the three-day week imposed by the Tory government in response to the historic 1973-4 miners' strike, which was shortly to bring down Prime Minister Edward Heath; on a less impressive class-struggle front, TUC leaders were making it clear they were not prepared to back claims going beyond Phase Three of the Tory government's incomes policy.

In fact, in March 1974 union officials settled the Ford claim within Phase Three, even though the Tories had just been defeated in a General Election mistakenly called by Edward Heath on the basis of a "choice" between him and "the unions".[28] The Ford officials agreed that the claim could be revived if Phase Three was abolished by the new Labour government, but they seemed reluctant to respond to the more militant views represented by the increased number of convenors now on the committee. The five convenors' opinions were frequently ignored, and they still had no right to hold the officials to the demands of their members. Not surprisingly, Ford's shop-floor trade unionists were calling for a drastic reorganisation of the negotiating structure.

In early autumn, another wave of conflict surfaced as press shop workers at both Dagenham and Halewood struck, bringing production to a standstill. The workers had demanded increased shift payments and holiday pay at average earnings; the company refused, and the press shop workers walked out. Direct action won them a £4 night shift differential and time and half on shift pay. Other Ford workers across the company followed before long with a series of unofficial stoppages. For once Ford responded, taking advantage of the breathing space before the new Labour government began yet another incomes policy; management and unions finally arrived at a substantial wage settlement of 17 per cent, matching the staggering levels of price inflation[29] at the time. As Barbara Castle recorded in her diaries, 'Ford management decided to scrap their current annual agreement only seven months after it had been signed. This was widely interpreted as a breach of the TUC agreement with the Government to limit pay rises to once a year.' Labour Chancellor Jim Callaghan found the Ford deal 'very disturbing .... There is real fear of the power of the unions'.[30]

PTA steward and 1107 member Berlyne Hamilton remembers it differently: 'You just wanted a decent pay increase. We ended up with 17%, the biggest pay increase in the British Isles ....' But by this time the Labour government was already making ominous noises about industry-wide pay restraint under its proposed 'Social Contract'. The top-level deal, which centrally involved TGWU leader Jack Jones, was rapidly renamed 'Social Con-Trick'. As Arthur Flicker, an AUEW steward in the Press Shop, commented: 'We work for a living – we do our best, and we do that for less money than in the rest of the motor industry. If the social contract means that our lads have got to work for less money, it means the social contract has got to go'.[31]

'A Bit of an Obstacle'

Yet 1974's 17 per cent pay agreement also included clauses requiring improved 'efficiency' – speed-up, lower staffing levels and harder work. In October, FNJNC union leaders signed a Joint Statement on Efficiency which emphasised the need for workers to 'use the appropriate grievance procedures' to deal with workplace issues – instead of, for example, walking out. The company called on the Ford unions to ensure that 'all employees ... provide full cooperation towards achieving efficiency of operations', and in early 1975, Bob Ramsey set out two of the main components of this new approach: 'to provide a vastly expanded company information programme' and 'to analyse the basic causes of disputes through greater involvement of employees at plant level'.[32]

In fact, this period began to see what some have analysed as the greatest threat to union strength in the workplace[33] – shop floor trade union reps, including convenors and even stewards, becoming gradually drawn into 'cooperation' with management. This process involved more formal recognition of stewards, off-site meetings with management in luxury hotels, office facilities and – perhaps most importantly – time off for trade union duties. This last concession was included, among a number of other new 'rights', in the 1974 Trade Union and Labour Relations Act (TULRA) and 1975 Employment Protection Act, as Labour's side of the Social Contract; the quid pro quo expected of workers was pay restraint, introduced first of all in Jack Jones' across-the-board '£6 limit' and later in a series of percentage pay norms violently resented by workers and culminating in the famous Winter of Discontent (see below).

In fact Labour's legal provisions – even the much-needed 1974 Health and Safety At Work Act – inevitably increased bureaucracy and 'legalism' in the workplace. As Paint Shop steward Berlyne Hamilton put it, 'When they established the HASAW, that to a certain extent turned out to be an obstacle because ... if you give people wrong advice you can be prosecuted. The union will represent you, but with the whole idea that you could end up going to prison. So that in itself started creating a bit of an obstacle.'

As seen earlier, Fords was to some extent in the 'vanguard' of these moves to formalise relationships with workplace representatives. In the words of Steve Hart, a shopfloor Ford worker in the 1970s who rapidly became a full-time TGWU official, 'Ford ... had learned the lesson very quickly .... Once the convenors were on the negotiating committee ... in the mid-70s, [management] decided that the key thing was to develop relationships with convenors and they boosted the JWCs[34] and made them very similar in feel to ways Works Councils operated in Germany ... in terms of boosting the Works Committee and boosting the convenors into very powerful people ... in the '70s, they moved to try and incorporate convenors into their whole picture'.[35]

Neddy Steps In

This point is backed by Ronald McIntosh, then head of the government-industry-union National Economic Development Council (commonly known as 'Neddy'). In his diaries for 2 April 1975, McIntosh reports 'I had lunch with Bob Ramsay of Ford at the Cafe Royal. He [complained of] the constant interruptions due to industrial disputes of one kind and another. These pushed their productivity right down and Ford's overriding aim was to reduce or eliminate them. They had come to the conclusion that to achieve this they needed to involve the shop stewards much more in the running of the plant and to give them much more information than hitherto ...'.[36]

As already seen in the attempt made to introduce 'Briefing Groups', this information-based approach was beginning to be central to the company's industrial relations strategy – and was to pose considerable challenges to trade union independence. A confidential memo to management suggested establishing Departmental Groups which would bring together supervisors and foremen with shop stewards 'at all ... levels in the organisation – from Joint Works Committees to ... Joint Working Parties ... and finally as members of the Trade Union Side of the NJNC ... Shop stewards will inevitably become "partners in control" ...'.[37]

These proposals might have sounded innocent, even positive. But they threatened the crucial independence of shop floor organisation which had now served the Ford workers well for almost ten years since the defeats of the late '50s and early '60s. Meanwhile, Ramsey's despairing description of current shop floor relations in Dagenham and other plants as 'perpetual chaos every day of the year'[38] was eloquent testimony to the sustained militancy of workers on the shop floor.

Yet Ford management was now determined to push this perspective. In 1975, the 1955 Ford Procedure Agreement was amended for the first time to provide that in future most problems would be resolved by shop stewards at plant level without intervention by the FNJNC. The company also introduced – again for the first time – a 'status quo' provision (common in the best organised sections of the engineering industry) which specified that no major changes to working conditions would be made until the negotiating procedure had been exhausted – though the FNJNC union leaders also agreed to a 'no-strike clause' specifying no strike action while this process was taking place.

All this diplomacy seemed to have little effect on the shop floor, where according to one observer

> more and more employees were resorting to direct action – walking off the job, working to rule, banning overtime, indulging in acts of physical violence or occasional vandalism, threatening to occupy factories and offices and even, on at least one occasion, holding a manager hostage in his own office .... The attempt to send home workers laid off in the middle of the night shift simply served to extend the area of conflict and to produce solidarity action where none had previously existed.

This writer might have been thought to be an outraged shop steward, but was in fact the senior Industrial Relations Manager Sander Meredeen.[39]

Guerrilla Tactics ...

In fact, Ford's attempts at 'management-worker co-operation' were made during a period when workers at Dagenham were engaged in almost continual direct action, including occupations, to wage war against management's own 'militancy'. As convenor Henry Friedman recalled a few years later, 'the most persistent cause of intense and sometimes violent conflict' in the period was still the issue of continual unpaid layoffs; not surprisingly, 'workers, particularly when on night shift, increasingly objected to being taken off the payroll and sent home shortly after arriving for work'.[40] And those objections led to increasingly militant action.

In September 1973, at the same time as Ramsey was optimistically planning labour-management 'cooperation', laid-off workers in the Body Plant locked managers in their officers and staged protest marches through the plant, setting off fire alarms and breaking windows in their rage. That November and the following June PTA workers physically blocked production lines in protest against layoffs. In October 1974 an occupation at Swansea over redundancies and lay-offs galvanised workers at Dagenham, and management began erecting barricades around their offices against the threat of similar action. Yet although Body Plant convenor Danny Connors called for an occupation of the plant at a mass meeting, the vote was split

50-50. As Dagenham activist Ed Emery put it, 'They called an occupation ... But nobody came'.[41]

In early May 1975 Body Plant workers at Dagenham barricaded themselves into the plant after management announced that 137 men would be moved from the area to form a 'labour pool' used to replace workers who had left the company. The transfer would mean an increase in workload of up to 50 per cent for some of those remaining on the line, and a group of doorhangers and fender fitters struck in protest. This action was supported in many other sections of the Body Plant, but the convenor refused to call a plant meeting; instead he suggested that the two work groups should get their workloads checked by the supposedly 'impartial' time and motion department. When the workers rejected this advice, the company immediately sent home the entire B shift from the Body and PTA plants until the following week. At this, workers forced the convenor to call a plant meeting which ended with a vote for an indefinite occupation until the company agreed to no job cuts; the plant was barricaded with oil drums and pallets.

Though this occupation was soon over, the strike action continued and by mid-June was leaving more than 6,000 workers idle; lay-off pay had 'run out', and as always workers were being refused unemployment or social security benefits. Workers' argument that the company had deliberately provoked the dispute was backed by an interview in the *Observer*[42] in which a Ford spokesman confirmed that they had chosen this moment to 'crunch' the Body Plant 'renegades'. In that same week, the AUEW and T&G had made the dispute official; but all their suggestions for a resolution, including job re-timings by independent consultants, were rejected by management.

In the meantime the stockpiling of parts gave the company the opportunity to ride out further strikes, most sparked by relentless increases in speedup. Throughout this period, management continued to 'turn the screws'; workers complained of having to 'run all day to keep up with the line', with older men taken off line jobs being brought back on – 'and sweating'. A sympathetic Jaguar worker described the assembly line at Dagenham as 'the fastest line in Britain', at 70 cars an hour.[43] And the 'sweating' was routinely twinned with its opposite: no work, and therefore, often, no pay – let alone information. As PTA steward Berlyne Hamilton remembered, 'You as an ordinary workers wouldn't know anything about why you were laid off'.

'A Rampage of Destruction ...'

But it was not the PTA that eventually erupted. On 6 October 1976, day shift workers in the Body Plant found a message from the night shift when they came in to work: 'Co-workers, we solicit your support in this hour of crisis. Let us unite in demanding a right to work from the company rather than being sent home whenever it suits the company. Today it's our turn. Tomorrow it will be your turn. United we stand, divided we fall.'

This 'crisis' had been provoked by yet another lay-off just before midnight, when the shift had been operating for only two hours. The stand-down was caused by a door-hangers' dispute over manning levels, but rather than direct their anger against their workmates the workers surged into the yard outside and began throwing their tea mugs up at the windows of management offices in a protest which rapidly turned into a riot. Frederick Creamer, a Body Plant steward and TGWU 1/667 activist, vividly described subsequent events in a story published years later: 'I told my fellow-workers to stay by the barricades we had built and to make sure the security guards didn't remove the oil drums or wooden pallets. They had taken us up to an hour to place along the car factory gates. I then hurried along the edge of the factory wall to the other building .... As I got closer, I saw the night sky lit up by flames ... the store's depot was on fire .... About eight feet above me ... a white china mug flew across the roadway and smashed into the office windows. I stood transfixed as mugs rained down into the windows .... The aim of the people throwing them was as good as a trained marksman, and they were putting out the remaining windows one by one ....' The rest of the account is a vivid description of 'total and utter chaos'.[44]

Two hundred police arrived almost instantly, only to have hoses turned on them by the furious workers, who then set fire to two vans, forming a barricade across the factory gate. Ford management spoke to the workers through loudspeakers, urging them to 'go home and not jeopardise the company's future', but this advice was greeted with a barrage of glass and furniture taken from the canteen and hurled at police and union officials.

The action created a sensation in the press, provoking headlines like 'Rioters smash up Ford Plant' and 'Rioting car workers go on the rampage'. The *Daily Mirror* described 'a rampage of destruction at Ford's Dagenham works .... Bottles and bricks were thrown through the windows, and rioters ... ripped off pieces of the roof and [threw] them to the ground.' Despite hundreds of police surrounding the area, 'the rioters found their own hose pipes and turned them on the police'.[45]

What the press did not report was the subdued, miserable end to the workers' outbreak of fury. As Fred Creamer recalls: "Between us, [the shop stewards] managed to get most of the men together for a mass meeting. Instead of the heaving, scrambling horde we had witnessed minutes before, now there were [exhausted] people lying on tables .... This meeting was very quiet compared to the packed and angry meeting three hours earlier, when we had agreed to occupy the plant …. The group was called to order and the crowd shuffled forward …. I looked at the men massed in front of us, and found it hard to believe that they were the same people who had been wreaking havoc only moments before. These men were responsible and hard working. They had been driven to these acts by their frustration at the company's indifference and its policy of laying off staff without pay or explanation ….'

Yet Ford management showed zero sympathy for their employees' long-held frustration. Instead, the company sacked 10 workers, suspended others, and picked out 22 for further investigation. There was little support from shop stewards, who 'dissociated themselves from the 1976 riots … and expressed their disapproval of this kind of violence'.[46] Nor did workers agree to strike in support of their suspended workmates, despite evidence from canteen staff that one of them, a door setter, was simply trying to prevent more damage. Management was triumphant; having sacked eight door hangers, they threatened that if the union prevented re-manning the section the whole plant would be laid off.

Yet the following week, after door-hanger Ken West was suspended for his part in the riot, his fellow workers stopped work in his support; shop stewards and district officials prevented the company from employing enough scabs to fully 'man up' the section, and when other sections blacked any cars produced by scabs, the door-hangers were reinstated, although West remained suspended pending an inquiry.

'From Dominica to Dagenham …'

It was during this turbulent period that 1107 activist Alf Richards first became a steward in the Engine Plant. An early fighter for equal opportunities, Alf was motivated first of all by discrimination within the company's redundancy policy: 'It got to me that the opportunity for redundancy or early retirement was not given to the West Indian community. We were told we didn't have the service. The company had been on site for 60+ years so the workforce at the start was naturally British, white – immigrants came from the 1950s, but most of them were not given a fair crack of the whip – opportunities were limited.'

Redundancy pay was not the only area of discrimination: 'There was unfairness re immigrant workers – they were always paid the lowest grade, opportunity for promotion was not forthcoming. When we all started we were on the same grade, but I noticed that the majority of immigrants, though they could be a hard worker, a good timekeeper, when it came to regrading they were left behind. Promotion to staff was more or less nonexistent'.[47] Alf's quiet but persistent organising on this issue was an early sign of 1107's principled stand on equal opportunities at Dagenham.

Meanwhile solidarity between workers over racist attacks soon extended beyond the plant. According to future 1107 chair Mick Gosling, PTA workers walked out in support of Asians under attack in Brick Lane in the mid-70s: 'They said "Right, we're going out" and there was a spontaneous walkout for that day'.[48] Steve Hart recalls that the 1107 branch discussed 'anti-racist issues, the Anti-Nazi league – we had a lot of campaigning in the plants around the ANL.' Yet the problems of racism at Dagenham that would lead to serious scandals in the 1990s were already beginning to surface. By July 1978, Asian and black workers were forced to take one-day strike action against racist attacks. TGWU steward Shel Uddin voiced their concerns – 'We demand protection' – but commented that 'It was good to see white workers coming out as well, and many more supporting our action'.[49]

Jupiter Harry, a West Indian who started work at Fords in 1972, became a steward at the suggestion of a white worker: 'There were no black stewards then, though I suppose about a third of the workers were black.' Later he wrote a moving article, 'From Dominica to Dagenham', in which he commented, 'One thing I've learnt, and that is that working people in Dominica are very much the same sort of people as the working people in Dagenham. The white workers *seemed* so different when I first came here, so stuck up, so snooty. But when you come to know them, work with them, strike with them you find that they've been *conditioned* to think in that silly racialist way. They're really not very different at all. They want the same things, and they can't get them for the same reason ...'.[50] The unity created by the common experience of work was the positive side of the coin – the more negative aspects began to emerge in the 1980s and beyond.

'Absolute rubbish'

In the meantime, union leaders were continuing to support the Labour government's 4.5 per cent ceiling on pay, the latest phase of the now hated 'Social Contract'. True to the stand of his leader Jack Jones, the TGWU's Moss Evans had described any talk of breaking the government's pay code as 'absolute rubbish'. As a result, Ford workers were losing money. Over the previous two years Ford cars had gone up in price by around 40 per cent, the same amount as the rise in the cost of living; but their producers' wages had only increased by 16 per cent. In addition, despite the brave fight for parity in 1971, wages at Fords continued to lag behind the rest of the car industry by £15 a week on average. Yet the company continued to reject all union claims above the £2.50-£4 allowed under the Social Contract, and was even seeking to take into account the cost-of-living payments which workers had been receiving since August under the current agreement.

Workers at Dagenham launched a campaign for a £15pw increase and a 35-hour week, promoted with stick-on badges and a 2p bulletin, *Fordworker*. The claim was to be presented to a national conference of Ford shop stewards in Coventry on 17 April 1977. This event, which attracted over 300 stewards, discussed an alternative proposal for a 15 per cent (as opposed to £15) increase, with Body Plant convenor Danny Connors arguing that this demand would achieve the broadest possible unity. But many stewards argued that this was not enough. One compared his recent rent increase, his electricity bill and food prices with the 15 per cent demand and said it could not match up to the huge increase in living costs. Another Dagenham Body Plant steward argued for the £15 (as opposed to 15 per cent) increase now being demanded by rank and file supporters of the *Fordworker* bulletin.

A Historic Victory?

The struggle around layoffs also continued during most of that year. Following on yet another layoff of the PTA day shift, the fight was on; at a 3000-strong mass meeting on 30 June, PTA workers agreed on the demand for a guaranteed 40-hour week or 80 per cent lay-off pay. They also voted to implement an agreed policy of picketing all five plants on the Dagenham estate if any section was laid off for disputes over which the workers had no control. The meeting rejected the ineffective agreement drawn up between trade union officials and the company on the issue; TGWU official Fred Blake[51] was met by a shower of leaflets and jeered off the platform, while PTA convenor Brian Elliott commented that 'Our committee feels the case for lay-off pay has not been met. The officials want to sell the workers of the PTA down the river.'

In the summer of 1977, the agreed action was put into effect, bringing the whole of Dagenham to a halt. Almost immediately after the picketing started, stewards could report that 'Fords UK is grinding to a standstill, and their European operations are being severely affected.' The action itself had 'united both day and nightshift PTA workers as never before' and had also gained support from workers in the Foundry, Engine and Body plants. As one steward exulted: 'The PTA pickets have shown that the [demand for] 80 per cent layoff money without strings can be won. It will be a historic victory against one of the most vicious and calculating companies in the world'.[52]

Yet the action had been taken in the face of fierce opposition from trade union officials and some convenors. The PTA shop stewards' committee issued an Official Statement accusing Dagenham trade union officials of having 'done everything they can over the past two weeks to demoralise us and drive us back to work'. Among other accusations and questions, the document asks 'Why has Brother [Mick] Murphy not fought to make the PTA dispute official, in line with the clear policy of his own union branch, the TGWU 1/1107 (Ford Central Branch)?'[53] It was an early sign of the radical spirit – based in the PTA – that was to transform the 1107 branch (see next chapter). By contrast, 1107-er Johnny Davies, deputy convenor in the Engine Plant, encouraged transport workers to cross the picket lines. More predictably, Ford management were also doing everything they could to undermine the action, including trying to set other plants against the PTA by offering a package deal on layoffs; this offered minor concessions in return for agreement on a still harsher disciplinary code.

In spite of his role in breaking the strike, Johnny Davies reflected in an interview: 'If you take the problems in Fords, they blame the workers, but ... a lot of the disputes in Fords were brought about by the company. They would build a lot of stock up and then they would start rumours – We're going to start laying people off. And people got upset about that and strikes began. Because the company in those days would send you home. It'd be in the middle of the night – don't worry about how they were going to get home in the middle of the night ....'

Meanwhile, outside events were pushing the Ford workforce towards a much bigger confrontation in which 1107 would be a central player. At the TGWU conference in July, 'Terrible Twin' Jack Jones saw defeat at the hands of delegates who overwhelmingly voted against his latest proposed pay limit. Steve Hart recalls that '1107 moved that motion that defeated Jack Jones. We put through our branch a motion opposing the Social Contract that got passed by union conference in 1977 ....'

Rank and file fury over the pay limits was by now clear to both government and Ford management. By mid-October, there seemed to be some hope that the company might be prepared to pay over the odds; the government was 'going easy' on Ford to encourage the company's plans for a new engine plant in South Wales. But by late October militants were describing that year's pay settlement as a wage cut. Ford unions had accepted a company offer worth about 9 per cent after deductions – effectively a cut of 7 per cent, given that inflation over the last year had been running at 16 per cent.

'You'll Need a Union Here ...'

In spite of the problems, the Dagenham plant was a fortress of union organisation by the late '70s. Ron Doel, a future 1107 branch secretary, started work in the PTA in 1977:

The plant was 100% union – not just the T&G and AEU ... there were about six or seven unions when I first started, but the particular union membership wasn't important really – you all had your own union but it didn't come into play when you needed someone to represent you because the steward would represent members from any union. [At the] two-day induction there was always a slot for the union to talk to people and they used to say to people "You may not believe in the union but believe me you'll need a union in here". And within the first day of going on to the shop floor you'd signed the form to join the T&G. It was never any trouble signing people up into the trade union – working in here you knew you had to have a good strong union – from things like getting signed off to leave the plant, to your workload .... Part of the steward's function was to make sure people weren't overloaded. The main union in the production area would have been the T&G, though you'd represent anyone – what trade union they were didn't really come into it. But the biggest membership there was of 1107, so we had the biggest number of stewards – about 60.[54]

Yet by October 1977, Dagenham management were again on the offensive against workplace organisation. Shop stewards were sent a letter telling them not to leave their jobs on union business or carry out stewards' activities in working hours, despite the fact that this had happened by agreement between management and stewards for years. The notion of 'Workers' Participation' was fashionable at the time, yet as Body Plant convenor Danny Connors noted in a pamphlet published by the Institute for Workers' Control (IWC), 'If you were talking genuinely about workshop democracy, then ... we should have at least an hour a week to be able to sit down with our blokes without their pay being stopped'. Connors made the fundamental point that trade unionism in the plants already included key elements of worker democracy: 'Our lads give up half of their dinner time in order to be able to take part in some sort of discussion.' He related this to the issue of industrial democracy – workers' control of the industries in which they worked – which was central to IWC policy: 'In my view genuine industrial democracy should start on the shop floor and we should have some sort of facility for meeting lads on a regular basis during working hours'.[55] But the 1974 TULRA, in spite of its provision of many workplace trade union rights, had not included any right to hold union meetings in the workplace during working hours.

In fact, when Body Plant stewards Tom Bermingham and Dave Wray tried to hold a shop meeting to discuss the clampdown on steward activity, they were threatened with the sack; a few months later, in January 1978, Bermingham was indeed sacked for 'cutting a hole in the body of a car'. When another worker came forward and confessed to this, management sacked him as well and refused to reinstate Tom. His department came out on strike, with other departments expected to follow -despite a lack of clear support from the senior convenors or Joint Works Committee. Meanwhile, management made it quite clear they were prepared to see the whole of Dagenham shut down if they could 'clear out some shop stewards and break shop floor organisation'.[56]

Although 400 workers had walked out on behalf of Tom Bermingham, by late January some were keeping the line going with the help of senior convenors and full time officials; in spite of his support for shopfloor meetings, convenor Dan Connors argued that if everyone returned to work it would be possible to negotiate. A majority then voted to go back, and by 5pm Bermingham was out of a job and out of the plant.

The next steward in line was Dave Wray. The company argued that by calling a meeting to discuss Bermingham's sacking, Wray had 'violated' the warning they had issued to shop stewards not to hold meetings in work time. At the same time management announced they would refuse to recognise another shop steward, Mick Hurd, who had been elected just before Christmas. Mick Murphy, now a T&G official, and senior steward Sid Harroway argued at a departmental meeting that it was better to persuade their members to remove the stewards' credentials rather than letting the company do it, since this would allow Wray to keep his job. After a bitter meeting, the department agreed; meanwhile, engineering union official Jack Mitchell allowed management to take away shop steward credentials from Mick Hurd.

But within weeks Dagenham workers were taking action over yet more shop steward victimisation. On 8 April 1978 all production was stopped when PTA workers went on strike in support of Stan Squires, a T&G steward and key 1107 activist dismissed after an argument with a foreman who was, they said, obviously drunk. The foreman was a member of ASTMS (Association of Scientific, Technical and Managerial Staffs), which had recently succeeded in organising the Ford supervisors in an example of the growing strength of technical and white-collar unionism at the time. ASTMS gave the company an ultimatum – sack Squires or they would strike. Management opted to get rid of Squires, whose members immediately came out on strike; other sections of the PTA voted not to scab or to touch any scab work, and all production in the PTA and Body Plant came to a halt. Within days, management had laid off the Assembly Plant, an action which effectively shut down the factory. Workplace conflict at Ford was clearly yet to be resolved.

Management Achievements

In June 1978 stewards from all 23 Ford plants met to decide that year's pay claim. Yet with only 110 of a possible 1500 stewards present, there was little opposition to 'rubber stamping' a claim already decided by the convenors. No amendments were allowed, and 'some of the more militant stewards left as soon as the pubs opened'. Their cynicism and the poor attendance was explained by PTA steward and 1107 member Martin Jones, who claimed that stewards were 'only allowed to rubber stamp a claim already decided by the convenors [with] no amendments allowed'. Jones argued that the convenors' motive was 'political .... The present agreement runs out on 21st October and there is almost certain to be a general election in the autumn. [Prime Minister] Callaghan says this is the election of the century, a Labour government must be returned – so the convenors are prepared to stifle the shop stewards' movement'.[57] The convenors pushed through an eight-point package which focused on fringe benefits rather than pay.

Nor were the convenors alone in their inclination to keep down workplace action. In July a secret report revealed yet another company strategy for tightening management's grip on the shop floor. This document, leaked by Dagenham activists, outlined new industrial relations strategies and also showed how full-time union officials were cooperating with the company in devising methods of 'squeezing' the workforce towards maximum productivity. Between the first and last quarters of 1977, warnings to workers had gone up by 250 per cent and suspensions had trebled. Management listed its 'achievements' in the Dagenham plant as:

1. closing the River Plant press shop with trade union agreement and without industrial action.
2. Increasing the Cortina line speed from 45 jobs per hour to 55; agreement to run Cortina estates down the Fiesta solder line despite trade union resistance.
3. Agreement by the FNJNC trade union side that employees were not entitled to trade union representation as a right.
4. A militant shop steward [Tom Bermingham] sacked with little opposition from trade union officials, and the removal union credentials from his co-steward [Dave Wray], sanctioned by trade union officials.

Ford management must have been congratulating themselves that they had suppressed the beast of trade union militancy at last ....

And then came the winter.

'We Smashed the Pay Freeze'

In the last week of September 1978 Jupiter Harry, now a senior TGWU shop steward in the Body Plant, could report: 'See you at Christmas! That was the cry as we streamed out of the gate. The men had known that there might have to be a strike. They know damn well that the company can afford to pay...'.[58]

Steve Hart, then still a shopfloor worker in the Engine Plant, recalled the early hours of this famous dispute, widely seen as launching the 1978-9 Winter of Discontent:

> I remember we gathered in the canteen and we just started chanting *Out Out Out* – 1000 people, 2000 people, and they were just sitting banging the tables and shouting *Out Out Out* – the feeling was fantastic. It wasn't the convenors who were doing it, it was the lay members saying "We've got to go." We all walked out at about 1 o'clock in the morning – and that was that – the other plants, the Assembly Plant, the Body Plant – also walked out that night. And that was the start of the dispute .... We were off, we were out, and we stuck out for the nine weeks.

Roger Dillon, soon to become a highly effective shop steward and key 1107 activist, had just started work at the plant. For him, the strike was an initiation:

> The first week I was there they had a mass meeting and they went out on strike – I was there for about four days and we were out on a 9-week strike ... it came as such a shock – one minute I'm working away and the next it was "Oh there's a mass meeting" – and you see these hundreds of people all walking in one direction and it was just like if you go to a football match – and then you'd end up in this massive area, the loading bays and the despatch area – and you'd have maybe a thousand people there and all you heard was *Show of hands* because in those days it was just before the law came in about ballots and – "Right, brothers, we're out".

This explosion of militancy was the fallout from years of resentment against both company and union leadership. And the 1978-9 Ford strike rapidly became a standard-bearer for anger by workers everywhere against the government's 5 per cent pay limit. As the conflict developed, public and private sector workers, including convenors at Metal Box and Glasgow District Council, soon declared their solidarity. A NUPE branch chair wrote from Edinburgh, 'We're looking to Fords to smash the 5% limit. It would make a world of difference to us.' By 30 September, when the strike began, dockers at Harwich had already agreed to boycott all Ford equipment; seafarers also refused to move Fords goods, despite being threatened with mutiny charges.

While some 'Ford wives' tried the old tactic of a back-to-work protest, others from Dagenham, Langley and Southampton organised a counter-demonstration. As one argued – giving some insight into the impact of working at Ford on family life – 'If they accept 5% this year, what will we get next year ...? [Bosses] have never had to scrimp and save to make sure their kids get a decent coat for the winter. Mike works three shifts, 6-2.30, 2-11, and nights 10-6. It has a dreadful effect on him ... He comes home from a shift like a bear with a sore head ... he shouts at the children ... It takes him a good couple of hours to get back to normal. It's the pressure. To live like that has to be worth more than 5%'.[59]

By the end of October, almost all the engines produced at Dagenham had been used; 1,700 workers had been already laid off at the Belgian Genk plant, and 1,200 in Amsterdam put on a one-day week; and on 4 November, after all the British Ford plants had been halted for six weeks, union negotiators turned down a 15 per cent package which included both productivity increases and another version of the hated 'penalty clauses'.

This relatively strong stand by the officials may have been influenced by the rank and file Ford Workers' Combine Committee. As one activist put it, 'The best way to influence the decisions of convenors and strike committees is to have an active rank and file organisation breathing down their necks ....' And not only the Combine Committee but an even more grass-roots organisation, the Ford Workers' Group, played a part in maintaining the strikers' stand. As Steve Hart recalled, 'The Ford Workers' Group was a rank and file left-wing group which started pursuing the arguments for a strike and ... making the case for a very big wage claim ... [T]here were two different [strategic] lines going at the time and I argued at the Ford Workers' Group ... that as it was an ambitious claim from the official unions it would be sensible for the FWG and the official unions to align their demands – rather than counterposing one against the other. And I think that worked very well – all pulling in the same direction.'

The strike stayed solid into November, with workers turning down another offer on the 10th. As Jupiter Harry reported: 'It was really fantastic – more than 2-1 against the company.' Dell Gordon, a TGWU steward in the PTA, commented, "The vote last Friday was really great. I was a bit surprised what with it coming up to Xmas. But I didn't want to go back with those penalty clauses included ... I'd rather go back on straight wages than those kind of anti-strike clauses, and I think most people felt like that.' Another 1107 member, Bob Overstall, noted: 'Most of the people thought it wasn't on .... The penalty clauses were a bit naughty. They would force people to come in when they were ill .... Ford had said this was positively their final offer, but the lads wouldn't be blackmailed back to work'.[60]

We Smashed the Pay Freeze!

Based on this staunch solidarity, on 22 November the Ford workers won a 17 per cent pay rise which 'drove a coach and horses through Phase Four'.[61] As Terry Duffy from the AUEW commented – perhaps inventing the historic phrase – 'Even the lads sweeping the street wanted 17 ½ per cent when Fords had got it ... and that caused a winter of discontent'. 1107 activist Pete Singh remembers his father proclaiming 'We smashed the pay freeze!', and in fact the Ford workers' killer blow to Phase Four of Labour's incomes policy was the spark for an almost uninterrupted wave of strikes throughout the autumn and winter of 1978-9.

But despite its historic significance, the strike was not a total victory. The pay rise averaged £10.50, not the £20 claimed, and £3.52 of this was based on a 'Supplementary Payment Plan' with provisions closely resembling the hated penalty clauses. PTA worker and 1107 activist Matt Salisbury reported that 'We receive the £3.52 if we work "normally" .... All workers laid off due to unofficial action would lose the whole week's bonus. At present there are numerous small stoppages in Fords. Workers complain about oil on the floor, about heat and cold, about draughts. They stop for say, half an hour, with the knowledge that at worst they will lose 80p or so. With the new penalty clause they are bound to lose the £3.52 bonus as well ....' He put down acceptance of the inadequate offer to the fact that 'Everyone simply needed some money for Christmas'.[62]

Getting the Genie out of the Bottle ...

But nothing could undermine the massive boost of defeating the government's pay policy; and Ford activists' organisation continued in other important directions. In October 1979, twenty-five Ford workers from Britain, Spain, Germany, Holland and Denmark met to discuss the setting up of an International Fordworkers' Ring. Contacts between the countries had arisen from practical acts of solidarity; for example, Dutch Ford workers had raised £1000 for the 1978 strike fund. The conference discussed strategies like swapping information between countries and plants, building strike funds and solidarity stoppages.

This international perspective points to the political awareness of those most central to the 'Winter of Discontent' triumph: workplace activists. As one steward put it, 'There were more Che Guevaras in Dagenham than in the Caribbean'. Ford Workers' Group supporter Rod Finlayson recalls, 'You had those politically-conscious people being elected as shop stewards, working together with workers, inspiring workers .... They'd hand out leaflets saying "Get united, come to a meeting" – the Ford Workers' Group was trying to unite left wing and militant people on a trade union programme.'

Such organising was easily accepted by less consciously political workers at Ford. In the words of one worker interviewed during this period, 'Certainly left of centre groups would be at the gates at shift times selling their papers and giving their leaflets – Maoists, Communists, revisionists, all sorts. There used to be a guy outside the factory selling the Morning Star, and various people selling the Socialist Worker magazine. There was always plenty of political activity down there, much of it well to the left of the left of the left .... It heightened the scene. It was very good. It kept the main trade union people on their toes'.[63] This worker was clearly not 'political', but many so-called ordinary workers were themselves politicised – permanently – by the experience of working for Ford in the 1970s. As steward Dave Wray commented on his own radicalisation, 'Once you've got the genie out of the bottle it's difficult to get it back in again.' By no means all 1107 stalwarts would have described themselves as inspired by this 'genie'; but it was the same key processes of workplace resistance and direct democracy that were to achieve a 'revolution' in the 1/1107 branch during the next decade.

NOTES

1 John Mathews, *Ford Strike*, London: Panther Books, 1972, p. 77.
2 Mathews, *Ford Strike*, p. 92.
3 Mathews, *Ford Strike*, p. 77.
4 Mathews, *Ford Strike*, p. 123.
5 Mathews, *Ford Strike*, p. 126.
6 All quotes from Colin Beadle, 'No Cracks at Ford', *Socialist Worker* 20 February 1971, p. 8.
7 Mathews, *Ford Strike*, pp. 131-2.
8 Beadle, 'No Cracks at Ford'.
9 Beadle, 'No Cracks at Ford'.
10 This nickname was common throughout the 1970s to describe the two union leaders, who at first were much more left-wing than their predecessors.
11 Mathews, *Ford Strike*, p. 141.
12 Punctuation as in original.
13 Mathews, *Ford Strike*, p. 143.
14 Paul Foot, *The Postal Workers and the Tory Offensive* – see Mathews, *Ford Strike*, pp. 144-5.

15   Mathews, *Ford Strike*, pp. 146-7.
16   Mathews, *Ford Strike*, p. 161.
17   Interviewed 5.1.2011 (see Bibliography).
18   'Fords: News From The Shop Floor', *Solidarity* Vol 6 No 10, 26 June 1971, p. 14.
19   T.C. 'The Ford Fiasco', *Solidarity* Vol. 7 No. 6, p. 5.
20   Colin Beadle, 'Crunch at Ford', *Socialist Worker* 17 February 1973, p. 9.
21   Cf Sheila Cohen, *Ramparts of Resistance: Why Workers Lost Their Power, and How to Get It Back*, London: Pluto, 2006, pp 13-29. The Upsurge is usually dated 1968-74, but there are many examples of exceptionally militant workplace union activity both before and after these dates.
22   M.F., 'The Ford Fiasco', *Solidarity* Vol. 7 No. 6, 22 April 1973, p. 5.
23   Interview carried out on 17.11.2010 (see Bibliography).
24   'Ford: Sacked man is victim of big production drive', *Socialist Worker* 29 September 1973, p. 16.
25   'Union tells how Ford worker was harassed', *Morning Star* 25 September 1973, p. 1.
26   Interviewed 16 November 2010 (see Bibliography).
27   Henry Friedman and Sander Meredeen, *The Dynamics of industrial conflict: Lessons from Ford*, London: Croom Helm 1980, pp. 234-5.
28   Cohen, *Ramparts of Resistance*, p. 29.
29   Levels of inflation rose to almost unprecedented levels in the 1970s and early '80s: from 8.7 per cent in 1973 to 13 per cent in 1975 and 12.5 per cent in 1980 (Department of Labour).
30   Barbara Castle, *The Castle Diaries 1974-76*, Weidenfeld and Nicolson 1980, pp. 188, 194.
31   'Ford: No Wage Cuts Here', *Socialist Worker* 28 September 1974, p. 1.
32   Friedman and Meredeen, *Dynamics*, p. 240.
33   A much-quoted article by a left-leaning industrial relations professor, Richard Hyman, argued this position in the late 1970s: Richard Hyman, 'The Politics of Workplace Trade Unionism: Recent Tendencies and some problems for Theory', *Capital and Class*, 8 (Summer), 1979, pp. 54-67.
34   Joint Works Committees – committees of all shop stewards within a specific plant.
35   Interviewed 15 February 2011 (see Bibliography).
36   Ronald McIntosh, *Challenge to Democracy*, London: Politico's, 2006, p. 200.
37   Friedman and Meredeen, *Dynamics*, p. 348.
38   Friedman and Meredeen, *Dynamics*, p. 243.
39   Friedman and Meredeen, *Dynamics*, p. 243.
40   Friedman and Meredeen, *Dynamics* p. 267.
41   'Ed Zell' (Ed Emery), 'The Dagenham "Occupation"', *Solidarity* Vol 8 No. 2, 31 May 1975, p. 5.
42   Quote from *Observer* in 'Pickets on Ford Plant' *Socialist Worker* 14 June 1975, p. 14.
43   'Dagenham: Ford's turn the screws', *Socialist Worker* 5 July 1975, p. 14.
44   Fred Creamer, 'Riot', in *Life's Too Short: True stories about Life at Work*,

Bantam Books, 2010.
45 Patrick Long, Stuart Grieg and Jill Palmer, 'Fires break out – then hoses are turned on Police', *Daily Mirror*, 29 September 1976, p. 4.
46 Friedman and Meredeen, *Dynamics*, p. 268.
47 Interviewed 17 November 2010 (see Bibliography).
48 Interviewed 21 February 2012 (see Bibliography).
49 Shel Uddin, 'Strike against racism', *Socialist Worker* 22 July 1978, p. 1.
50 Jupiter Harry, 'From Domenica to Dagenham', *Socialist Worker* 4 November 1978 (italics in original), p. 5.
51 The National Union of Vehicle Builders, Blake's union, had merged into the TGWU in 1972.
52 Peter McMonagle, Bob Overstone, Roma Samy, Hafizur Rahman, 'For years we have been treated like cattle … ' *Socialist Worker* 25 June 1977, p. 2.
53 Reprinted in 'Diary of the June 1977 Dispute', *Red Notes* June 1978, p. 24.
54 Interviewed 7 May, 10 June 2010.
55 Bernie Passingham and Danny Connors in *Ford Shop Stewards on Industrial Democracy*, Institute for Workers' Control Pamphlet No. 54, October 1977, p. 15.
56 Ford stewards, 'Ford sack shop steward' *Socialist Worker*, 14 January 1978, p. 15.
57 Martin Jones, 'Ford: Keep your eye on that £250m profit', *Socialist Worker* 10 June 1978, p. 14.
58 Jupiter Harry, 'From Domenica to Dagenham', *Socialist Worker* 30 September 1978, p. 5.
59 Florence Stubberfield, 'Fighting Wives of Fords', *Socialist Worker* 28 October 1978, p. 4.
60 Plant Reports: 'Dagenham' by Dell Gordon, T&G steward, PTA, *Socialist Worker* 11 November 1978, p. 5.
61 Alan Thornett, *Inside Cowley*, London: Porcupine Press,1998, p. 272.
62 'Carry on Working', Mat Salisbury, *Socialist Worker* 2 December 1978, p. 4.
63 Dave (no surname), interviewed for a history project at the Valence House Museum near Dagenham.

Chapter Five

THE EIGHTIES: STORMING 1107

One rather important event had taken place a few months before the start of the new decade; the election of a new Conservative government under the leadership of Margaret Thatcher. Not everyone saw the implications at the time. Steve Hart recalls that 'the active minority were worried, but the sense in the plant as a whole was that this was a result that they wanted – probably following our [1978-9] strike they felt that Labour had not been at all supportive.'

Yet Thatcherite anti-union laws limiting solidarity and undermining workplace trade union democracy were to have a devastating impact on even strongly-organised workplaces like Ford's Dagenham plant. In a whole range of ways, Thatcherism was the beginning of the end of independent class-struggle unionism – at least for the duration. As shown below, by the mid-to-late 1980s workers were citing aspects of Thatcherism, from secret balloting to the new obsession with 'home ownership', to explain what was seen as an ongoing loss of shopfloor power.

Yet it was during the early years of Thatcherism that some key players in the transformation of 1/1107 were drawn into active workplace unionism. Future branch secretary Ron Doel became a steward in 1982 or 1983: 'I was just 20-odd years old, used to stand up for myself a bit ... I said, I'll give it a try. I tried it and I excelled in it – just looking after people like you would look after yourself really.' Roger Dillon, the Ford 'novice' quoted in the last chapter, quickly became absorbed into the plant organisation as an 1107 activist and, before long, steward. As he recalled, 'Coming to Fords, being part of the union was the thing to do .... And in those days when people took industrial action it worked.'

Yet key 1107 activist Jim Brinklow, an experienced trade unionist who started work in the PTA in 1980, remembered Dagenham then as 'an awful place trade union wise ... you couldn't tell the difference between the trade union people and the bosses because they were all booted and suited the same ....' It was an interesting comment on the apparent growth of 'union-management cooperation' at Fords.

In fact, management aggression was more typical. In November 1980, Employment Relations Director Paul Roots wrote to all 57,000 Ford workers condemning work stoppages as causing the company's 'low productivity' and announcing that 'the company intends to discipline strikers who stop work unconstitutionally' (i.e. before having exhausted the company's procedure agreement).

The introduction of new technology was another aspect of Ford management's drive for increased productivity – whatever the impact on workers. Electricians' steward Mick Hadgraft remembered the 1982 launch of the Ford Sierra as 'accompanied in the Body Plant by a swathe of robotisation'. The innovations led to one disturbing episode in the early 1980s when the company destroyed lineside 'cribs' – small stations where workers kept their possessions – in order to adapt the line for robotisation. 1107 activist Pete Singh confirmed that 'Management took out all the cribs by the line … they threw away a lot of people's possessions – there was a stoppage of work over it …. We got better facilities, but they wouldn't have given us that without the punch-up [stoppage].'

Storming 1107

At this point, the 1107 branch was still dominated by a more conservative – and allegedly corrupt – leadership. As Jim Brinklow recalled, 'Our branch was basically in the control of right-wing elements, and they were as corrupt as anything – like gangsters. There was financial corruption, corruption all around.' Yet from the early to mid-80s, 'We gradually took over the branch …. Then we turned up mob-handed and voted them all out and voted people in that were going to do a job ….'

By this time one of the central forces in the reformed branch, Steve Riley, was coming to the fore. Pete Singh remembered that 'In February 1983, when I was transferred from the Foundry to the PTA, my shop steward was Steve Riley – he took me under his wing and basically gave me a top-up about how trade unions work …. Steve had so much respect from the workforce that they wouldn't go to any other steward, they'd go to Steve …. He was just a natural leader.' Jim points out that 'Steve was on the national committee of the T&G – our union is basically lay-led – so he was a union activist [as well as] a shop steward.' It was Steve who, as Ron Doel confirmed, 'led the takeover [of 1107].' Another key activist, Rod Finlayson, remembered 'Steve Riley and company storm[ing] 1107 – they brought hundreds of people up and won the election and Davies never came back'.

Ron listed the 1107 'vanguard' activists: 'Jim Brinklow was on the committee, Allan Martin, Ted Amos. Ned Leary[1] was the treasurer, I was the minutes secretary ....' Serious reforms were needed: 'When we took over the branch the finances were very poor given how many members we had – 4,500 to 5,000 – there was only about £200 in the account! We built it up to £30,000. We kept it up to a healthy rate until the plant closed[2] – we had to keep tighter control.' But the branch reformers were not alone; as key 1107 activist Mick Gosling added, 'The real rocket force that ... challenged the branch [ex-leadership] was the PTA shop stewards' committee .... At the meeting where we all got elected, they turned up in force and [the action] was organised and very disciplined.'

On the controversial issue of the branch finances, Mick was careful to point out that 'Re. the old 1107 leadership, some stuff is un-provable, for example where the branch secretary's funds were going – there were rumours that they were going to massage parlours .... At that time there wasn't a check-off, so people's dues were collected by stewards and 16% was supposed to go to the branch secretary – and we could never understand quite where the money was because it never appeared to be in the account ....'[3]

Rod Finlayson also described the alleged financial corruption of the branch under the previous leadership: 'That rotten group emptied the branch funds of £14,000 .... When Riley took over and started saving money the 1107 funds went up by thousands of pounds.'

Trim Shop steward Dora Challingsworth, herself a member of the 667 branch, was equally positive about the transformation of 1107. Speaking of the previous leadership, she commented, 'They done a lot of fiddling. The Engine Plant thought they was gods – they was in charge of everything. But there was a big blow up – you got some in the PTA that had a bit of sense and thought "Right, that's it, they're not getting away with that" – and that's what happened – 1107 was stepped out from the Engine Plant. The [previous leaders] were still in 1107, they couldn't do nothing about that – but they just didn't go to the meetings or anything, they didn't get involved any more'.[4]

After Japan – What?

The new 1107-ers came to power with a fighting stance. The November 1984 issue of the branch newsletter, under the headline 'Ford Can Pay – Ford Must Pay!', damned the 'final offer' of 7 per cent recently accepted by trade union officials and some convenors on the FNJNC. A more fundamental problem with the offer, as *Fraud News*[5] spelt out, was that 'they intend ... to kill us with AJ ....'

This is an early reference to 'After Japan', a range of changes in work organisation based on the supposedly harmonious management-worker setup in Japan (where, in fact, a highly militant trade union movement had been crushed after the Second World War). Secret minutes obtained by the stewards had revealed that under AJ a range of new tasks was to be imposed on line workers, including identifying defects and carrying out repairs, keeping their areas clean and tidy and equipment in good condition – all this on top of their own work. These proposals – along with the new 'Just-in-Time' strategy of limiting parts storage – would, of course, mean the loss of more jobs, yet they were also linked with the introduction of 'Quality Circles', the cosy management-worker discussion groups already opposed by the Dagenham rank and file.

As TGWU official Steve Turner later commented, 'Ford was at the forefront of many of the industrial changes that were coming about at the time, trying to drive home a new agenda of not working "smarter" but working a lot harder. Driving home efficiency, taking out sanity time from the job, dehumanising work ....' The company was also moving towards contracting out of jobs and replacing job grading with flexible work practices.

1/1107's response to these initiatives included support for the national Ford Combine, launched in 1984, which brought the branch into contact with not only other Ford plants but political activists and sympathetic researchers across the movement. As Mick Gosling recalled, 'We were receiving information all the time about what was going on in other areas. Management couldn't understand it .... "How the hell do these people know about what's happening in Japan or Australia?" And it was because we had other information from people like International Labour Research, CAITS[6] etc. .... Managers were coming up to us asking for copies of *Fraud News* .... We had connections in the US, all over Europe.'

Gosling adds that 'We were so locked into the membership on the shop floor that people trusted us, they believed in us and that's why they always elected us into positions inside the official trade union structures, as well as saying "We'll quite happily roll along with more open-ended stuff" which was what the Ford Workers' Group and the Combine was all about.'

It was at about this time that Mick was transferred from the Engine Plant to the PTA, giving him a glimpse of a very different experience of work and workplace trade unionism. 'The PTA was a world in itself ... although many of us were in the same union branch, the 1107, the difference in character between the Engine Plant and the PTA was extraordinary. The PTA had the roughest jobs – the graft on the line and the continuous speedups were unbearable – you had about 56 seconds to do the job, and all the time the pressure was coming down to do more. People were ground into the dust ....'

In a global company, the move towards combine organisation was logically extended to organising internationally: as Mick put it, 'The stewards at Dagenham were extremely aware of the fact that the Sierra was also manufactured at Genk, and it is in response to the threat of any lost production at one plant being made up at the other that Ford unions worldwide were seeking to form an "international combine" so that this could not occur ... Via the branch, we started putting pressure on about forming an international unofficial combine – then we said "That's not enough – we want an official international Ford workers' combine." And we pushed for that and that was when there was the first worldwide international Ford Workers' Combine meeting in 1985.' As Rod Finlayson reported, 'The first Ford workers' world conference was a magnificent achievement .... We had shop stewards, convenor-level workers from Japan, Malaysia, South Africa, the United States, Mexico, Brazil ... Joe Gordon spoke for us – Steve Riley, fair enough, stepped down for Joe Gordon .... So we had a black guy speaking for Britain.'

The Sewing Machinists Finally Win – Sort Of

It was in this environment of union activism that sewing machinists at Dagenham and Halewood came out once again over their regrading claim, still unresolved despite the historic 1968 strike. As *Fraud News* noted, 'For sixteen years, the Sewing Machinists have patiently pursued their claim for recognition of their skill. They are the only workers at Ford who have to get a certificate of competence to do their job, but do not get C grade .... Sixteen wasted years have taught them that the only way to get their rights is by fighting for them. That's why the machinists at both Dagenham and Halewood walked out last Thursday.'

On 24 November 1984, the 300 sewing machinists at Ford Dagenham – soon joined by those at Halewood – had voted unanimously for an all-out strike and walked out for the day to lobby the Ford pay talks in London. One factor in their favour was the introduction of some elements of 'Just-In-Time' production, meaning there were fewer made-up seats in the plant when the strike began; the action had an almost immediate effect in Europe due to the low stocks. Although trains were coming to Dagenham with parts, PTA workers refused to handle them, and the plant was soon shut down.

Meanwhile, the sewing machinists had produced and distributed a leaflet explaining their case to workers in both plants. As their shop stewards reported, 'All 24 Ford plants are behind us. Once the men hear about us, they support us .... We've got all the lorry-drivers backing us.' The myth that the historic 1968 strike had achieved 'equal pay' was demolished: 'Those girls 16 years ago came out for the same as we're out for now and they were pulled back to work on the promise of equal pay. But equal pay with who? It could be equal pay with a janitor. We want equal pay with skilled workers'.[7]

The workers were out on strike for three weeks before their dispute was mysteriously made official – perhaps because it was so effective. A 1985 Parliamentary Committee report records Dagenham management admitting 'We had got the outside-UK manufacture of vehicles percentage of our total requirement down to 40 per cent .... Unhappily, because of the machinists' strike, we had to go back ... and say "Sorry, that 40 per cent is now 44 per cent". That is the kind of impact [this] kind of thing ... has on our business'.[8]

Meanwhile, management at Halewood faced stubborn resistance when they tried to train men to do the women's jobs. One machinist reported: 'We haven't had any aggro with the men. Fords are trying to wind them up, but we've had good support from everyone.' She linked their struggle with the claim for a lineworkers' allowance: "If we win, the line workers will need to come out on strike for their claim – and they deserve it. The conditions they work in are awful'.[9]

Dagenham machinists' steward Dora Challingsworth emphasised the degree of solidarity from workers both in and out of Fords. Referring to the historic 1984-5 miners' strike, which activists at Dagenham staunchly supported, she recalled, 'The coal people were out on strike too and they had pickets out, we had pickets out and we had a right laugh .... Ford's tried to fetch work in on the railway .... But the men in the PTA wouldn't use it'.[10] Mick Gosling remembers that 'We supported the 1984-5 sewing machinists' dispute wholeheartedly ... there was absolutely no animosity towards the women whatsoever', while Joe Gordon – TGWU convenor of the PTA in the 1980s – noted that 'Most members were fully behind the sewing machinists ... There was no hatred for the women but for the company.'

Early in January the familiar escape clause of an 'independent inquiry' was used to get the sewing machinists back to work. A tripartite committee of TGWU officials, Ford management and the government's Advisory, Conciliation and Arbitration Service (ACAS) was set up to assess the claim. The sewing machinists were understandably reluctant to accept this outcome, and did so only under pressure from the union. But the Inquiry finally 'won the women their grading grievance and recognition as skilled workers', according to Halewood militant John Bohanna.[11]

A commemorative plate jointly produced by the two TGWU branches involved, 667 at Dagenham and Halewood's 562, was inscribed 'Ford Sewing Machinists win upgrading and skill recognition'. But the triumphant announcement of victory that should have belonged to the Dagenham sewing machinists' stewards was robbed from them by management and male trade unionists; Dora Challingsworth recalls 'I was annoyed about that. The convenor was up London and he'd phoned in to the management to tell them that we'd won, and the management went out on the floor and told the women!'

Meanwhile, the increasing number of women now working at Dagenham in direct production were welcomed and encouraged by the branch. As 1107 activist Terry Turner recalled, 'Ford were always pumping their thing about the "Ford Family" – they meant it in one way, we took it in another, because we were fraternal and sororal or whatever the word is. We embraced women just as we embraced people of colour ....'.[12]

Engine Plant 1107er Ted Amos agreed: 'It went very well. If the job was a little bit over the top for them the guy next to them would help her out. Everybody wanted to help ....' Women workers became 'militants' with the rest; as one commented, 'This is the first time I've ever worked anywhere where there have been strikes or anything like that. I never thought I'd strike but if we didn't ... things would be a lot worse. It is strenuous now ... but it will be a lot harder if the line is turned up'[13].

But not all was positive. Mavis Martin, an assembly-line pioneer and 1107 activist, recalled the problem of pin-ups, not really dealt with until the 1990s: 'Oh, that was terrible ... guys would come round with the toolboxes and as soon as they were opened up they had all these calendar girls ....' Sexism expressed itself in other (predictable) forms: 'I found a girl crying one day ... this foreman [had] tried to force her in the lift and in the car park .... She told me the things that went on on the line with this guy and other women – he would tell them if they didn't do what he wanted he would put them in a rotten job and all the rest of it ....' But on the whole her experience was positive: 'I loved the guys, we used to get on really well – they were great once you got to know them, they were your friends ....They were very helpful, very good to me'.[14]

The Future Is Uncertain ...

In 1985 the (then left-wing) Greater London Council carried out a Public Inquiry into Fords. Its report began with a quote from the PTA convenor,

Joe Gordon, which emphasised the onset of significant job cuts: 'We have seen a massive investment in new technology in the assembly area, but very little in manufacturing. The future of our press shop, wheel plant [and] forge ... are uncertain. [The workforce in] our Dagenham Engine plant which was one of the largest in the world, producing over 4,000 engines per day, has now fallen dramatically to just over 1,700 ....'[15] The report itself went on to confirm that Ford had 'cut employment at its London plants by one-third in the last five years, and is introducing extensive automation ... while attempting to reorganise labour relations. The contraction of Ford at Dagenham has enormous social costs both for the local economy and the wider economy of London ....' Prophetic words.

The GLC Inquiry showed that the future of the press shop and toolroom were also now in doubt with the development of new technology like computer-aided design and manufacturing (CAD/CAM). The historic wheel plant – once Kelsey Hayes – was to close in 1985; in the River Plant, a move to plastic seating materials threatened the jobs of the ever-defiant sewing machinists. In general, the decline of employment at Dagenham in the early-to-mid 1980s produced shocking figures; while in February 1979 total employment at Dagenham was 28,583, by the end of 1985 it had fallen to 14,700 – a drop of almost 50 per cent. In addition, while Black workers had been 'heavily recruited' in the late 1960s and '70s, when wages were relatively low, the report calculated 'a loss of 3,007 black workers' jobs at Dagenham' since 1979.

Meanwhile, Ford employees were working harder than ever. TGWU official Steve Hart reported that 'Even according to Fords' own work study system, many of our members are working at 98, 99 and in some cases 100% of their physical capacity.' The beginnings of 'Employee Involvement' (see further below) were charted in the Inquiry, with Deputy Convenor Tony Baker commenting that despite its attractive image, 'The corporations ... have not been prompted to invest in EI by some newfound concern for workers' needs, but as a convenient way to tighten up control over the workforce. Nonetheless, union leaders are still binding to the concept for their own reasons. For many of them EI is a job security strategy ...' Like 1107 activists (see below), Baker was not convinced: 'EI and QWL [Quality of Working Life] eat away at the power of the unions.'

Finally, Steve Riley made a poignant contribution: 'Conditions at Dagenham are now reminiscent of slave labour, with men[16] feeling that they are no more than slaves to the company machine, with no hope for the future ... [In] 1979 the average work load ... was 75%. Today many workers are close to and on the 100% mark. That means from bell to bell, every second of the working shift is used .... It is often difficult for the public ... to understand some of the disputes that have taken place ... around what seem to be trivial problems of a few minutes' relief, but when you look at what the production worker has to endure it is not very difficult to understand why.'

It was Steve's intense understanding of and empathy for workers' problems that made him a pivotal force in workplace trade unionism at Dagenham, particularly in the PTA. In the early-mid 1980s, it also put him at the centre of the long-overdue transformation of TGWU 1/1107.

'1107 – We Were There'

The new 1107 demonstrated its radical priorities at an early stage; branch activists were among the first in Britain to embrace an 'equal opportunities' perspective. Jim Brinklow recalled that 'We'd had a couple of disputes in the plant involving racism, and as a result of it decided to set up these Equal Opportunities Committees .... It was done eventually on a nationwide basis – all the plants had to set these up. They were joint between union and employer.' But the reform did not come without, as Pete Singh would put it, a 'punch-up'. As Jim Brinklow recalled, 'When two foremen were discovered distributing a racist leaflet, we went on strike, we stopped the production line. We said to the company, something's radically wrong here when you have two foremen distributing stuff like that. As a result Ford set up an equal opportunities committee .... They began advertising jobs in ... the black press.'

As one *Guardian* writer commented much later, 'This is what anti-racism looks like. Equal opportunities are not handed down from on high by Westminster bureaucrats; they have been fought for by ordinary men and women'.[17] In this case, the 'ordinary' fighters were night shift workers at Dagenham who had walked out on unofficial strike over the racist leaflet, demanding the sacking of the two supervisors concerned (one of whom, Tony Lacoma, was a notorious and high-level member of the National Front who later blew himself up planting a bomb in a left-wing bookshop.[18]) Jim commented, 'That shook the company, they realised they would have to do something – so they signed an agreement, set up monthly meetings of the Equal Opportunities committee.' Summing up the dynamics, he concluded 'It's on the ground floor it all happens – pass what laws you like but unless workers take direct action ...'.

In November 1985 Dagenham management wrote to all its employees to tell them 'how seriously the Company takes its commitment to Equal Opportunities, and what we are planning to do in the Plant to create greater equality of opportunity ....' The letter notes ruefully that 'it has now become clear to us that although we have good policies about what <u>ought</u> to happen, what <u>does</u> happen is not good enough.' The letter proposed setting up a joint Equal Opportunities Working Party with the JWC and ASTMS (the union representing supervisors) and pledged to 'continue to investigate the sources of any offensive material ... and watch closely for any signs of organised racist activity.'

It was clearly not enough. In November 1986, Fords 'told union leaders that it will consider their request for a new company-wide equal opportunities policy involving joint union-management ethnic monitoring ....' At the time just over 38 per cent of Dagenham's 12,000 workers were Black; yet 'figures for recent recruitment at ... Dagenham showed that 9 per cent of the white applicants got jobs, but only 3.5 per cent of the black applicants were successful'.[19]

Racist recruitment practices were entrenched – among management. As one worker put it, 'Dagenham has hundreds of black workers, but they are confined to the unskilled jobs. The skilled workers are all white .... When they go round the schools to recruit apprentices they go to white areas first to make sure they don't get any blacks applying until all the jobs are gone.' On the shop floor, on the other hand, 'There is racism but with most of the blokes it's superficial ... they play cards and dominos and get on with the black workers'.[20]

But serious problems remained, particularly in Dagenham's truck fleet, where hourly-paid jobs were jealously guarded from 'intruders'. One indication of the unusually serious problems of racism here came in May 1988, when Jim Brinklow reported to a grievance procedure meeting that a Mr Ward had applied for a driving job the previous November but had never received a response. The minutes of the meeting record Jim's diplomatic approach: 'Mr Ward was black and it had crossed their minds that the Truck Fleet mainly consists of white employees ....' The union side of the meeting 'would like to know that there was no bias against people from ethnic backgrounds ... Mr Ward had quite a wide experience of driving and they would like to know why he was rejected'.[21] The minutes convey embarrassed management shuffling, but no clear answers.

One early Equal Opportunities committee meeting also raised the issue of sexual harassment in the plant. Following on an allegation by a woman worker against her foreman, management announced that 'policy guidelines as to what constituted sexual harassment would be jointly issued.' But this was not enough for Joe Gordon, who 'was concerned over the actual process of dealing with sexual harassment' – an important distinction. As a (female) personnel manager noted, 'in one case a woman had complained that the accused men had responded in an unsavoury way to her allegations', but Jim Brinklow pointed out that 'This was an automatic response' by those so accused. Policies, while essential, were clearly not enough in themselves.

The branch contributed to increasing awareness of all these issues, and the establishment of related structures, within the TGWU at national level. As Mick Gosling recalled, 'In the 1980s, 1107 put through the motion that led to the establishment of race equality committees and the Women's Committee inside the T&G. We had to fight every inch of the way to get that, but we did it and that's now accepted as standard.' On this and other issues, 1/1107 was by now playing a historic role as one of the most active and 'political' of all TGWU branches, leading not only on shopfloor demands but also on wider political issues; campaigns on equal opportunities were matched by solidarity with struggles across the movement in this tempestuous period.

As TGWU full-timer Steve Turner enthused on the topic of 1107, 'Good branch? It was the best of the movement. It was the politics. Steve [Riley] was a good branch secretary. He was also on the executive of the union so … nothing was happening in the union that wasn't discussed in the branch. Although a lot of people don't go to branch meetings, stewards and activists go – and there were an awful lot of activists, political activists, in the plants at the time. Dagenham was a place where people could find work, certainly in those days, and a big immigrant community was employed there and they came with their own politics, their own background …. And [1107] was a hotbed of activism ….'

Many activists spoke of the mid-1980s boycott of South African parts at Dagenham, organised by the 1107 leadership. Jim Brinklow remembers, 'We refused to handle parts – it was that action that made Ford pull out of South Africa'. As Mick Gosling emphasised, 'What we were doing was not only boycotting parts [but] saying we won't *produce* any parts if they're going to export anything to South Africa – so there was triple-level boycott action on and that was taken down the line by the shop stewards – they said no more producing parts – bang. And the people said fair enough – we're not doing it. I think management was going ape-shit ….' For Terry Turner, 'One of the things I'm proud of is the work that we did on the boycott for South Africa …. It was an absolute war of attrition at Fords to get that done and we did it.'

By early 1987, the *Guardian* could report that this shopfloor pressure had forced Fords to 'phase out all trade with South Africa …. [The] decision represents a major step forward for the campaign for direct trade union sanctions against South Africa ….' As Mick had pointed out, the campaign also worked in reverse; in late December 1986 Engine Plant workers had 'successfully demanded the withdrawal of South African-made blocks', and in January 1987 'mass shop floor meetings in Dagenham's huge assembly plant decided to block supplies to the KD export plant unless trade with South Africa was stopped.' Clearly it was this guerrilla action, far more than any TUC resolutions, that had led to 'Ford management signal[ling] its intention to climb down from its "constructive engagement" stance'.[22]

Staunch 1107 supporter Alan Deyna-Jones summed up the cross-union spirit of the branch: '1107 spread their wings a bit, helped other trade union members. The banner of the 1107 was always there on marches and rallies all over Britain, supporting all other workers like the nurses, miners and bus drivers. They also took the lead re other issues round the world …. Other branches would say 1107 was "too far left" but the branch was concerned with every worker, all workers. 1107 was different. We stood up for what we meant. We didn't go shouting from the rafters – we were there. 1107 – we were there.'

Best Thing Since Sliced Bread?

The branch was not short of issues to discuss – and fight. The 1985 agreement had reduced the number of job classifications from 550 to 52 through 'flexible working practices' despite shop floor opposition blocking some of these changes. Ford's ultimate aim was 'a redesigned production system based on team working' and 'numerical flexibility through the introduction of temporary workers',[23] though the plan to introduce temps was dropped due to effective workplace opposition, and they were never used in the PTA. Yet, as Jim Brinklow recalled,

> the company drive for flexibility was a constant struggle. They were forever demanding changes – the company was always on to us about Japanisation in the '80s, it was the best thing since sliced bread. They brought in "After Japan", quality circles, trying to get us to think differently. Our response was to look at what was going on elsewhere. We had contacts in the US and Canadian plants, we could see what was going on there. Management would say Why don't you want quality circles? And we were saying quite plainly, Because quality circles are designed for workers to start blaming each other if the thing ain't right ….
>
> Then it was teams, teamworking, all that. The team would have a certain workload and you might have say eight people in a team, and if one of those people didn't turn up, the seven was expected to do the work of the team. And if that person didn't turn up on a regular basis because he had a problem they would then start seeing him as a liability. That's

divisive and that's why we said "We're not going to have teams." You know very well the members don't really want to work like this.

As 1107 stalwart Allan Martin remembers, 'The branch position was against Quality Circles – it was for exposing all this as a farce because you were led to believe that you were having an influence on the quality of the product but of course you weren't. I found it quite easy to expose this …. The manager at the meeting would say "We're going to make this decision collectively" – but they were just trying to guide you down a particular road …. The Engine Plant [union] leadership's comment was, "We're all going to lose our jobs if you listen to anyone from the [1107] branch, they're all a lot of left wing loonies …." But we did our best to fight it.'

PTA steward Pete Singh expressed the 'loony' cynicism of the branch: 'After Japan, Employee Involvement, Quality Circles … at the end of the day it's just cosmetic, because all they're concerned about is numbers, not quality – when there's a defect they're not bothered – they just want the line running … Meetings, groups, exercises etc? Making aeroplanes and things like that? I went to a couple but basically it didn't interest me. I just sat there drinking my cup of tea all day – I didn't want to know. It's just brainwashing. Part of a team, this that and the other but when it comes to it the company will drop you as soon as they can.'

A detailed account of early attempts to woo workers to 'joint' approaches came from branch chair Jim Brinklow:

Management had a film with scenes of mass meetings, filmed in black and white and put across as "the bad old days" – and then the other half of the film was all bright and colourful because everybody was "cooperating". When the film ended they asked for comments – I said "What's all this nonsense about showing all the black and white stuff and the 'bad old days' – what about your part in all this? Are you all goodness and light?" I really tore into them.

All this was part of their "hearts and minds" programme. They were taking people away all over the place, places like the Grand Hotel in Brighton – getting shop stewards to go to meetings where they did play acting and things like that – role playing – and our committee had steadfastly stood against all this crap, said it's all bloody propaganda, it's mind games. One time early on, prior to going there we had a debate and the shop stewards' committee split virtually 50-50. Joe [Gordon] was for going, so we said OK we'll go, but we won't be split up into groups, we'll stay as a committee [and we'll] … wreck the meetings.

So we was expecting Joe to get up and say No we're not splitting up into groups – we'll stay as a committee and that's it – but he didn't. He just sat there and accepted what the company said. That's really what did him in I think.[24] Anyway, I went into my meeting and this geezer got up and started speaking, and I said "Who are you? I've never seen you before." He said to me "Who are you?" I said "I'll tell you who I am. I'm the Deputy Convenor, I've been *elected* to come here." So it started getting out of hand …. And my superintendent, who wasn't a bad bloke, jumped up and he said to this bloke I think you'd better leave because there's going to be no meeting with you there.

I went to another meeting and the garage steward was sitting there with a magazine and a pair of scissors and he was cutting out pictures. And I was absolutely furious. I said "What the fuck are you doing?" He didn't know who to be afraid of more, the bosses or me. I said, "I'm going to go back into the plant, and I'm going to tell your members what you're doing …." And the look of terror on his face – he knew that if I did that, they'd have him out. So I said "Pack it up and get a bit of bloody dignity inside you." Anyway, we ended up wrecking all the meetings and we spent the rest of the day in the swimming pool.

Yet despite the opposition, management continued to move towards its goals – with a little help from its friends at higher trade union levels. A newsletter put out by the Ford Workers' Group[25] on 27 January 1986 proclaimed, 'The company and the Officials have stitched us up again: REJECT AND WALK!!!' According to *Fraud News*, the officials had 'voted away hundreds and thousands of jobs … our right to … organise job allocation and mobility … [they have] done away with inspectors, maintenance skills, repair men, relief men, janitors, stockmen, general services, in fact everyone who doesn't work flat out … the way Ford wants.'

The lack of a 'say' by the rank and file was bitterly criticised: 'We vote with our feet – spontaneous down tools and out – "Wrong" say the officials. We vote with our hands – at mass meetings, usually with the majority wanting to take Fords on – "Wrong" say the officials "each plant equals one vote, no matter how many are in it." We vote in a ballot – kick out the offer and strike – "Wrong" say the officials ….'

A Place Like This

In a mid-1980s interview,[26] 1107 leader Steve Riley contrasted this gap between the workforce and their full-time officials – 'the union'[27] – to workers' closer relationship with their shop stewards: 'I think the members see the steward as someone who is part of them … and isn't necessarily in tune with the union. I think their perception of the union is very much like their perception of the company: them and us. They see the union as being quite aloof and not doing very much for them.' Steve recognised that growing workplace bureaucratisation had had an effect: 'There's natural resistance coming from the shop floor. But if an area stopped work – say over flexibility – the JWC[28] would have to go down and tell them they can't strike over it because it is a national agreement. And that again fits into the perception of "them and us" …. To a large degree the company is getting its own way …. A lot of new starts are already saying "What's the union here for?" People feel like they are trapped in here, and so the few things that they can say no to become very important … and the less of those you've got the worst it gets. The members think "The union can't do anything about it …".'

At the same time, the new policies of 1107 were beginning to make a real difference to the branch/workplace relationship. Engine Plant steward Ted Amos commented, 'I think the branch became a lot better at solving the problems we got in the plant. The branch would call meetings and put round leaflets, inform members, which Davies never used to do …. The [workplace leadership] were looking after themselves in the [Engine] plant and they didn't seem to be bothered about problems outside.'

Rank and file members were less positive. Asked whether he was interested in union meetings, one worker on the Fiesta Final line answered, 'There are no union meetings – we never really know about any of them …. We get a leaflet every now and again but it doesn't tell us what the union is doing ….' He commented, 'The union can't do more for us because the blokes aren't behind the union like they used to be – it all comes down to politics really – everyone's buying their own house, people can't afford to strike ….' Yet the same worker added, 'You've got to be in the union … you've got to lean on something, the union is the only thing for the working class.'

Another assembly-line worker commented, 'The union in the plant's all right – but too much politics – they don't contact the workers, just make their own decisions.' This remark stood in ironic contrast to the previous comment on the very influence of wider politics on the shop floor, yet reflected many workers' suspicion of a wider 'political' stance reflecting issues outside the workplace.[29] At the same time, 'I support the union. It's for the workers. I would always support them, stay united …. It's worse now because of the Tory government. The union can't do nothing now, can't help us. They're doing their best, but because of the laws, etc., they can't help us.'

The same themes of weakness caused by the Thatcherite anti-union laws (particularly on secret postal ballots) were raised by a number of workers. Yet equally common were comments like 'You couldn't do without the union – it would be terrible without them – in a place this size, you've got to have a union, even if you don't agree with all their views, because management would run all over you.' In an interesting reference to current events, one interviewee commented, 'One day [the union] might get strong again. There could be a surge up in union power like in [Polish] Solidarity'.[30]

The time and place of meetings was undoubtedly a problem. As one worker among many commented 'I'd be prepared to be more involved if meetings were at a suitable time.' Another commented, 'Now you have to work really fast, there's no time to stop – at the end of the day I'm completely knackered. If I wanted to go to a meeting I couldn't go. Too tired ….' But whatever the lack of involvement in branch meetings, the phrase 'You've got to have a union in a place like this' cropped up constantly. One worker on the Sierra Final line claimed to be 'Hardly involved at all … I'm not a great believer in the union' – yet in the next sentence he claimed, 'It's a case of having to be in the union in a place like this, you've got to have a union in a place like this – they could take advantage if you've not got the backing of the union …. I believe you've got to have a union in a place like this.'

In a later interview,[31] Steve Riley addressed the issue of union branch 'versus' plant organisation at Dagenham: 'There isn't the sort of structure you have at other workplaces where there is only one union – here the shop stewards' committee is really the "branch". It's detrimental because the stewards think they don't have to go to the branch – but branch organisation is very important. Purely trade union problems are dealt with through the branch – disputes within the T&G and so on – following through [national] trade union policies – the only way that will happen is through a branch.'

As he acknowledged, 'Until very recently, if you asked the majority of members in my branch what branch they were in, they would say, I think I'm in the T&G – We have even had people say I'm in the PTA'.[32] But since the recent transfer of leadership, 1107 activists had been working hard to increase membership involvement and education: 'We've introduced education for branch members and shop stewards on economics, political history etc. They can't take time off and the company won't pay them, so if they attend at least four branch meetings a year we will cover their pay …. Through our branch we have sent members on basic branch members' courses, and the situation has improved. The majority of people now know which branch they're in and have a very basic idea about the structure. But there is very little involvement.'

Unorthodox Tactics ...

As management aggression continued, stewards and activists in 1107 sometimes used unorthodox methods to combat the class enemy. Pete Singh vividly recalled the 'Maverick' incident: 'There was a case called the Maverick where I was in a bit of trouble. It was Friday afternoon – '85, '86 – and we were having a drink down in the tracking pits – four of us – out of the blue two superintendents, two security guards and a foreman came down and basically said "You're drinking" and we didn't say a word .... They said "Well we'll sort this out after dinner." So we got hold of Steve and he says to us, "You're in a bit of trouble ... let me think about it over the weekend and I'll get back to you." So we came back to work and he said "Don't worry ... I want you to go to every off-licence you can and find any black can of non-alcoholic lager you can find and bring it to work." We went all over and finally came to this off-licence, and I saw this black can – we looked at it and it said "Non-Alcoholic Lager" – it was called "Maverick". Anyway we brought it in, and Steve said "Oh well done" and took it in to management who were rubbing their hands basically – "We've got 'em" – and Steve said "That's what they were drinking – non-alcoholic lager." They were just gobsmacked. Steve said "Here's the proof – this is what they were drinking." So with that basically they dropped it.'

Ron Doel also remembered and celebrated the 'Maverick' incident: 'Me and Steve Riley and Jim Brinklow went about saving these people. We looked for black cans, because the extra-strong lager, Kestrel, was in a black can. We eventually found some low-alcohol lager in black cans and we put the case up that they were drinking, but it was low-alcohol – so we got them off. The low-alcohol lager was called Maverick, and later on they had a model called the Maverick. I could swear it was named after that.'

In fact, there was indeed a Ford model called the 'Maverick', but of an earlier vintage, produced as early as 1969 in the US. Yet the name also comes up in a diary entry by Margaret Thatcher. Discussing her goal of privatising British Leyland in the mid-1980s, she writes: 'Before we had got to grips with the GM offer [for British Leyland], code-named "Salton", the still more intriguingly code-named "Maverick" [project] put in an appearance. At the end of November [1985] the Chairman of Ford of Europe [announced] that Ford were considering making an offer for Austin Rover ...'.[33] Given the date, there is more than a suggestion that the strategy was named after the stewards' cheeky manoeuvre.

As the 'Maverick' issue shows, activists were as capable of bending the stick to protect their members' interests as was management in advancing theirs. Yet Dagenham workers were up against a highly organised and determined opposition; workplace trade union organisation was continually under attack during the period. Ford's next strategy, contracting-out of work, now began to make itself felt; Jim Brinklow remembers 'constant battles' on the issue. 'The biggest problem was with the jobs in sub-assembly areas that people could go to when they come off the line ... if those were contracted out there would be less jobs for people to go to .... You can only work so many years on the line, and then you're knackered. That was why it was important for us to hang on to as much as possible.' Ron Doel confirmed this, recalling that when he started work at Dagenham 'I was lucky, I was put in the seat area ... If I'd had to work on the line, I don't know if I would have survived.'

Flexibility and Mobility ...

As well as contracting out, the main issues raised by members with their stewards under the 1985 agreement were allocation and organisation of work and transfer of labour. PTA convenor Joe Gordon[34] saw these as clearly related to the deal, which had integrated the principles of flexibility and mobility of labour and 'outlawed' demarcation between skilled jobs. The effects of the newly-negotiated working practices were many: 'We used to have line inspectors, 'B' grade operators working on the line, and a repair man – the inspector would mark up defects and pass to the repair man.' Now all three 'B' grade jobs had been integrated into one. For doing their own inspecting and repairing, 'B' grade workers had received only the basic 4 per cent increase, although line workers had also received another 2 per cent with the final achievement of the line workers' allowance. Overall, though, the deal made conditions 'a lot harder. A guy used to be able to come into work and he'd know for example he was going to be fitting alternators. Now he's not just fitting, he's also inspecting, repairing and sweeping his own area.'

The greater flexibility was having an impact on custom and practice rights. For example, there had been an acceptance that workers could be 'loaned out' to other areas no more than three times; now, they could be moved any time. Previously, workers could not be taken off a job once they had been working there for one hour – now they could be taken off at any time of day. 'If the foreman says you'll work here now, then over at the trim for two hours, then somewhere else, there's no comeback.' Stewards had previously taken up such issues on a daily basis, but were now technically helpless because of the agreement.

The stewards' less central role was particularly problematic in relation to the introduction of lead operators[35] under the deal; the company was now organising working lunches for lead operators and their groups where, Joe noted, 'people talk about issues the shop stewards should be dealing with.' 1107's position was to refuse to cooperate with these meetings, and shop stewards had been going along only in order to sabotage them. Recently a whole section, Fiesta Line One, had refused to attend.

Joe noted that 'People didn't believe there'd be problems at first – it takes a while for them to register this is happening.' Like many of his members, he felt that the failed 1984-5 miners' strike, added to by the printers' defeat at Wapping in 1985-6, had 'knocked the confidence of our members – the miners' defeat was a defeat for themselves– they just can't see themselves winning …'. The two-year pay deal had added to this demoralisation: 'There was a massive vote to reject it … the majority to accept was only about 200.' But Joe now felt the members were in a mood to fight back: 'Members are arguing and resisting – they're stopping work over fumes etc., too many cars coming down the line – people are fighting back a bit.'

'Best In Class …'

The next pay offer – 4.5 per cent, based this time on a three-year deal – was announced in late 1987 and saw immediate walkouts. This proposed package included more highly resented 'strings', including further proposals to select some shopfloor workers to act as 'group leaders' (often termed 'team leaders' elsewhere in industry). As the *Financial Times* commented 'The company's three-year offer is … not merely an attack on working practices … but an attempt to lay open the way for a transformation of the organisation of Ford factories which could take several years'.[36]

Several years it would take. Workers in the UK – particularly at Fords – were holding the line against such changes more strongly than in either Europe or the US, where workers had accepted 'teamwork' (Genk and West Germany), 'flexible work teams' (US), deskilling (West Germany), Employee Involvement – 'well advanced in the US' – and Quality Circles in West Germany and Spain. Three-year agreements such as Ford UK workers were currently resisting had also been accepted in West Germany, Spain and the US.[37]

Yet Dagenham workers' opposition to the proposals was based on bitter experience; as one assembly-line worker commented on the 1985 'strings': 'Flexibility means that every 102 seconds a car comes by, and not only do you have to screw something into the car, but in between you have to tidy up, check your tools, repair things and check you've got enough parts. You do not have a single job any more. If there is no work on the line they move you to where there is work. You are working the whole time'.[38]

Perhaps because of this bitter experience, 11 November 1987 saw the 'Worst day of industrial unrest for years'[39] as more than 17,000 Ford workers across the country struck against the offer. Activists lobbied the pay talks, waving placards bearing the slogan 'Best in class, Left on our arse'; 1107ers in the PTA voted to lobby the next set of talks and brought together stewards across Dagenham to talk about making the forthcoming strike solid in all sections. Their strategy of using both official and unofficial channels to spread the strike action worked to ensure that militants were not left isolated.

Ford had increased the pay offer from 4.25 per cent to 5.5 per cent, while union officials Jimmy Airlie (AEU) and the TGWU's Mick Murphy had indicated their willingness to go along with some changes in working practices, including use of temporary labour and the redeployment of skilled workers to work on the assembly line. Yet the pay increase was not enough to stifle opposition to the deal, and a ban on overtime was imposed in the body and assembly plants at Dagenham.

By late January 1988, Ford workers were ready for action whatever their officials' attitude; almost 90 per cent voted to strike for 10 per cent and a one-year agreement. On Monday 1 February, the night shift at Dagenham PTA walked out after a 1,500-strong mass meeting; their placards lambasted Murphy's and Airlie's treachery. Mick Gosling recalled 'People on the Sierra line were walking and we went down the lines pulling people off …. That was the start of the dispute and it spread like wildfire all over the country. Within two days the whole of Ford of Britain was shut.' According to one study, 'Ford appeared to be taken by surprise by the 1988 strike and by the strength of opposition to the new working practices.' In addition, J-i-T meant that 'the effects of the UK strike were substantial and were felt almost instantly …. European-wide integrated production inadvertently provided an significant shift of power to labour'.[40]

Workers demanded a vote there and then; if the ballot went against the deal they would walk straight out again. The *Daily Telegraph* reported 'Men on the picket lines … claim[ing] that their strike action was more to do with "class and conditions" than it was about money.' Two Engine Plant workers had described the company's use of 'Japanese' production techniques as 'all one-way traffic. They are pressing home automation and extra work, but at the same time we are losing out over pensions and conditions. Of course we want more money, but we want improved conditions and terms of employment – that is what has brought us out'.[41]

Despite the company's complaints of low 'efficiency', a confidential report exposed at this point in the *Financial Times* showed that productivity at the Dagenham PTA and Body plants was expected to be higher than at Nissan's famously 'lean' plant in Tyne and Wear.[42] At this Mick Murphy was forced to eat his words, appearing on TV to declare a national strike due to start the following Monday.

Ironically, the 'Just-in-Time' techniques the workers were resisting now came to their aid; Mick Gosling recalled that once the strike began 'The whole of Ford of Europe was stalled because of this Just-In-Time system.' Even before the strike had begun, the *Financial Times* was predicting that production all over Europe would be at a standstill in days rather than weeks. The deeper integration of Ford operations in Europe, which made many European operations dependent on supplies from the UK, now also 'strengthened the unions' hand'.[43]

The surge of militancy galvanised the press; the *Economist* reluctantly admitted that 'Suddenly, the government's trade-union laws are beginning to look vulnerable …', while in a gesture of support hardly imaginable today, Labour employment spokesman Michael Meacher expressed his support for the Ford workers.[44] One magazine described the Ford strike as part of a 'rising wave of industrial unrest, recalling memories of the "winter of discontent" …';[45] and in fact the late 1980s saw a spate of disputes by groups of workers from seafarers and signal workers to BT and ambulance workers, as well as at Fords.[46]

The strike was also honoured with a mention by Mrs Thatcher, who 'told' Parliament that the Ford workers 'must be intended to presume the consequence of their own action and to take responsibility for it, be it on themselves, on other workers here or overseas, or on inward development'.[47] Whatever this meant, it was overshadowed by the unfortunate consequences of a banner held by some Dagenham pickets which proclaimed 'We're Brits not Nips' in a reference to 'Japanese' management strategies. Needless to say, the papers made the most of this, though the comment was immediately condemned by 1107 activists.

Notoriously Militant

The 1988 strike was supported enthusiastically by 1/1107 with posters, leaflets and badges. Commenting on a photograph of a worker holding up a placard proclaiming 'Bollocks to the Strings!', Jim Brinklow recalled, 'That photo was taken at a lobby in London during the '88 strike. We used to do things like this to get the support of our members. We had these stickers with "On the money" – that was our slogan at the time.' Another 1107 product, T-shirts sporting the slogan 'Notoriously Militant', referred to 'when one of the papers dubbed us the notoriously militant 1/1107.'

Ron Doel also remembered the origins of the 'notoriously militant' tag: 'We used to hold our meetings at the school over the road .... We used to have smoking then – even the school allowed smoking. So Steve [Riley] was smoking a cigarette, there was a can of Coke by his side, and a reporter burst in from the Daily Mail asking questions. No one talked to him. The next day an article appeared saying the reporter had attended a meeting of the "notoriously militant" 1107 branch, the ashtrays were overflowing, there were beer cans everywhere etc. We've called ourselves "notoriously militant" ever since.'

Yet despite the undoubted militancy of the branch and Ford workers in general, by mid-February the strike was once again 'sold out' as union officials agreed to recommend acceptance of a two-year deal with an unimpressive pay increase tied to increased flexibility. The climbdown from three years was said to stem from Detroit, where executives were 'concerned about the rapid effect of the stoppage on other plants'.[48] But while Mick Murphy greeted the deal as a 'historic settlement', Dagenham workers felt differently; as one commented: 'The deal's outrageous ... Management have got everything they wanted'.[49]

The agreement introduced not only quality circles but, as threatened, the new position of 'group leader', for which some workers would be paid an extra 10 per cent to chivvy their fellow group-members. As one worker commented, group leaders would work to encourage production workers to share management's viewpoint – as well as putting 60 per cent of the existing supervisors out of a job. One supposed concession in the deal was that the detailed negotiation of changes in working practices would be carried out at plant level, a policy Joe Gordon opposed as allowing management to 'go as far as they want in individual plants – whatever practices the company could see were not giving them flexibility and mobility were open to them'.

Although Ford had been forced to give up the three year deal it had argued was 'central to our plans', the two-year agreement was no better in content, offering a 14 per cent increase which amounted to half a per cent per year more than the previous deal. As one worker put it 'We've been sold down the river for half of one per cent'.[50] The key point was that all the 'strings' stayed in place, at least in principle (see below); once-militant union leaders like the AEU's Jimmy Airlie had openly supported the increases in flexibility.

Mick Gosling was mortified: 'We only had to just say No once more and we'd have won the whole lot .... We got stuffed.' Joe Gordon agreed: 'In the plant the feeling will be sick. They've come back with the same thing and conned the membership into accepting it.' Introducing a political dimension, another activist commented 'We pushed Thatcher off her pedestal for a moment, but the officials picked her up and dusted her down again'.[51]

War-weary Dagenham workers accepted the deal; the PTA was the only plant with a majority against. Ironically, implementation provoked a wave of short unofficial stoppages across Dagenham. Yet, as Allan Martin recalled, 'The strings did come in .... People were generally worried about their employment and felt if we didn't start to give a little bit then they might close down .... People were seriously worried about their jobs. And it was done by little bits, little bits .... When we first got Group Leaders their role and responsibility was very minor. There was a fear that they would be underpaid supervisors – well, now that's what they are – but at the beginning it was done very very slowly ... and they gave these roles to respected people, people of whom workers thought "Oh, he's done a lot of service, that guy..." But later they replaced them and brought in younger people .... It was very cleverly done.'

Meanwhile, ever-growing pressure towards union-management 'co-operation' was pressuring even the most dedicated activists to go along with the illusion of what were termed (by management) more 'constructive' ways of 'doing business together'. This terminology is featured in a Memorandum of Understanding issued in September 1988 which notes that 'the Trade Unions have affirmed their commitment that employees will not be involved in unconstitutional action' and that the (unspecified, but clearly unconstitutional) 'events of the last few weeks' called for a more 'constructive way of doing business together'. The document concludes 'We jointly expect employees to co-operate by working around the problem' rather than, presumably, walking out. It was signed by PTA area manager J. Body and at least one prominent 1107 activist, pointing to the marked increase in shopfloor union 'cooperation' in even this combative era.

The Sacking of an Activist

Meanwhile, flushed by their victory in shoehorning in the deal, Dagenham management were preparing to get rid of one of 1107's leading activists. On 10 December 1988 Mick Gosling was called into his supervisor's office to face a lineup of senior management who accused him of 'inciting people to take unofficial action'. Mick was told he could keep his job if he signed a document denouncing all unofficial stoppages and accepting that if he took part in or encouraged any future strike – even if official – he would be sacked. Not surprisingly, Mick refused to sign.

There was no rhyme or reason for sacking Mick other than his position as a politically conscious, militant activist. As the PTA stewards' bulletin

Under Pressure pointed out, the unofficial action cited by management had involved 'over 80 workers ... following [a supervisor's] ... search of a workers' tea box last July 1st. No one was warned or threatened with disciplinary action at the time ....' The charge was clearly absurd; management could only turn to the fact that Mick had a university degree to support their claim that he was an 'outside agitator'. In fact, Mick was able to prove at his first disciplinary hearing that management had known about his qualifications for years.

The 'graduate' argument clearly could not work, but the *Sun*, eagerly weighing in on the side of Ford management, now reported that Gosling had been sacked because he had skipped work to attend a political meeting addressed by Irish activist Bernadette McAliskey. In fact, the meeting was held *in* Ireland; as workers joked, 'Gosling had had difficulties finding parking space for Concorde in the Dagenham car park'.[52] The absurdity of the accusations made it obvious that Mick was being punished for nothing more than being a militant activist. Yet, on the advice of local TGWU officials, the convenors' and stewards' committee decided not to call an immediate strike.

The following week Ford management refused to allow the plant to hold a mass meeting; the stewards' bulletin *Under Pressure* condemned this 'disgusting undemocratic manoeuvre' and pointed out that this was 'the FIRST TIME a mass meeting before a ballot has been denied'.[53] 1107 activists were clear that the real motive behind the attack on Mick was suppression of the constant unofficial strikes which had cropped up in the wake of the 1988 deal. As one put it, 'Unofficial stoppages over the past year have made the national agreement ... unworkable at a local level – that is what Mick's sacking is really about.' Workers and stewards were clear that, as 1/1107 activist Ned Leary put it, Mick was being 'made a scapegoat to frighten off everyone else.' The victimisation was being compared to that of 'Red Robbo' – British Leyland convenor Derek Robinson, who had been sacked along similar lines in late 1979 as a symbol of Thatcher's determination to get to grips with workplace militancy. In parallel, Mick's sacking was seen as 'the biggest attack on the union for years at Dagenham'.[54]

Support for Mick was impressive, with Ford plants all around the world, including Brazil and Argentina, mobilising to protest; 42 Labour MPs signed an Early Day Motion demanding his reinstatement. But Dagenham management were not the type to give in easily. As one manager had snarled at Mick's disciplinary hearing: 'Unconstitutional action gets up my nose in an extreme fashion and I am going to stamp it out.' In early March 1989, management finally got its way; Mick's appeal was lost, and with it his job.

'This manager's our best union organiser ...'

Other forms of management aggression – and worker resistance – continued on a daily basis. In July, the PTA was shut down after one manager searched a worker's bag and locker, alleging possession of drugs. His section immediately stopped production and demanded an apology. Meanwhile, the PTA stewards' committee refused to implement the policy included in the 1988 agreement of 'remanning', i.e. requiring workers to scab on any strike by covering strikers' jobs during unofficial action; as a result, the walkout stopped the entire plant. This would normally have meant all PTA workers would be laid off without pay, but fearing this could escalate a dispute with the rank and file already on the offensive, management kept other workers on full pay. As one paint shop activist commented, 'This manager's an animal, but he's the best trade union organiser we've got in the plant'.[55]

Meanwhile, a rise in confidence at Dagenham expressed itself in a series of sectional walkouts – almost one a day since the August shutdown, all unofficial. Most involved only a handful of workers and lasted less than an hour, but even these short stoppages cost Ford hundreds of cars – and meant the plant consistently failed to reach its daily production targets. It is notable that due to this kind of guerrilla warfare management had not yet dared to attempt to force through the strings attached to the two-year pay deal.

However, Dagenham managers had been told in no uncertain terms to sort the assembly plant out, and in January 1989 Ford Europe delivered its own sucker punch, announcing that the company would be moving production of the Sierra to Genk. The motives were fairly clear; as the *Financial Times* pointed out, while the basic wage at Dagenham was £227.35, at Genk it was £184 (though for a shorter working week). More importantly, Genk's 8,950 workers were represented by only 24 stewards, a ratio of 373 to one, while Dagenham stewards represented an average of 55 workers.[56]

Overall, comparisons between Genk and Dagenham revealed considerable advantages for Dagenham in terms of workplace trade union democracy: 'Most negotiations at Genk are channelled through just four senior stewards who meet management once a month. At Dagenham, there are four joint works committees, with a combined membership of 64. Changes to working practices at Genk evolve through regular discussion with the committee of four. At Dagenham change is agreed in periodic bursts through national pay negotiations in the cumbersome, 70-strong national joint negotiating committee ....'[57]

This, of course, was a crucial principle of shopfloor trade union democracy, to be valued by workers if not *FT* journalists. But on that very issue, an important exception must be noted which revealed the ongoing lack of such grassroots democracy in the Engine Plant. According to veteran steward and 1107 stalwart Ted Amos, 'You tried to do the job as steward but it was a bit hard because each [TGWU] assembly-line steward in the Engine Plant was given what, 200 men in his department – and an electrician, he'd have five. And the electricians had the same vote as I did. You're outnumbered. The [skilled workers] thought if they got ten more stewards in Assembly, that'd be 10 more votes against them when they come to meetings.

'It wasn't that there wasn't enough people to stand for steward – no. They had smaller constituencies in the PTA – about 60 per steward – if you've got somebody like Steve Riley, he would fight for that, but John Davies wouldn't fight for that. You'd go in in the morning and before you even got out of the car park you'd have about ten guys who wanted to see you and that was how the day went – 200 men with problems – it was your whole life really – the whole time you were mobbed by members.' The significance of this restriction of workplace union democracy is revealed in our Conclusion, which shows that such inadequate 'representation' dominated the union organisation in Dagenham after the closure of the PTA.

Regarding working practices and labour-management cooperation, the Financial Times analysis quoted above again described Dagenham as 'lagging behind': 'Workers at Genk first joined quality circles in 1979, but Dagenham stewards still oppose the company's Employee Involvement programme.' In 1987, Bill Hayden, Ford of Europe's new vice president for manufacturing, had produced a report which sighed, 'Despite successive campaigns on quality awareness, for a substantial number of [UK] employees an enduring commitment to "building quality" has yet to be achieved ....' Worker representatives at Genk had also agreed to the introduction of temporary workers as long ago as 1982, while 'the British unions have always rejected' this.

Yet the article notes that 'all these differences do not prove that Dagenham is less efficient ... The gap [between Dagenham and the continent] has narrowed significantly.' By contrast, 'A crucial factor was probably that ... Ford will find it less difficult to introduce a 24-hour production system at Genk by moving from two-shift working to a three-shift system. Three-shift working will allow more intensive use of capital, but also mean the Sierra will only have to be engineered for one plant'.[58] As this spells out in journalist-speak, the transfer of the Sierra was decided by the company's one and only true love – profitability – rather than being based on the 'inadequacies' – aka effective workplace unionism – of the Dagenham workforce.

Although Dagenham management claimed that only 500 jobs would be lost – and these through natural wastage – the TGWU thought differently. National official Jack Adams argued prophetically 'We fear Ford is laying the basis for the total closure of the body and assembly plant in Dagenham'.[59] In this climate, as so often, union officials put jobs before working conditions; Adams announced that the union would discuss the introduction of flexible shift patterns if Ford would keep the work at Dagenham. Meanwhile, instead of old-fashioned industrial action, the TGWU was recommending a 'community-based campaign' to boycott purchase of the Sierra if it was moved, along with the launch of a petition to be signed throughout Dagenham.

'You'll have another dispute on your hands ...'

Company priorities were indicated in other ways; in spite of the health and safety legislation, Dagenham was still a criminally dangerous place to work. In March 1989, a Ford fireman dragged two men from a fume-filled demineralisation tank. As the *Dagenham Post* reported, stressing the bravery of the 'bighearted Ford fireman' rather than the criminal irresponsibility of management, the men were working without any breathing apparatus.[60] Perhaps it was this economic approach to safety which contributed to – yet again – record profits in the financial year 1988-9.[61] In fact, the same month it was announced that 'Car giants Ford have been forced to pay £2million compensation to workers deafened by noise', while the TGWU pointed out that the company had 'known about noise risk for at least 30 years but failed to ... give enough protection'.[62]

Yet the union spoke with forked tongue; that October the T&G sent a leaflet to its members at Dagenham 'suggest[ing] that they should work harder, improve quality and give up wildcat strikes'. As usual, such finger-wagging was prompted by fears of job loss or – worse – total closure. Although, in a prophetic denial, the *Economist* reported that 'Ford insists publicly that there are no plans to close the plant', the journal was prepared to play the prophet of doom, pointing out that 'the Japanese have come .... By the mid-1990s, Nissan should be producing 200,000 vehicles a year .... Toyota is planning for 200,000 at Derby and Honda 100,000 at Swindon'.[63]

Yet despite these stern warnings, shopfloor militancy remained strong, as shown by the fact that – incredibly – management was still unable to fully impose the strings agreed years before in the 1985 pay deal, let alone in 1988. Unofficial strikes had continued despite the loss of the Sierra, and in early November, 300 Engine Plant workers downed tools in protest at the company's latest two-year offer; among other problems, the company had turned down the unions' demand for a cut in the working week from 39 to

35 hours.[64]

On 18 November 1989, Ford's final offer saw spontaneous walkouts; the company was offering nothing much more than another two-year deal of 9.5 per cent that year and inflation plus 2.5 per cent for 1990. PTA stewards called a strike for 24 November, the day the previous pay deal would run out. Workers were angry over plans to integrate yet more flexibility into the deal, and they were also taking the unions' demand for a 35-hour week seriously; the current 39 hours was physically exhausting and disruptive of family life. On 24 November almost 4,000 PTA workers voted for an unofficial strike over the shorter working week – and walked out.[65] Meanwhile, the Dagenham workforce showed its class solidarity by collecting £4,000 at mass meetings for the locked-out ambulance workers.[66]

As this makes clear, 'old-fashioned' collectivism and militancy was far from over as the 1980s turned into the 'post-modernist' '90s. And 1107 activist Roger Dillon -who received a series of letters from management complaining about his 'unconstitutional' activities in the mid-to-late '80s – could vouch for that. As he described a typical dispute: 'I had 70-odd members [meeting] on the lineside and a supervisor shouted some abuse over to the guys and the meeting turned into a full-scale rout – almost a fight. Then ... the meeting was deemed a stoppage and he said "Right, you're off pay." So people said, "Well, if we're off pay we'll leave now" – and the guv'nor said "Well go on then – leave."

'So we did go on strike and because the strike lasted two and a half weeks and was a very damaging one for the company, we managed to come to some agreement. But when they said they were going to discipline me, the union said "Well you'll have another dispute on your hands then – he's a very popular man. In fact we can't go back to work unless you tell us he's safe ... " And that really upset management because they thought they really had me at that point – but because they wanted us all back to normal working as quick as possible, I was saved. In fact, I didn't even get a disciplinary.'

In a last word on the still impressive levels of resistance in the 1980s, Roger commented: 'The politics on the shop floor was very simple – everybody accepted that you took strike action to get more money – everybody was ready for it .... Most people was clear what the fight was about in those days – you did it because in those days if you picked up a newspaper there was always somebody winning something in an industrial action – Not any more, it's a completely different world.'

As this suggests, the persistence of workplace struggle even under Thatcher was an impressive contrast to twenty-first-century patterns of victimisation and suppression of struggle – and a tribute to the power of the unofficial strike, which was almost to disappear in the 1990s.

NOTES

1. A staunch 1107-er, Ned tragically died in his mid-fifties a few years before this history was written.
2. As shown in Chapter Six, the PTA was closed down in early 2002.
3. Interviewed 21 February 2012 (see Bibliography).
4. Interviewed 11 November 2011 (see Bibliography).
5. The bulletin of the Ford Workers' Group (see last chapter).
6. Centre for Alternative industrial and Technological Systems, active in the 1980s and '90s.
7. Julie Waterson 'Fords – 16 years on', *Socialist Worker* 1 December 1984, p. 15.
8. Minutes of Evidence taken before the Parliamentary Select Committee on Overseas Trade, 22 January 1985.
9. This and other comments from the film *Making The Grade*, Open Eye Video and Animation Workshop, dir. Greg Dropkin, 1985.
10. Sabby Sagall and Sheila Douglass, 'When History was Made in Dagenham', *Socialist Review*, October 2010, p. 21.
11. John Bohanna, 'Finally Making the Grade', *Red Pepper*, February 2011, p.
12. Interviewed 27 April 2012 (see Bibliography).
13. Quoted in Elane Heffernan, 'The Fight is on at Ford', *Socialist Worker* 13 February 1988, p. 5.
14. Interviewed February 2011 (see Bibliography).
15. *The Ford Report*, Greater London Council Industry and Employment Branch, 1986, p. 3.
16. Women were now being employed on the assembly lines for the first time since the war, but Riley's language reflects the more sexist culture of the period.
17. Daniel Trilling, 'The far right: the warning signs', *Guardian G2* 13 September 2012, pp. 6-9.
18. Unfortunately, due to the current shortage of left-wing bookshops in London, I have been unable to find out which one ...
19. Patrick Wintour, 'Ford unions urge drive on equality', *Guardian* 1 November 1986, p. 2.
20. Workers quoted in 'Non-Stop Hell on the Line', *Socialist Worker* 14 November 1987, pp 8-9.
21. Minutes of Stage IV Meeting, 20 May 1988.
22. Seamus Milne, 'Ford UL to stop exports to South Africa', *Guardian* 20 February 1987, p. 2.
23. Barry Wilkinson and Nick Oliver, 'Obstacles to Japanisation: The Case of Ford UK', *Employee Relations* 1990 (12) (1), p. 17.
24. See next chapter for an account of Joe's replacement as PTA convenor by Steve Riley.
25. See last chapter.
26. Steve and other stewards and workers were interviewed for the 1986-88 'Workplace Trade Union Democracy' research project, (see Sheila Cohen, 'You Are The Union' Workers' Educational Association Studies For Trade Unionists Vol. 14, No. 53, April 1988, and Patricia Fosh and Sheila Cohen,

'Local Patterns of Union Democracy' in Patricia Fosh and Edmund Heery (eds), *Trade Unions and their Members*, London: Macmillan, 1990.

27 As is clear from subsequent quotes, this term – 'the union' is used differently by workers at different times, applying to full-time officialdom, to the branch or to workplace representation.

28 Joint Works Committee, consisting of stewards from every section of each plant under the auspices of the convenor and senior stewards.

29 This issue is further explored in Sheila Cohen, 'Left Agency and Class Action: The Paradox of Workplace Radicalism', *Capital and Class*, Vol 35, Number 3, 2011, pp 371-389.

30 A few years before, in 1980-81, Polish shipyard workers had struck, occupied their yards and formed a new union, Solidarnosc ('Solidarity') in protest at the bureaucratic management of their work and trade union.

31 Towards the end of the research in 1988.

32 Other research shows this is far from unusual.

33 Margaret Thatcher, *The Downing Street Years*, New York: Harper Collins, 1993, p. 439.

34 Also interviewed for the 1986-88 'Workplace Trade Union Democracy' study.

35 These were often termed 'team leaders' at the time; possibly they were given a different title at Fords because of the trenchant opposition shown to 'team concept'.

36 Charles Leadbeater, 'Ford plans break with traditional work methods', *Financial Times*, 11 February 1988, p. 1.

37 Charles Leadbeater, 'The pressure grows on Ford UK to conform', *Financial Times*, 11 February 1988, p10.

38 Barry Wilkinson and Nick Oliver, 'Obstacles to Japanisation: The Case of Ford UK', *Employee Relations* 1990 (12) (1), p. 18.

39 Charles Leadbeater, 'Car industry suffers worst day of industrial unrest for years', *Financial Times* 12 November 1987, p. 12.

40 Wilkinson and Oliver 'Obstacles to Japanisation ...' *Employee Relations* 1990, p. 19.

41 A.J. McIlroy, 'Japanese democracy needed, say pickets' *Daily Telegraph* 6 February 1988, p. 5.

42 Charles Leadbeater, 'Ford plant may beat Nissan productivity', *Financial Times* 12 February 1988, p. 7.

43 David Felton, 'Integration of Ford plants speeds lay-offs in Europe', *The Independent*, 12 February 1988, p. 2.

44 'Who's embarrassed now?' *Economist*, 13 February 1988, p. 21.

45 'Strikes May Herald a Budget re-think', *Financial Weekly* 11-17 February 1988.

46 Sheila Cohen, *Ramparts of Resistance* ..., London: Pluto Press, 2006, pp96-8.

47 Roland Rudd and Michael Dynes, 'Thatcher warning of economic damage as Ford strike deepens' *The Times* 10 February 1988, p. 2.

48 David Felton, 'Ford to offer strikers new deal', *The Independent* 16 February 1988, p. 1.

49 Elane Heffernan 'Anger over sell-out' *Socialist Worker* 6 February 1988, p. 15.

50 Elane Heffernan, 'Anger over sellout', *Socialist Worker* 6 February 1988, p. 15.

51 Quoted in Elane Heffernan 'We've been conned' *Socialist Worker* 27 February 1988, p. 14.
52 Sean O'Neill, 'Ford Scapegoat Fights Sacking', *City Limits* 15-29 December 1988, p. 5.
53 'Vote Yes For Your Rights', *Under Pressure* Ballot Special (nd).
54 Judy Hirst, 'Ford sacking fuels factory trouble', *City Limits* January 1989, p. 5.
55 *Socialist Worker* 9 July 1988, p. 15.
56 At least in the PTA and Body Plant – see Ted Amos' account below and the Conclusion for an account of the much higher member-steward ratios for semi-skilled workers in the Engine Plant.
57 Charles Leadbeater, 'Dagenham's decline is Genk's gain', *Financial Times*, 30 January 1989, p. 10.
58 Leadbeater, *op. cit.*
59 Quoted in Leadbeater, *op. cit.*
60 Tim Murray, 'Firefighter's Heroic Rescue at Fords', *Barking and Dagenham Post,* 22 March 1989, p. 5.
61 'Unions demand share of £673m profits', *Barking and Dagenham Post*, 10 May 1989, p. 7.
62 'Ford pay £2m to deafened employees', *Barking and Dagenham Post*, 10 May 1989, p. 56.
63 'Detroit, Damocles and Dagenham', *The Economist* 28 October 1989, p. 35.
64 Simon Beavis, 'Ford walkouts mark pay talks', *Guardian*, 7 November 1989, p. 2.
65 Mark McCord, 'Strike costs car giants £9 million', *Barking and Dagenham Post*, 29 November 1989, p. 17.
66 Roy Jones, '33,000 to ballot at Ford', *Morning Star*, 21 November 1989, p. 1.

Chapter Six

NINETIES TO NOUGHTIES: THE BEGINNING OF THE END

In January 1990, Ford workers were forced to take unofficial action yet again after the FNJNC seemingly ignored a 85 per cent strike vote over the '89-'90 pay claim. The 1107 shopfloor newsletter *Under Pressure* warned that Ford's 'flexibility' proposals would mean shift pattern changes, altered starting and finishing times, no worker choice on overtime, vending machines to do away with tea breaks, and much more.

At the end of January officials organised a new ballot, but not surprisingly, stewards feared that the vote would be much smaller this time. As one disillusioned worker spelled out the process: 'Some think "Well, what's the point in going out for weeks just to get an extra couple of quid?" ... so the officials engineer a lower vote ... and then they say take the offer' [1].

1107 secretary Steve Riley argued that Ford was trying to get workers to fight amongst themselves: 'The strings in the offer aim to get different groups fighting for different things – they want the shop floor to see this as a strike to benefit the skilled men only.' Meanwhile, the 1980s claim for a lineworkers' allowance – promoted by 1107 – came back into play. As Ron Doel commented, 'People on the line have the most awful jobs – the hardest and the lowest-paid – That's why the line-workers' allowance became a big issue in the early '90s'.

In early February, a majority voted to accept the offer. Yet more than 100 skilled maintenance workers had already walked out at Dagenham,[2] and within days electricians across Fords were on indefinite strike against the requirement to form 'Integrated Manufacturing Teams' alongside semi-skilled workers. In an additional inter-union complication, the new Electricians' and Plumbers' Union (EPIU), a left-wing breakaway from the EETPU, did not support the strike, and its members were crossing the electricians' picket lines; workers from Spain and Germany were brought over to break the strike, but themselves refused to cross. On 17 March, the EETPU gave up and ordered its members back to work.

In April, Ford UK decided to switch a £225m engine investment to Germany 'after months of strike action [at Dagenham] in support of wage claims and shorter hours'.[3] Yet Dagenham workers continued to fight back; according to the *Financial Times*, the company had 'agreed productivity deals at 11 of its 12 UK plants. The exception was ... Dagenham'.[4] Semi-skilled TGWU 1107 members were mounting a rebellion against the 'efficiency' deals the company was now requiring on a plant-by-plant basis. Signing these deals was a condition for workers to receive the extra 3 per cent (about £6 pw) agreed in January, along with back pay. But in spite of a projected loss of £130 per worker, no one was cooperating. It was hardly surprising; management was asking for a lot in return, including the contracting-out of seats, cutting dinner breaks, putting janitors' jobs out to contract and replacing catering workers with vending machines.

At the end of June, catering workers themselves voted to strike after Ford put their contract out to tender. It was not only the catering workers who were angry; as the *Daily Mail* reported in April, Dagenham shopfloor workers had 'rejected an efficiency plan because it would mean the end of the traditional tea trolley'.[5] In fact, according to one 'tea trolley lady', after vending machines were installed workers welded three of them on to the roof: 'The three machines were outside the tea crib where in the early morning we used to do the bacon rolls and make the sandwiches – that was where the tea trolleys went out from. Then when they shut the tea crib the workers welded the vending machines on to the roof as a protest'.[6]

The general unrest sparked stern – and, as it turned out, prophetic – warnings. In June the *Daily Mail* carried the headline 'Ford gives Dagenham deadline for closure', reporting that Ford directors had published an internal document threatening that 'the Fiesta assembly line at Dagenham ... will stop ... unless standards are raised ... Even the left-wing transport union warned its Dagenham members ... that the plant's future may be under threat unless wildcat strikes stopped and work rate improved'.[7] The *Financial Times* echoed the warning, announcing that 'The very survival of the Dagenham car assembly operations is at stake' and underlining that 'It is the car assembly operations, not ... the Dagenham engine production operations, that are at issue'.[8]

'Reinstate Steve'

In this context, Ford moved to undermine workplace organisation within the assembly plant. In December 1990, Steve Riley was threatened with the sack for what management called 'malicious compliance' with a foreman's instructions. Steve had been asked to remove some faulty tyres and shown where to put them. But there was a barrier in the way, and when Steve rolled the tyres towards it he was charged with gross misconduct. As 1107 activist Terry Turner recalled, 'They had been looking for a way to get Steve. He was supposed to have put on wheels in an "unsafe manner". We were called in to give evidence and we said "It's standard practice to get rid of wheels in this way". But they suspended him, and the whole area walked out …. He was reinstated. They would have sacked him if the blokes hadn't stopped. On a daily basis, our job was dependent on our blokes standing behind us.'

As Jim Brinklow reported in a written complaint, Steve's foreman had been involved in 'continuous harassment and victimisation of S. Riley as a shop steward … he … has lied to the company in an attempt to set [Steve] up and … avoid criticism to himself for not doing his own duty …. This is a matter of record from a previous … procedur[al hearing].' TGWU District Officer Steve Hart made the same point: 'It is my view that Brother Riley would not be suffering this disciplinary action if he were not an active trade unionist, shop steward and [TGWU] General Executive Committee member.' Hart, by no means an 'irresponsible' activist, made clear his 'agreement with Bros Brinklow and Riley in seeking … a workplace ballot for indefinite strike action … in Brother Riley's area.'

By early 1991, as Dagenham activists reported in a cross-movement trade union magazine, Steve's shift and section had given 'decisive support against persistent attempts to victimise him. Workers on Steve's own area voted 87% in favour of strike action should management try to enforce their final written warning.' This was 'all the more significant in that management has forbidden any mass meetings in the plant over victimisation', a ban imposed during the move to sack 1107 chair Mick Gosling. With 1107's help, Steve had now managed to reverse this decision. As the stewards commented, the failure of management's determined move to sack Steve was 'testament both to his effectiveness as a steward, and to their own record of action to destroy effective workplace organisation in their factories'. Steve himself emphasised the importance of bringing back mass meetings to counter such threats to the workforce and plant-based trade union organisation.[9]

Too Political for Me …

But 1107 was not active only in fighting management aggression. The branch's leading role in introducing equal opportunities policies became still more important as increasing numbers of part-time women workers started on the assembly lines in the early '90s. According to Engine Plant 1107er Allan Martin 'Sexism was an even bigger problem than racism – there was a lot of people who were aware of racism and knew it was wrong, but the attitude to women was "They shouldn't be here – their place is back at home" …. The feeling I got from people was that they were frightened of women coming in …. There was the feeling "They're going to get the easy jobs, they're going to be looked after" ….'

Management was no better: 'A couple of women spoke to me about the pinups and I said, "OK, we're going to have to sort this out." So I went to see a manager and said "I want both of us to go round and take this stuff down. Not just me – a joint approach" – and he refused. He said "No no, I'm not going to get involved in that stuff, it's too political for me – if you want to go around and take them down it's on your own head." He didn't want to know …. And then when I complained to the Engine Plant JWC their view was "Well this is a workplace, this is not home, and if women don't like it tell them to go elsewhere." Our [EP] JWC would just take the mickey out of you if you said you wanted to do something like that.'

Many of Allan's points were borne out by Janet Marlow, who started work at Dagenham in 1990: 'The men were unanimous – if someone had made suggestive comments or a woman had been touched up it'd be her fault because she was wearing makeup. There was a hell of a lot of sexism – just walking through the plant there was catcalls, whistling – and bizarre ideas about women – the number of times I was told "Well I'd never let my wife work here", or "My wife is too good to work here" ….

'When I started the amount of pornography everywhere was unbelievable – the benches would be covered in pornography … strippers would come in when a man was retiring …. It was probably a lot worse in the early '80s, but even in 1990 porn was everywhere … then by the time I left in '95 it had gone – and it was the unions that got rid of it.' The 1107 branch was active in combating sexual abuse of women workers: 'I can remember an incident in the women's changing rooms where men burst in – and the union got those men sacked.'

Yet the company's move to introduce part-time women workers on to the assembly lines was controversial not only due to basic 'sexism' but because of opposition to part-time working – though this was not always clear to the women involved. As Janet recalled, 'When I first started the union were against part-time workers and I saw that as not understanding my position – "This is really handy for me as a woman with children" – but they explained that the problem is that a part-time worker's never going to get a full time contract – also it affects your sickness conditions and your holiday pay. I saw the logic in it then, but the way it was presented was "We're against this sort of work, and you took it" – so the women workers felt that we weren't really liked, but as we got to know the workers we realised what their position was. It wasn't that they were personally against you – it was the fact that the company was manipulating and exploiting people through not providing sickness pay or holiday entitlement, taking on hundreds of part time workers and doing people out of jobs. The union were about people having a proper job ….'

'They weren't people that could be bribed …'

For this and other reasons, Janet spoke warmly in support of 1/1107: 'Jimmy Brinklow came into my induction and he not only sold you the union but also suggested strategies on how to cope with the boredom of the job. His argument was that really you could get a monkey to do this job so you don't have to feel pressurised – he said to me "You can only do what you're doing, and this is where the union comes in". 1107 were enormously respected. The PTA stewards had the reputation of being very militant – they really did look after their members. If the line was going too fast they would get it time-checked. You didn't get the feeling there were any little backdoor deals going on – they weren't people that could be bribed by the company – so you'd automatically get the tag "militant", wouldn't you, for that! Sometimes you get people get in positions of power and they become like the people they're supposed to be challenging – you never got that with the 1107.

'They wanted people to go along to their meetings, and they were very good at attending marches – they went up and supported the miners [in the 1992-3 wave of protest over pit closures]. But workers never complained about the union being "too political", no. Never ever …. You had your goodies and baddies and the union were the goodies and management were the baddies and that was really apparent.

'They were very good at getting the men to support them – they were very good speakers – Roger Dillon could hold a crowd, he could sell an idea … Steve Riley was very good as a convenor, he was a very intelligent man as well – all of them were very intelligent – and they were good at leading by example. The stewards would take management on and there would be huge stand-up rows – Roger explained a lot of it was "theatre" – it gave a vent to the men's feelings. 1107 won an enormous amount of respect from the men. And I couldn't ever say that Steve Riley wasn't supportive or didn't put women's rights forward because I know that he did and I know that Jimmy did and I know that Ron did and I know that Roger did and Ned – and they were a good crowd.'

Janet added that 'The 1107 did try extremely hard to get women to stand as a women's rep, but they had a lot of difficulty in getting people to come forward ... also I don't think you'd have ever got a woman beating a man if they went up for a steward's job, just because of the percentage of men as opposed to women.' Allan Martin was critical of the union-management Equal Opportunities committee for neglecting this point: 'The Committee questioned whether it should be all white stewards representing the plant – yet there wasn't one woman on that [stewards'] committee, but that was not seen an issue and it should have been.'

No More 'Sweet Nothings' ...

As Janet's tribute to Steve Riley implies, by late 1991 he had replaced Joe Gordon as PTA convenor. While the change of leadership was welcomed by 1107 activists, the *Daily Mail* took a different view. With a headline quipping 'Now it's the Life of Riley in Dagenham', the article, featuring a sinister-looking photograph of Steve frowning through a cloud of a cigarette smoke, began with a stern critique of 'disruption' at the plant and continued: 'Like a time-warp from the Seventies, the spectre of industrial might ... has emerged at Dagenham with a factory-floor coup that has dumped the moderate convenor and replaced him with Steve Riley.' Steve had apparently 'in a classic trade union coup ... ousted veteran convenor Joe Gordon', who was said (with the *Mail*'s tongue well in its cheek) to have 'had the temerity to negotiate with management on a range of Japanese-style improvements'.[10]

Specifically, the 'last straw' driving Joe out had been his agreement to the outsourcing of overalls cleaning to Sketchley; the Dagenham *Post* ridiculed this as a 'row over laundry', but in fact older workers had until then been given these jobs to relieve them from the assembly line. TGWU official Jack Adams had backed Joe over the outsourcing, but shop stewards called a vote of no confidence in him as convenor, and 'hard-liner' Steve was elected.[11]

Given the opposition of both branch and stewards to contracting out, Joe's replacement seemed justified. But, in contrast to the paper's portrayal of scheming conspirators, 1107 activists were positive in their comments on the ousted convenor. As Jim Brinklow put it, 'Joe Gordon was a good convenor, no doubt about that.... He was a progressive convenor – he had a lot of influence because of his Blackness amongst the other black workers there.' Terry Turner agrees: 'I liked Joe Gordon, but the company got too close to Joe as a global company with years of experience of sweet nothings.' The comment recalls Jim's questioning of Joe's openness to 'Employee Involvement' as spelt out in the last chapter.

Management's First Big Break ...

Meanwhile, management aggression – and official trade union moderation – continued. The 1990-91 pay talks were still going badly, with Ford stalling on the unions' demand for a shorter working week while simultaneously announcing 1,000 redundancies. By the last week in November, the company had offered only 'marginal' improvements. Yet T&G full-timer Jack Adams argued that the pay offer was 'not one we could confront the company on …. The industry is not in a very good state … '; and, at the beginning of December 1991, Ford workers voted four to one to accept an offer of 5 per cent that year and 5 per cent or inflation plus 0.5 per cent next year.

In fact, 'old-fashioned' militancy was under increasing threat from seemingly benevolent management policies like the Employee Development and Assistance Programme (EDAP). This scheme, originating in the US, aimed to encourage workers to take up various kinds of education and training beyond their current jobs. Despite the positive image, 1107 was 'lukewarm' towards EDAP. As Jim Brinklow pointed out, 'It was never a demand of the unions – [Ford] threw it into the ring …. The big plants forked out loads and loads of money [for EDAP], several hundred thousands of pounds …. We were suspicious because we thought it might mean they were getting rid of training programmes.'

The 1107-ers' suspicions can perhaps be justified by a later interview with Ford manager John Hougham, who praises its impact in lessening shopfloor conflict: 'It was our first big break … EDAP was seen as an enormous catalyst in changing Industrial Relations in Ford because it was non-confrontational. In 1990, the pay negotiations lasted six months as usual. In 1992, they lasted 24 hours. The press … asked Jack Adams, the union negotiator, why it had ended so quickly and he said: "I think it's working together on this programme. When you're working with managers like that, it's much harder to hate the bastards!"'[12]

"Something Goes Bang ..."

It was probably easier for shopfloor workers to hate them. Top Dagenham manager Terry Belton interrupted the 1991-2 Christmas break with a letter telling workers to improve quality and work harder; another letter set out the 'need to achieve a 36.4 hour car by 1993'. This was despite the continued imposition of job cuts; the Dagenham manual workforce had fallen from 5,896 to 5,015 by the end of 1992. At the same time the company was breaking two agreements: one which had provided the hard-fought-for 100 per cent lay-off pay, and another which had promised no compulsory redundancies.

After Ford unions announced a strike ballot, voluntary redundancy provisions were extended to 30 March 1993, and the 100 per cent lay off pay provisions were restored. At this 'the unions' response was ... [to] make it clear that they would cooperate with voluntary redundancy rather than fighting for jobs.' As one Dagenham steward commented, 'When the ballot was announced there was a good response ... with even people who've been quiet for a long time saying "We've got to do something", but then the wind was taken out of their sails with the unions calling off the ballot.' The problem was the 'lure' of voluntary redundancy – a lump sum combined with the relief of getting off the hated line.

But shopfloor resistance could not be wiped out altogether. Matt Conklin reported that in 1992 'Our whole line went out [because] people there for only a year were facing redundancy. Fords were contracting out to bigger conglomerates .... They told a guy in his 20s, just married, that he was redundant .... The workers were whooping and hollering to go out on strike – "We won't accept compulsory redundancies".'

Yet the drip, drip of lost jobs from all parts of the company went on. In March 1992, Ford management finally got rid of all its directly-employed 'janitors' (cleaners) as part of its strategy of contracting out all services not directly related to production. Predictably, the private firms paid far lower wages, and activists were now working to get the cleaners into the TGWU and back on equal rates of pay with Ford workers.

Another blow was short-time working, with Ford workers across the country put on a three day week in August; two months later a total of 1500 jobs were axed from Dagenham and Halewood. Not content with this, Ford threatened to make the redundancies compulsory unless workers accepted a six month pay freeze. Yet there was resistance in the air; Andy Richards, the chair of the national Fords convenors' committee, warned that Ford would face strike action if it imposed the freeze.

In fact, within a week of Ford's announcement, workers across the company were attending mass meetings to discuss the threefold assault facing them: compulsory redundancies, a six month pay freeze and a cut in layoff pay. At Dagenham, a plant-wide meeting backed the stewards' stance against both redundancies and pay freeze. In fact, a 'Consultative Survey' of the plant carried out by the company found – no surprise – an 'overwhelming majority' against the company proposals. As one Dagenham worker put it: 'Only about three people out of 4000 voted for the company and I think they must have ticked the wrong box'.[13] Yet at the same time, *Fordworker* reported, 'Everything seems to be on hold until after [union leaders] have had talks with the company at the end of the month.' Meanwhile, Ford was announcing that if it did not get enough voluntary redundancies by 11 December, workers would simply be sacked. Not surprisingly, stewards who campaigned for a strike were winning support, boosted by the threat of a 40 per cent cut in layoff pay. Fords were, it seemed, well and truly on the warpath.

In January 1993 the threatened cut in layoff pay was withdrawn. But yet another job loss announcement – 4,215 jobs to go, with the brunt of losses at Dagenham and Halewood – galvanised militants. While trade union leaders had now called off the strike ballot because enough 'volunteers' had come forward, one letter in *Fordworker* pointed out 'This is not voluntary redundancy. They scared everybody and made them panic. I was given a letter saying I would go on 30th December if there were not enough volunteers .... I got no support and no information from the union. There was no sense of urgency about the strike ballot. I was just left in total limbo, not knowing whether I would have a job or not.'

There was worse to come. In March 1993 a leaked Ford document revealed plans to contract out all its general services, affecting truck drivers, maintenance and office workers. Over 1000 jobs were at risk on top of the redundancies already demanded. Yet the document also revealed Ford's fears about the workers' response: 'A British truck fleet dispute would probably result in the progressive closure of all Ford European manufacturing plants within three days.'

The document provoked strikes by hundreds of drivers, with boiler workers and security guards walking out the following day. Stevedores at Dagenham jetty struck in support, stopping any goods moving on the water. As one Dagenham worker put it: 'We showed them the power is there. Ordinary workers said they weren't going to take it .... That's what really frightens them'.[14] The document had made clear the company's fears of a 'high risk of significant disruption' across the company, and in fact within a week Ford's plans for compulsory redundancies had been dropped.

No Longer the Butt of Jokes ...

Only months later, *The Sunday Times* could proclaim 'Ford backs Dagenham .... The future of Ford's Dagenham plant ... has been secured into the next century.' The paper reported Albert Caspers, Ford of Europe's manufacturing chief, commenting that Dagenham could be the lead factory when the new Fiesta was produced in the mid-1990s. The article commented that 'The decision seals an astonishing turnaround by the plant ... which many believed doomed only three years ago .... A Ford spokesman said

"Since the end of 1990, Dagenham has halved the productivity gap with the continental factories – a considerable achievement"'.[15]

In May 1993 Ford of Europe CEO Jacques Nasser 'laughed off' the 'whispering campaign' which said that a British plant would have to close, pointing to a 'Dagenham revival' in which productivity had risen 50 per cent inside four years. The plant was now guaranteed a new Fiesta model in July. As this report notes, 'From being the butt of jokes, Dagenham is now a leading production centre in the Ford empire … It is a remarkable success story …'.[16] Hardly a description of a factory whose main assembly facility would close in less than ten years.

Yet by the autumn the company was at it again, with up to 450 jobs to go at Dagenham. Although the redundancies were presented as 'voluntary', workers felt, as before, that the company was holding a gun to their heads – this at a time when Ford worldwide had made £333m profit in the first three quarters of the year and productivity had increased by almost 12 per cent. In fact, British Ford workers were estimated to work 170 hours a year more than those in Germany, while – despite the brave fight for parity in the 1970s – UK Ford wages were still lower than at Rover, Vauxhall or Jaguar.

Yet the 1993 pay offer was the lowest for 20 years, at 2.5 per cent that year and 3.5 per cent the next. The offer also eliminated some allowances, like those for dirty working. That October the 1107 branch produced Briefing Notes for shop stewards on the wage claim, focusing on the issues of voluntary redundancy and SERs (senior employee retirement provision): 'The only way the company can achieve voluntary redundancy is to offer better S.E.R. terms. This they have consistently refused to do …. The reason for this is that it's much cheaper to reduce layoff pay and use layoffs as a mechanism for reducing mann[ing].' The branch also noted that 'a main problem is the new efficiency of multi-skilling, ie a worker doing mechanical and electrical tasks … jobs will be reduced as a result.' Yet by the end of November 1993 a majority of Ford UK workers had voted to accept the offer, although at Dagenham a clear majority voted against.

'Using Worker Knowledge …'

In November 1994, Dagenham and Halewood shop stewards wrote a detailed overview of Ford's efforts at improving productivity and strategies of resistance. Commenting 'We are well down the road of "Lean Production", the article noted the introduction of Total Preventative Maintenance (TPM) at Dagenham's Engine Plant, meaning 'teams of highly-skilled and … semi-skilled workers interchanging production and maintenance tasks … [which] cuts out a tremendous amount of labour. Maintenance shifts have been cut from three to two ....'

The article made it clear that although Just-In-Time had helped workers in previous strikes by limiting availability of parts, the system had now 'cut out a lot of jobs. Ford has committed to a 10 per cent reduction in the labour force year-on-year ..., Just-in-Time is also linked to the widespread outsourcing of functions like stores, janitorial duties, heating, lighting, scrap recovery, seat production and many more. The ultimate aim is to reduce the plants to "core" production responsibilities only'.[17]

The 1995 pay round began with the joint unions' claim for a 10 per cent pay rise and two-hour cut in the working week. A new publication, 'Dagenham Trade Union News', compared Ford UK pay rates with those in Europe, Japan and the US, showing that Britain was bottom of the league. Meanwhile UK Ford Chair Ian McAllister had seen his salary rise from £140,591 in 1993 to more than double in 1994, at £347,453 (an item the bulletin reported under the heading 'No Comment').

As the joint unions noted, 'The average worker at Ford is exasperated at hearing phrases like "world class" and "continuous improvement" when ... their pay and conditions are anything but "world class" and have shown no real "improvement" in recent years ... ' Citing an Incomes Data Services study which showed that 'only Toyota pays its main assembly workers a lower basic grade rate than Ford', the FNJNC pointed out that 'The company's own data show it was £150 cheaper to build a Fiesta in Dagenham last year than at Cologne .... An employee in this country works nearly 21 days per year longer than his/her German counterpart.' Over and above this, '1994 saw overtime increase substantially in every one of your [UK] plants. Our members are being caught in a vicious pincer grip where without overtime [they] cannot get a decent pay packet.' The document called for a two-hour cut in the working week – as well as creche facilities, a demand first formulated by the 1107 branch.[18]

By the end of the month, outrage at a stingy offer – 4.75 per cent that year and 4.5 per cent or inflation the next – galvanised hundreds of workers at Dagenham and Southampton to walk out on unofficial strike. The walkout was described by many journalists as the first unofficial action for years, although as shown above this was far from being the case. The scale of the strike, however, was exceptional. Under a large photograph showing 1/1107 'usual suspects' Pete Singh, Steve Riley, Alf Richards and Ron Doel, the *Financial Times* reported that 'Dagenham ... the country's biggest Ford plant – was the first to be hit by an unofficial stoppage when several hundred production workers walked out ... after spontaneous shopfloor meetings .... The stoppages recalled the wildcat strikes and other militant union tactics of the 1970s and 1980s'.[19]

The 'disgruntled of Dagenham', as the *FT* called the strikers, had gathered at an impromptu meeting on the morning of 23 November to 'swear and moan about the pay offer' in the words of one worker: 'There were no proper meetings about it. People were just upset. Then some of them just walked out and others started to follow.' Steve Riley, who arrived to find workers walking out, confirmed, 'It was spontaneous ... it all happened very quickly. .... What happened reflects the strength of feeling over this offer.' Even workers who had stayed in the plant supported the walkout. As one commented, 'Everybody is upset. We deserve a 10 per cent rise because of the amount of work we do. As soon as they heard about the pay offer people did not want to work. In fact they did not even start ....'

In spite of this outburst of militancy, Ford management refused to increase the pay offer – or cut hours – when trade union leaders met them early in the New Year. In response, 300 Dagenham drivers walked out; as one commented, 'What we did was for us, the assembly plant, the engine plant and everyone in the factory. Ford are really taking the Mickey. They go on about us being the best plant in Europe and they still treat us like shit.'

Driven By You?

Meanwhile, the branch's continued attempts to secure genuine equal opportunities received a grotesque setback with the 'whiting out' episode of the mid-1990s. 1107 activist Alf Richards recalls the company 'putting out an advert – "Everything we do is driven by you". The Fords publicity people wanted a large group of workers in the poster .... Then in Poland they coloured out all the Black faces.' Another 1107 activist, Matt Conklin, confirmed the story: 'Ford advertising showed Black members in England, but in Poland their faces were "white" – their hands were still black ....'[20]

Workers interviewed by the *Independent* described their shock and hurt at the racist doctoring. One described herself as 'humiliated and angry' when she saw that 'she had put on 10lb and turned white', while a male worker who saw his face and arms replaced with those of a white man 'immediately thought it was racist: "Why didn't they just use a different picture?"'.[21]

As Roger Dillon summed up the story, 'We'd had this big drive about equality so instead of being all white workers on a new company brochure we had Black workers on there – people were quite pleased and proud about it. All the people in the picture came from our plant. And then this guy came in and said "Have a look at this" – he said "They've put a different head on it."....

'And I went Oh shit – because I knew what that meant ... Riley said,

"You deal with it". So I sat down with people and I tried to keep order – 200 people was going to walk out of the garage, and I got up and said "Look, we only discovered this last night, there's some serious meetings going on and we're doing everything we can – If you walk out, I'm not sure I can protect you …. You haven't got a right to take independent unofficial action." But the fact of the matter is there's no way the company would have taken them on over a race issue like that. Years later I regret it … there was going to be a massive walkout from the plant and I stopped it, which I wish I'd never done now.'

Roger's early move to suppress the walkout was indicative of the more 'cooperative' attitude management had succeeded in instilling in even the most militant workplace reps. As Steve Riley stated at a special JWC meeting on 31 January 1996, 'the JWC had worked very hard … to keep the incident within procedure', though 'he warned … that this would not be possible for any length of time.'

Later that year the TGWU represented a group of black and Asian workers who complained of racism in the selection procedure for truck drivers; two truck fleet assessors had been heard to say it was not their fault 'if Pakis can't drive'. TGWU officials said they would cooperate with management to break any action by lorry drivers to control job allocation; in response, more than 300 drivers announced they were leaving the TGWU for the United Road Transport Union (URTU). As the *Daily Mail* pointed out approvingly, 'Since the Tory industrial relations reforms, dissident union members have had the power to fight back against arrogant union bosses who do not represent their interests';[22] in this case the 'arrogant boss' was mild-mannered Bill Morris, the first Black trade union general secretary.

1107 activist Alan Deyna-Jones described how 'The 1107 committee backed the case of one of my members against racial discrimination in Fords Truck Fleet …. Part of a wake-up call to Fords and their policy on Diversity' – a reference to the company's adoption of the now-fashionable yet superficial concept of 'diversity management'. And indeed, soon afterwards Ford was forced to pay more than £70,000 in compensation to seven non-white employees who had proved that the company had denied them jobs as truck drivers on ethnic grounds.[23] Although about 45 per cent of production workers at Dagenham were from ethnic minorities, they 'account[ed] for just 1.8 per cent of the coveted drivers' jobs' which, at £32,000 pa, were paid twice as much as those of shopfloor workers at £16,000.[24]

Eternally Working Within the Plant ...

Yet racism or indeed sexism were not the only sources of discrimination in the plant. Trevor Tansley, soon to become an 1107 activist, played a courageous role in introducing the issue of sexual orientation on to Dagenham's equal opportunities agenda. He recalled that 'When I started in the Engine Plant I was organising a group called GLOBE for gays and lesbians at the Ford Motor Company – we were working with the company trying to include sexual orientation politics on the Equal Opportunities agenda, domestic partner benefits – because [unlike conventional partners of Ford workers] our partners couldn't buy a car. We had all these issues, and not only that we had issues with the union as well! I was dismissed basically by the Engine Plant convenor Harry Harrison – he told me to get out of his office and said he didn't want nothing to do with it. I wrote to [General Secretary] Bill Morris – he supported me and so did [TGWU official] Steve Turner, and we worked with Fords to implement this sexual orientation policy and it came out very well.'

Trevor had found a sympathetic response from the TGWU at regional level: 'I got elected on to the Vehicle Building and Automotive Committee .... The Engine Plant leadership didn't like it, because being on the committee put me at a more senior level than them – and suddenly within a year I got elected off the Engine Plant shop stewards' committee. So instead I got involved with the 1107 branch and became an equalities rep.'

Trevor's experiences again revealed the widening gap between union activities in the Engine Plant and the approach of 1107 activists in the PTA. As Trevor recalled, 'The Engine Plant convenor and the PTA convenor never spoke, never got on. 1107 was very active in the PTA and very strong and we always thought that the union committee in the EP was working with the company more. One shop steward I knew was kicked out of the committee because he was getting more active and stirring up the workers to fight back. 1107 was a lot stronger in the PTA – most of the assembly line workers wore 1107 T-shirts, they were proud of the branch, there was a lot of support for it.'

By contrast with the lively, 'political' PTA, 'When I went to union meetings at the Engine Plant all they spoke about was how many engines they'd built. I felt very strange sitting there listening to talk about production levels ... I'd never ever been at a union meeting where they talked about production – "Why has production slowed down, why are we having problems with production?" Talking about supply issues at JWC meetings ... and I would say "This is more like a Ford management meeting than a union meeting". They never discussed issues within the union, meetings with the TUC, marches, what was going on outside, cutbacks and so on – all they discussed was production levels – it was a joke.'

'Trade Union As Institution'?

Yet only weeks earlier a picture of worker-management harmony had been presented by rising star Tony Blair, then shadow Employment Secretary, when he commented that 'Ford in Britain has been transformed through proper cooperation between unions and management'.[25]

And in fact, beneath the militancy a growing culture of 'management-union cooperation' had infected even 1107 activists. Despite his basic support for the November strike, Steve Riley had also commented, 'It is a shame that people felt they had to take this action …. The trade union has procedures and we hoped employees would stay in line with them. People should not stop work until you get to an official position after a ballot.' Roger Dillon admits that 'Really the company did get a lot of control of us, we were used as a police to say to people "Don't walk out, let the company deal with the individuals, let's have a bit of order here, I'm doing the responsible thing".' As Matt Conklin recalled, while praising 1107 activists' militancy in defence of their members, 'There were procedures everywhere …. Trade union as institution, the procedural system, health and safety – it all adds up. You're constantly using the Blue Book[26] to defend people.'

Yet 'wildcat' action persisted, as indicated by a management memo to employees which commented plaintively (and ungrammatically) that 'We are having another major mis-understanding that I would like to ask your help on, this is what I will call casual work stoppages. We have people stopping work for many issues ….'[27] One of those 'issues' continued to be pay. As TGWU official and FNJNC chair Tony Woodley put it in presenting the 1997 claim, 'Ford workers [are] not being treated fairly … we are treated as the poor relations of Europe'.[28] When Ford offered an 'insulting' 2.75 per cent increase, Woodley fumed 'Is this an offer or is it an insult? It's deeply disappointing and totally unacceptable …. We are not going to tolerate this any longer'.[29]

In fact 'lightning unofficial strikes' flared up in the PTA on 3 October, and a week later Dagenham and Halewood were halted by walkouts over a new overtime scheme which would substitute 'time off at a later date' for overtime pay; workers would have to store up to 100 hours before they have to be paid for overtime.[30]

Smart at Getting us to Work Harder …

Pay was not the only issue affecting workers. As Ron Doel recalls, 'Another battle was about quality and numbers. We would say, "You're not sincere about quality, you just want the numbers."' And in the mid-late 1990s Ford were working on quantity in no uncertain terms. The process was described by Steve Turner: 'They were looking at every single job performed by every single employee trying to eliminate what they defined as being waste …. Basically it was trying to make you work "smarter not harder", as they put it – and we would claim that it was a real tribute to their engineering how smart they were at trying to get us to work harder.'

The drive for ever-increasing labour intensity was coupled with a treacly 'teamworking' approach: 'They'd try to socialise in the plant – they'd get people to wear name badges so the manager could walk round and become "part of the team" and say "Hello John, how are you, how's the kids". So people switched jackets and he'd be walking round saying "Hello John" and he was talking to Peter – because of course management didn't really know anybody. They'd try and get you to put peer pressure on others to attend work …. They tried to introduce … bonuses for the best-achieving teams in the plant and all that sort of bullshit, pitting workers against workers.

'The union did a lot of training on "New Management Techniques", and we used to try and ensure that the stewards were the key people in the "team", so whenever there was a team briefing going on it was the union that was doing the communicating, and the workers saw the union as opposed to the company as the channel of information …. The company were trying to isolate the stewards, make them look as if they were no longer the conduit for information and if the members wanted to know what was going on they had to go to the team leader. It was all company information, not union information …. There was a very sophisticated strategy deployed to try and understand where the union had influence on the shop floor and how they could remove and undermine that influence.

'So we used to work with the teams and work with our members – it was all very well-organised, 1107 in particular was very very well organised …. Stewards would intervene at the team meeting and say "Well this is really an issue for the joint stewards' committee, and we're meeting the company on Wednesday." That killed it straight away – these management techniques only work if people engage with them, and people weren't engaging with them. There's not a lot of trust between a line workforce and the company's managerial structure, and we had built up a lot of trust …. It was incredibly difficult for the company to try and isolate the union in that plant. There was a constant battle right through the '90s for the control of the shop floor and control of work. And in the PTA in particular, where the 1107 was well-organised and there was a very effective shop stewards' committee, they understood where it was going, and we didn't bury our heads in the sand, we tried to organise strategies.'

In 1998, the branch was involved in a highly effective action to unionise 'outsourced' workers. As Steve Turner recalled, 'Johnson Controls, a US company, shut a plant producing seats in Southend and brought it to Dagenham .... They refused to recognise the union and brought in a workforce on Workfare, getting dole plus £4 .... We demanded pay parity – the assembly plant voted by 96% for strike action. That was how we organised Johnson Controls .... We took a group of exploited vulnerable workers and made it a dignified place of work .... They ended up as the best organised group of workers with the support from 1107.' Ron Doel agrees: 'It was one of our proudest moments. A huge cheer went up ... when we concluded the agreement .... We took them from nothing to a really organised workforce.'

As this indicates, even in the late 1990s shopfloor militancy at Dagenham was far from being a dead letter. Yet contrary to popular belief, such activity had little or no effect on the company's investment decisions; in 1998, Ford 'committed to maintaining carmaking at Dagenham and ... making the plant the lead factory for the new Fiesta', and in 1999 went 'even further ... announc[ing] a £452m investment plan for the [Dagenham] factory including a new Fiesta-derived vehicle. Several industry experts thought the decision surprising, given the decade-long saga of Dagenham closure rumour ... But Dagenham appeared to have been guaranteed a foreseeable future'.[31]

Yet such 'guarantees' had little impact on reality at Dagenham. The March 1999 issue of *Under Pressure* quoted Steve Riley insisting that 'We are not going to sit back and allow Dagenham to become the Buffer Plant for Europe'. This followed company assurances of 'job security well into the next century' for its Cologne and Saarlouis plants, while at Dagenham 'questions were asked which the company were either unwilling or [unable] to answer'. As the bulletin comments, referring to the 'partnership' approach then favoured by both TUC and Labour government: 'Partnership. What Partnership? .... Despite the company's rhetoric about working together ... the company have not thought it necessary to even consult us.'

The 'partnership' image was further damaged with a night-shift 'mini-riot' at the end of September 1999 when 'numerous problems throughout the day meant night-shift workers had to down tools and ... angry workers went on the rampage – causing damage to about 50 vehicles ...'.[32] A similar spirit was shown when 350 toolroom workers walked out on a wildcat strike over a bonus dispute – the day after AEEU General Secretary Ken Jackson had proclaimed at the TUC that year that strikes in general were 'a thing of the past'.

Sukhit Parmar

But in the same year, 1999, a far more sinister form of conflict came to a dramatic head at Dagenham, with a campaign of relentless and sadistic attacks on Asian Engine Plant worker Sukhjit Parmar. As Steve Turner recalled, 'Sukhit Parmar suffered the most disgraceful treatment at the hands of his supervisors and work colleagues – he had food kicked out of his hand into his face – he was told to go into an oil mistifier unit where you were meant to have full face protection and it wasn't provided – he was just locked in this bloody machine while people were laughing. He was called a Paki – there was this whole catalogue of harassment, abuse, intimidation, physical assault against him …. The company were aware of what was going on and they did absolutely nothing to prevent it. It was an absolute disgrace ….'

Sukhit Parmar himself commented, 'I can barely touch the surface of what happened to me over four years. On one occasion I was dragged across the shopfloor by the collar by a man shouting "You Paki bastard". The harassment was from a small gang who would intimidate others. Between them they managed to create a racist environment in parts of the Engine Plant. The foremen and Group Leaders were the worst.' Although Sukhit complained over and over about the harassment, Ford management refused to take it up. 'I would go to the office, but they would not even take down my statements. The union in the Engine Plant is very close to management ….'[33]

The TGWU at both plant and district level rapidly moved to secure redress for Sukhit by bringing an employment tribunal case in his defence. Yet the response of Engine Plant convenor Harry Harrison, was hostile to say the least; he 'opened his remarks with the comment, "Well, that's a load of old bollocks". This was followed by a very heated debate with all those present during which it was made very clear … that Mr Parmar would not be getting the support of the [Engine Plant] JWC and Convenors ….'[34]

Nevertheless, following Steve's intervention, in February 1998 the company set up a formal investigation into Sukhit's allegations which identified Engine Plant foreman Joe Hawthorn and group leader Mick Lambert as having 'a case to answer'. The investigation took a snail-like nine months – only to conclude that 'due to the time that had elapsed' the Crown Prosecution Service would not be proceeding with criminal charges against Hawthorne or Lambert. In fact, the intervention only prompted further acts of extraordinary racist venom, including graffiti which used Ku Klux Klan 'graphics' and threatened to send Sukhit to join 'nigger Lawrence' as a target of racist violence.[35] According to Parmar's steward, 1107 activist

Rod Finlayson, who defended him stoutly from the start, the victimised Asian also faced attacks in his own neighbourhood.

Yet further recommendations to the Crown Prosecution Service were again met with a failure to act 'due to time delays'. Finally, the week before the Employment Tribunal, Ford took action; on 17 September 1999, three days before the tribunal was due to start, Mick Lambert was dismissed. The Engine Plant convenor, who had represented Lambert, 'immediately appealed this decision'.[36]

As Sukhit later recounted, even after Ford finally agreed to an internal investigation '[Racist workers] created such an atmosphere of intimidation that even some white workers went off sick. Then they organised a strike against me and another Asian worker. They refused to work with us – and they got management's backing. They were not even taken off pay. They spent a week in the canteen with free food and tea from Ford.

'Management then put pressure on me. When we had meetings it was like a public inquiry and I was on trial ... I faced pressure from the management and the trade union leadership in the Engine Plant. They shouted at me and bullied me. I was told I was "not bomb- or bullet-proof" ....'[37]

Although an industrial tribunal pushed Ford to take action against Hawthorne and Lambert, a new smear campaign began in the Engine Plant against both Sukhit and TGWU 1107. An official letter from the Engine Plant convenor accused the branch of 'misrepresentation and fabrication of facts', causing uproar among 1107 members in the plant.

At the same time there was widespread press condemnation of management's failure to address the scourge of racism at the plant. The *Mirror* sardonically matched the Dagenham slogan 'Everything we do is driven by you' with the quip 'Everything Ford does now seems to be driven by damage limitation'; the reporter quoted Steve Riley's comment that 'Ford is like an alcoholic. It is in denial about its problems ... So there is no will to find a way out.' On this basis Sukhit Parma had become 'a man who nailed the lie of the hunky-dory partnership with the workers'.[38]

At about the same time as Sukhit's tribunal was taking place, in late September 1999, Asian shop steward and 1107 activist Jaswir Teja was 'forcibly pushed' by a supervisor – ironically, while talking to a fellow worker about racist insults they had suffered. And, shortly after Sukhit's tribunal, another Asian worker, Shinder Nagra, began proceedings against Ford on the basis of almost identical allegations, despite his understandable cynicism about the possibility of any change at Fords: 'They are very good at saying "we've done this or that" but they don't put it into practice'.[39] Ironically, Nagra's own troubles had begun after he emerged as a key witness in Parmar's case, leading to a campaign of bullying which plunged him into 'an extremely hostile, hell-like environment'.[40]

Long-time PTA activist Berlyne Hamilton summed up the endemic problems, along with management's indifference and/or collusion: 'Management could not care less about racism. It has been going on for years. It is enshrined in the system.' In fact, he emphasised, 'the problem of racism is more from management than from the workers.'

By contrast, the 1107 branch had consistently fought racism at Dagenham in the face of management indifference and inactivity. At a special meeting on Equal Opportunities in February 1999, requested by the unions, Steve Riley reported that management had 'agreed that Equal Opportunities would be "re-launched" but then it just stopped.' Committee member Hari Chada observed that 'It seems the plant has no interest in Equal Opportunities …' while a management representative confirmed this impression by commenting that 'no one [in management] seemed to know what Equal Opportunities was.' As Steve Riley noted, it appeared that for management 'efficiency meetings take priority over Equal Opportunities meetings.'

At the end of September, the 1107 shopfloor newsletter *Under Pressure* reported that the company was still refusing the request for a special meeting on equal opportunities; this had been called to discuss basic issues like management's failure to facilitate regular equal opportunities meetings, while 'equal opportunities cases [are] being left to Employment Tribunals to resolve when [management] should be resolving matters with ourselves in Plant.' On this basis the JWC had now finally acted to lay a formal charge of institutionalised racism on the company, and had written to the Commission for Racial Equality requesting an investigation.

'I've Had Enough of Britain …'

It was not only the 1107 activists who were concerned about management's neglect of equal opportunities. For global CEO of Ford Jacques Nasser, the Parmar case had brought disgrace on Ford and on the company's equal opportunities 'image', for which Nasser himself had recently won a prestigious prize. As it happened, Nasser was already due to visit the UK, but the timing drew world attention to the Parmar scandal as Ford union leaders were summoned to meet the CEO. As one GMB official recalled, 'He talked about his personal experiences of racism. [The Parma case] hugely, hugely embarrassed him, both personally and as the head of one of the biggest companies in the world.' Another union official confirmed that 'Nasser was absolutely livid when … his company was accused of being racist and treating a black worker in this fashion. He said "I've had enough of Britain, I've had enough of this plant – all I ever hear about is problems".'

TGWU leader Bill Morris agreed, commenting that Parmar's case had exposed the 'callous and systematic failure' of Fords to take racism seriously; although management had promised 'zero tolerance' of racism, they had taken 'zero action. An agreement drawn up between Nasser and union leaders at the meeting pledged an 'urgent review of race relations … to try to create an atmosphere "free from harassment of any kind".' National and plant-level committees were to be set up in order to ensure the policy would be carried out. Part of the deal was ongoing talks 'to ensure that Mr Parmar can return to Dagenham's engine plant without fear of more victimisation'.[41] Not surprisingly, that clause was never implemented; Parmar, deeply traumatised, had no desire to return to the scene of his torment.

The agreement cemented Dagenham management's commitment to the newly fashionable concept of 'diversity' with the appointment of a Diversity Manager; meanwhile, the Commission for Racial Equality was concerned enough about Ford's lack of 'significant progress' to launch a formal investigation into the plant.[42] But it was never likely that the publicity surrounding the Parmar crisis would lance the boil of racism at Dagenham; only worker solidarity could begin to do that. And PTA workers did their part. In early October, a few weeks before Nasser's visit, more than 1,000 workers at the PTA had walked out in protest at 'institutional racism' and bullying of Black workers.[43] The unofficial strike followed … a "mini riot" after an Asian shop steward was allegedly pushed by a white foreman'.[44] Yet, while both significant and commendable, the action drew immediate official criticism, with one TGWU official noting sagely that 'An injection of confidence is needed to end the walkout madness'.[45]

Alongside the drama, 'normal' management aggression continued at Fords. Despite the debacle of the Nasser visit, a 'Special Equal Opportunities Meeting' shortly afterwards ended up discussing very different issues. Although plant manager Jeff Body commented that 'the company needed to take on the Trade Union's issues [on racism] and respond' his next sentence introduced a complete, and ominous, change of subject. Body maintained that 'the culture change needed to be within the Modern Operating Agreement[46] … this was the future enabling the Company to move forward … he had heard a number of veiled threats from J. Nasser at the meeting on Monday 25th October … Nasser had remarked that he could fix the North and South estate issues, the implication being that he could close one or the other of them ….'[47]

The 'South Estate' was the oldest area of the Dagenham factory closest to the river, which contained the Engine Plant, while the 'North Estate' held the PTA and Body Plant. Although Nasser's threat of closure was in part of course related to the crisis over racism, manifested mainly in the Engine Plant, his reference to the absence of a 'culture change' over 'modernisation' posed in practice a much greater threat to the PTA. Steve Riley immediately responded to Nasser's reported comments with a call to 'clarify the issue', adding that he 'did not believe that J. Nasser was saying that the plant was under threat due to Equal Opportunities issues.' Yet, needless to say, the ominous comment was never clarified.

Dagenham Doomed?

Meanwhile, the hidden current of class conflict continued to undermine the increasingly 'post-industrial' image of the plant. As the *Guardian* reported in an in-depth analysis of conditions at Dagenham, minor sabotage in the form of windows broken from the inside showed another side to the plant from the 'smart, smoked glass of the company offices [with their] suits and busy smiles.' While 'until very recently … [Dagenham] was close to being a model plant, with productivity improvements and "partnership contracts" between management and unions … Team meetings and picnic tables for the workers … ' the journalist also commented on the 'soullessness of the sprawling site' with 'no focus for a protest: just endless entrances and car parks, watched by security guards.'

Nor was 'soullessness' the only problem; the article points out that 'while [Fords] all seems perfectly New Labour: a well-intentioned corporation, a cooperative workforce … production stoppages were rippling through Dagenham, several a day … Shopfloor meetings were being held, up to a hundred strong. Cars were rolling off the assembly line unfinished ….' All this 'just as Tony Blair was telling his party conference that "the class war is over"'.

The article concludes with only too accurate a prophecy: 'Perhaps Dagenham is doomed. It has made Fords since 1931, and old factories are almost impossible to modernise …. The plant's labour relations may be the same. [In the '90s], thanks to a daily conveyor belt of meetings between unions and management, big stoppages had been reduced to almost zero. But now they're back, it seems …. As [Steve] Riley puts it: "Ford are good at partnership as long as it's to do with pure business"'.[48]

In fact, that autumn saw perhaps the worst ever pay offer – a three-year deal with a 2 per cent pay rise in the first year and inflation only for the next two years, along with yet more changes to working practices, including a threat to introduce annualised or 'corridor' hours.[49] In mid-November unofficial strikes hit once again, this time in both the toolroom and the paint shop; the toolroom workers walked out on the day of the pay talks over their claim for a bonus, while 200 paint shop workers also struck over management moves to 'stitch up' a shop steward who had been involved in a heated row with the foreman the previous week. In the same pay round, the three Visteon plants producing parts for Ford – which had once been Ford plants themselves – were hived off as separate companies. Ten years later, their eventual closure led to dramatic worker occupations.

The following week Ford's offer rose to 4 per cent that year with 3.25 per cent or inflation plus .5 per cent the next, with the 'three-year deal' apparently abandoned; Ford workers overall voted marginally to accept the offer, but it was overwhelmingly rejected at Dagenham, with 91 per cent against in the PTA, where workers refused to return to work after the ballot result. Engine Plant workers also walked out in disgust. Yet only a week later national officials signed the agreement, denying that there had been any problems with the ballot. As Dagenham steward Matt Conker put it, praising the famous demonstrations against the World Trade Organisation late that year: 'Seattle was the one bright light' of 1999.

'When they mend the roof ...'

But worse – much worse – was to come. On 18 February 2000, Dagenham Operations Manager Jeff Body sent a letter to 'colleagues' (aka workers) announcing that 'with effect from August 2000 a single shift operation is to be introduced in the Dagenham Body and Assembly Plants'. This would mean the loss of up to 1800 jobs, with the plants' whole future now in question. As the *Sunday Times* reported, chairman of Ford Europe Nick Scheele had announced that 'Ford [was planning] to accelerate the launch of the new Fiesta, but ... by Cologne, not Dagenham.' Asked about 'the 1997 deal with the unions', Sheele replied 'We have broken that agreement. We regret that ...'.[50] Whatever Scheele's 'regrets', outrage greeted the decision in both the plant and the surrounding area. The local *Post* reported Ford workers as 'angry' and 'hurting' as they 'took up their places on the assembly line ... knowing that their days are numbered'.[51]

Yet a clear 'divide and rule' issue was posed by the fact that the Dagenham Engine Plant was the only one in the world making diesel engines. As one worker put it, 'Ford wants workers in the Engine Plant to think their future is secure while it holds a gun to the head of workers in the Body Plant and the PTA'.[52] A PTA worker had once remarked, 'We'll know if they're going to save the PTA when they mend the roof'; not only had this not taken place, but it was becoming increasingly clear that 'There wasn't a lot of investment going in there'.

A Cruel Betrayal ...

By early 2000, it was becoming clear that 'Ford bosses [were] set to announce the end of car production at Dagenham'.[53] A Ford Employee Bulletin confirmed the company's 'intention to cease vehicle assembly operations at Dagenham by the First Quarter 2002, and ... its plans to transform the Dagenham Estate to become a ... centre for excellence of Diesel engines .... The existing Dagenham Engine Plant ... will be dedicated to engine machining for both present and future engine programmes ...'.[54]

Finally, the inevitable became a reality; it was announced that 1500 jobs at Dagenham would go after the summer break, when production would be reduced to only a single shift. Ron Doel recalled the date: 'On the 12th of May 2000 they announced the closure of the plant. I always remember the date – it was my 45th birthday.'

Announcements of the closure appeared in the press, with headlines like 'Disaster at Ford ... Broken and Betrayed' expressing the shock of onlookers at the decision. The *Mirror*'s report described 'Angry Ford workers vow[ing] to save Dagenham ... They denounced the decision to end 70 years of manufacturing on the site as "a cruel betrayal".' This description was endorsed by the knighted AEEU leader Ken Jackson, who declared 'Ford has broken its word. We are very angry and will do all we can to reverse their decision' – a pledge honoured in the breach, as it turned out. As the paper went on, 'The car giant confirmed that it was axing production at Dagenham with the loss of 1,900 jobs. The last Fiesta will roll off the assembly line in the spring of 2002 ....' One bewildered worker probably spoke for hundreds more with his despairing reaction: 'I've got a mortgage and three children. I just don't know what I can do'.[55]

As 1107 activist Matt Conklin recalled, 'I sat down with Woodley in Moscow Road – Pete Singh was there, Roger Dillon, Steve Riley – all of us were there .... It was a do or die situation.' But the sense of urgency seemed not to result in decisive action. The TGWU's Tony Woodley was quoted as 'warn[ing] of possible industrial action'; in June, Ford convenors and trade union officials met and resolved to fight the closure plan, pledging to hold strike ballots across the company. Yet no ballot papers appeared.

Later that month, union officials and convenors met New Labour Prime Minister Tony Blair to appeal against the closure, only for Blair to smirk that he 'couldn't interfere in business decisions'. TGWU steward Keith Gould recalled the meeting: 'We sat down and he come in, relaxed, in an open-necked shirt – and I pointed out that Dagenham was an efficient plant making a profit – we'd accepted the Modern Operating Agreement and we were prepared to do what was necessary – we said "You're the PM, you must be supportive, you can't allow this to happen" – but it was falling on deaf ears – he never made any promises, he didn't say anything.'

A Coup d'Etat

In the same fateful year, 1107 was hit by a major blow – the resignation-cum-sacking of Steve Riley. As 1107 activist Matt Conklin recalled, 'The message from management to Steve Riley was "We don't want you back in the plant".' Matt recalled some of the roots of Steve's unpopularity with the TGWU's powers-that-be: 'Steve Riley was a thorn in Bill Morris' side .... There was a meeting in the TGWU [education] centre in Eastbourne [where] Steve was pointing out how to fight management, lean production, Total Production Management – he said to Steve Hart "Why don't people see this – it's like the Emperor's Clothes – the guy is naked." Steve Riley understood power – he wanted things to be done and if not done he would blow up. His removal was a *coup d'etat* ....'

In a brief phone interview,[56] Steve himself expressed his bitterness over the circumstances surrounding the closure. In his view, the TGWU had made an explicit decision to 'save' Halewood rather than Dagenham: 'Halewood was going to close and they held ballots to save the plant which gave a 97% vote for strike action. [Unions] made a deal behind the scenes that Dagenham would close and Halewood stay open.' He added that 'The [Dagenham] closure was not a foregone conclusion but [union leaders] had a blacklist – If Riley stays, we won't fight the closure'.

As Ron Doel recalls, 'Steve had gone sick for quite a long time and there were rumblings within the shop steward committee, they wanted to get rid of him. I fought against that, and I made a call to Steve and told him the stewards were going to vote him out .... When the closure was announced the branch committee turned in on itself, and they replaced me [as convenor] with Keith Gould. When Steve finished as convenor he finished as branch secretary, so I took over.'

The Strike That Never Was

Despite the blow to workplace organisation posed by Steve's departure, resistance to the closure now mounted; over 700 workers lobbied a Ford NJNC meeting at the end of June, banging their placards and chanting 'We want a future' and 'No sellout' as well as demanding 'Nasser's head on a plate'.[57] Yet little inspiration – or action – was available from the union leadership.

It was almost the end of September before the announcement came that the Dagenham workforce was finally to be balloted for action against closure. About 1000 PTA workers had already struck for two hours before the meeting at which the ballot was announced. At a mass meeting the following week, Ron Doel quoted the Dagenham Labour MP Margaret Hodge's description of Ford workers as 'aggressive' and declared, 'We are certainly going to be aggressive to win this ballot and save our jobs.'

Yet the strike ballot was not scheduled to start until the 24 October, and was then postponed for a second time, to the thirtieth; even by the 4 November, trade union leaders had still not held a mass meeting. Activists complained that workers were being kept in the dark while Ford was 'pushing propaganda around the plant';[58] a letter from Dagenham manager Jeff Body containing two apparently contradictory statements –'The Company will not reverse its plans to cease vehicle assembly in Dagenham' and 'A top priority for the Company is the fair and proper treatment of its people' – bore out this point.

At last, on 15 November, mass meetings were held. But instead of one Dagenham-wide assembly, they were held separately at the PTA, Body and Engine plants, while – incredibly – no trade union leaders were in attendance. And so to the almost inevitable conclusion as, in the first week of December 2000, workers at Dagenham voted 1,439 to 851 against taking any action to save the plant.

It was a devastating – but understandable – result. As one PTA worker put it, 'I was hoping there would be a fight. But we never had any support from the trade unions …. All along, we haven't known what was going on or what they were doing …. We've been sat here in this plant, not knowing whether there was going to be a fight, no knowing what the hell to think'.[59]

As Dagenham TGWU official Steve Turner recalls, 'It was the strike that never was … The plant could have been saved'. There was over-capacity in the industry, but the most efficient way [to lose that] was not to close a plant in the UK …. Effectively it came down to the Dagenham workforce being the quickest, easiest and cheapest to sack. You couldn't imagine that the German government would have sat back and allowed them to close the plant. But we had a government that was more than happy to encourage the destruction of the manufacturing base of our economy. They did absolutely nothing to intervene.'

Though Janet Marlow had left a few years before the plant closure, she recalled that even then 'There were threats – the word redundancies was starting to be bandied about ….' Asked whether the PTA had been closed because it was more 'militant', Janet replied, 'I can really believe that, yeah, absolutely. I think the PTA was the most militant – and the men kind of revelled in that reputation ….'

Indeed, that reputation and that legacy would never be forgotten. As one sympathetic trade union official put it, 'Dagenham [had] the most sophisticated trade union structure that I had come across .... The history of motor manufacturing is a fairly brutal one and often the best-organised workforces are born out of necessity I guess, out of experience. They didn't need teaching about anything much, they understood pretty well their industrial clout, their industrial power – and I think you could argue over the years they'd used it very successfully.'

Cheaper and Easier in the UK ...

Yet in general commentators accepted that the closure of the PTA had more to do with Ford's financial priorities – and Britain's 'free market' policies – than with any direct desire for revenge on the militant workers of Dagenham. As 1107 activist Allan Martin commented, 'At the end of the day it was easier to close a plant here than it was in Germany .... Ford workers were cheap and easy to get rid of in the UK. It's not the same in Europe – there's more legislation. It's harder for them to shut down in Europe.'

EPIU steward Mick Hadgraft agreed: 'I think it was really just down to exit costs .... People say the unrest in the PTA influenced the company's views – but I think if they had felt that and still had a desire to make cars in this country there probably would have been some very high-profile firings and they would have got rid of [the activists] in that way. So the main reason for the plant's closing was really around exit costs ....'

Mick also accounted for the company's 'success' in diluting workers' initial fury over the closure: 'One of the things companies like Ford will do is they won't just close overnight – they come out with a long campaign in the press, arguments being leaked – by the time they got to the point of closure people were quite fatalistic about it. Plus by having strong organisation the PTA actually forced the company to make some quite impressive redundancy offers which I don't think would have been there if they hadn't built quite a fierce trade union campaign.'

A GMB official agreed: 'Once the redundancy payment figures were released, once people knew what they were getting, it was pretty much all over. There was a huge rush of people volunteering to take the money – and maybe Woodley knew that was going to be thrown at them and [decided] that once the money was out there resistance was futile. I don't have the answer to that ... but it was a bum call, it was the wrong call. Maybe the plant was just a pain in the ass to the T&G – maybe they were sick of it, sick of the militants. I don't know.'

A vivid description of the relief of some PTA workers in taking what looked like a huge sum of money – for some, enough to enable them to retire to the West Indies – came from Roger Dillon, who recalled the poignant reaction 'I thought I was going to die on that line ....' In fact, there were so many applicants for redundancy that a special JobCentre was set up in nearby Chequers Lane to process the claims. 1107 activist Matt Conklin was among them: 'Fords made me an offer I couldn't refuse. They gave me a big wodge of money – £33,000 ... I was getting £23,000 a year then.' But, he added, 'The money's not good enough with 20 years to go before retirement. The youngsters were sent away without a pension – £30,000 in your twenties is nothing unless you get a job.' In fact, even where other local jobs were available, at the beginning of the twenty-first century they were unlikely to pay as much as was still available in a huge, unionised plant like Dagenham.

A Lifetime Siesta ...

In the early afternoon of Wednesday 20 February 2002 'the last of 10,980,388 Ford vehicles to bear the stamp "Made in Essex" rolled out of the assembly shed in the form of a silver Fiesta ... sounding the death knell for 71 years of car production'.[60] And so the trendy label of 'postFordism' was made a reality for thousands of workers. As TGWU/UNITE researcher Andrew Murray wrote 'Times have changed, as Ford of Europe boss Nick Scheele told trade unions when he explained the company's decision to go back on its commitment ... to maintain car assembly at the Dagenham plant. He has since been promoted ... while thousands of workers in East London have been laid off, an eloquent enough commentary on the content of social partnership and the value of an employer's pledge'.[61]

Ironically, ex-General Secretary Ron Todd, not known for supporting the wilder activities of the PTA, was inspired to sum up the tragedy in a poem entitled *Death of Production*:

> Gone is the Paint Shop, no Robots await
> Gone is the Welder, no panels to meet
> Gone the Door Hanger, so decibels abate
> Gone is the Solderer, away from the heat.
> Gone is the Carousel, no more Tag Relief
> Gone is the Drag Line to Final Inspection
> Gone is a lifetime that now beggars belief
> Gone is our car world, with no resurrection
> Fords gather the profits in preference to honour
> While we who are left bid farewell to Fiesta
> We're now in Fate's hands, all hope is upon her
> For Ford has bequeathed us a lifetime Siesta.

But it is staunch 1107 activist Terry Turner who deserves the last word. 'When the PTA was finally shut, and I was one of the last people to leave the building, I walked around and it was dead. It was like the remains of a beached whale or a dinosaur. The things that were once full of colour, carrying work and cars everywhere, were now just dead and not moving. Like a huge animal and now its pulse had gone. The life coursing through its veins, the energy – everything had stopped. And the doors that used to open and close were now open and wind blowing through, and the temperature of the place just went. The life just drove out of it.'

NOTES

1 'We Can Win', *Socialist Worker*, 27 January 1990, p. 15.
2 Michael Smith, 'Strike hits Dagenham Ford plant', *Financial Times*, 1 February 1990, p. 9.
3 Dick Murray, 'Britain's not worth the risk', *Evening Standard*, 9 April 1990, p. 1.
4 'Line worker agreement at Ford', *Financial Times*, 10 October 1990, p. 13.
5 David Norris, 'Ford men throw out tea trolley deal', *Daily Mail*, 11 April 1990, p. 2.
6 Interview with Valerie Manningham at the Archives and Local Studies Centre, Valence House Museum, Dagenham, November 2011.
7 Paul Eastham, 'Ford gives Dagenham deadline for closure', *Daily Mail*, 21 June 1990, p. 9.
8 Kevin Done, 'Time to do or die at Dagenham', *Financial Times*, 26 January 1990, p. 20.
9 'Ford workers defend steward', *Trade Union News*, May 1991, p. 1.
10 Tony Maguire, 'Now it's the life of Riley at Dagenham', *Daily Mail*, 18 November 1991, p. 11.
11 'Shock as Ford men elect militant', *Dagenham Post*, 13 November 1991, p. 12.
12 *People Management*, '100 Years of Ford', 20 November 2003, p. 32.
13 'Ford Survey Says No', *Socialist Worker*, 17 October 1992, p. 15.
14 *Socialist Worker* 13 March 1993, p. 5.
15 Andrew Lorenz, 'Ford backs Dagenham', *Sunday Times*, 10 October 1992, p. 3.
16 Kevin Eason, 'Ford moves into top gear to fight back against Japanese', *Times*, 24 May 1993, p. 6.
17 Dagenham and Halewood TGWU shop stewards, 'Ford Workers Challenge the Productivity', *Trade Union News* 22, November-December 1994, p. 5.
18 Ford Hourly Paid Pay Claim 1995 (presentation by FNJNC unions).
19 Hugo Gurdon, 'Ford plants halted by return of the wildcat strike', *Daily Telegraph*, 17 November 1995, p. 6.
20 Ford has clearly learned little from this episode, despite its 'PR' efforts at the time. As late as March 2013 the company was forced to apologise after issuing 'an advert aimed at Indian drivers featuring a cartoon of Silvio Berlusconi

driving a [Ford] Figo with three gagged women in the boot' apparently with the intention of 'showing off its storage potential' (*Guardian G2* 26 March 2013, p. 3).

21 Barrie Clement, 'Ford workers angry as blacks are whited out', *Independent*, 21 February 1996, p. 7.
22 Ray Massey and David Norris, 'No truck with T&G', *Daily Mail*, 5 December 1996, p. 17.
23 Andy Beckett, 'Engine Trouble', *Guardian G2*, 6 October 1999, p. 2.
24 Liz Fekete, 'Black workers at Fords car plant challenge racism at the workplace', Institute of Race Relations 1 March 1997.
25 *Socialist Worker* 23 September 1995, p. 10.
26 In line with the US, from 1955 Ford produced a printed copy of its procedural agreement, entitled the 'Blue Book', every year.
27 Trim and Final Area Manager, 'What's going on in P.T.A', 1 October 1997.
28 Ford Trade Union News Issue 1, 4 September 1997.
29 Tony Woodley, 'Time to get serious' in *Fordclaim97: News from the Ford Trade Unions* p1.
30 'Ford Survey Says No', *Socialist Worker* 13 December 1997, p. 15.
31 Andrew Lorenz, 'Pile Up: The long-term future of Dagenham looks doomed ...', *Sunday Times*, 20 February 2000, p. 5.
32 'Night-shift "mini riot" denied', *Barking and Dagenham Recorder*, 30 September 1999, p. 3.
33 Interview with Sukhit Parma, *Socialist Worker*, 23 October 1999, p. 7.
34 Steve Turner, 'Racial Harrassment and discrimination in the Dagenham engine plant', South East District TGWU, 1 October 1999.
35 Barrie Clement, 'Systematic racism at car plant "was ignored by Ford" ', *Independent*, 24 September 1999, p. 6 (the reference is to teenager Steve Lawrence, murdered in 1993).
36 Steve Turner, 'Racial Harrassment and discrimination in the Dagenham engine plant', South East District TGWU, 1 October 1999.
37 Interview with Sukhit Parma, *Socialist Worker*, 23 October 1999, p. 7.
38 Anton Antonowicz, 'Any colour you like as long as it's not black ...' *The Mirror*, 15 October 1999, p. 30.
39 Daniel Foggo, 'The true face of racism at Ford', *Mail on Sunday*, 24 October 1999, p. 12.
40 Chris Kelsey, 'Indian wins discrimination case against car giant Ford', *India Weekly*, 17-23 May 2002, pp. 1-2.
41 Barrie Clement, 'Ford and unions agree plan to end Dagenham racism', *Independent*, 26 October 99, p. 10.
42 Seamus Milne, 'Asian Ford worker's years of torment', *Guardian*, 24 October 1999, p. 5.
43 Roland Gribben, 'Racial Tension is blamed for Dagenham row', *Daily Telegraph*, 6 October 1999, p. 33.
44 Rebecca Fowler, 'So who are the Ford racists?', *Daily Mail*, 9 October 1999, pp. 18-19.
45 Ray Massey, 'Walkout over "bullies"...', *Daily Mail*, 6 October 1999, p. 22.

46 While it is unclear when this agreement was introduced, its title suggests the usual late 20th century identification of 'modernity' with greater efficiency, aka heavier workloads.
47 Minutes, Special Equal Opportunties Meeting, 28 October 1999.
48 Andy Beckett, 'Engine Trouble', *Guardian,* 6 October 1999, p. 2.
49 In which employees are contracted to work a certain number of hours a year, meaning the working week can be increased or decreased according to demand and other production requirements.
50 Andrew Lorenz, 'Pile Up…', *Sunday Times,* 20 February 2000, p. 5.
51 'Unions' Anger over Broken Pledges', *The Post,* 17 May 2000, p. 4.
52 Sam Ashman, 'Ford: The Job Killers', *Socialist Worker,* 26 February 2000, p. 16.
53 *Socialist Worker* 'They are playing roulette with our lives', 13 May 2000, p. 1.
54 Ford Employee Bulletin (Dagenham), nd.
55 Clinton Manning, 'Disaster at Ford: Broken and Betrayed', *The Mirror,* 13 May 2000, p. 2.
56 Unfortunately, I was unable to otherwise contact Steve Riley during the writing of this book.
57 'Ford Workers Ready to Fight' *Socialist Worker,* 1 July 2000, p. 14.
58 *Socialist Worker,* 4 November 2000, p. 7.
59 *Socialist Worker,* 9 December 2000, p. 6.
60 Cahal Milmo, 'Last Fiesta marks the end of the party for Motortown', *Independent,* 21 February 2002, p. 8.
61 Andrew Murray, *A New Labour Nightmare,* London: Verso 2003, pp. 51-2.

Conclusion

POSTFORDISM: THE BATTLE FOR TRADE UNION DEMOCRACY

The late 1990s and early Noughties were the beginning of the end, and this is what the end means: a perfect, robotic workplace, a tidy union, the Brave New World of Aldous Huxley reborn. The pivot of union-as-institution overpowering, for now, union-as-movement; the crucial surge of the late 1960s to 1980s undermined by the reformist 'common sense' of union-management collaboration.

But it could also be the end of the beginning, as the pivot around which the issue of 'unions and unions'[1] always revolves – the roots of trade unionism in the workplace, the key sparks of exploitation and intensification of labour – reared its 'ugly' head once again in 2012, just as the story told here was coming to an end.

Our conclusion describes work life and trade unionism in the post-PTA Ford's Dagenham factory. Some of the paradoxical emotions sparked by its closure in 2002 were summed up by 1107 stalwart Jim Brinklow ten years later: 'I used to hate working here … But it breaks my heart to see it gone'.[2] And the same mixed feelings were expressed by two security guards I met on a plant visit in early 2012, both of whom had worked in the PTA before it closed. One recalled with a grin, 'It was like a prison down there. Alcatraz!';[3] the other man laughed in agreement, but added, 'It was a good place to work, though. The men were always nice to you.'

This two-sided response – the horrors of the job, the warmth of the workplace camaraderie – was a poignant summary of what had been lost, while very little, it seemed, has been gained. As our party enjoyed a post-tour lunch in the convenor's office, the Human Resource Manager described her daily labours with the phrase, 'My customer group is a unionised environment' and concurred with other managers that both quality and quantity had now been technically sealed within the computer-led organization of the assembly line. The plant was producing a million cars a year with, another manager noted, 'far fewer employees', while the decision whether to build a new engine in Britain or Turkey would not be affected by quality considerations, now universally built into the production process.

Walking back along New Road, a crack in the fence enabled me to squint through and glimpse a luxurious wilderness of plants. It was as though the site of the now demolished PTA had been turned into an ecozone, though I later learned the area was destined to house a new Tesco 'Distribution Centre' and, temporarily, a rehearsal site for the 2012 Olympics.

Green Credentials?

The self-consciously positive propaganda surrounding the Olympics was custom-made for the 'new' Ford culture. From the moment the PTA was demolished, Ford was squeezing as much favourable publicity as possible out of its 'green' initiatives, which included building a wind farm on the Dagenham estate. Three 120-metre tall turbines were approved by then-Mayor Ken Livingstone, who praised the company for 'making an important contribution towards making London a more sustainable world city'.[4]

More kudos followed when the Dagenham Diesel Centre (DDC) was opened in 2003 by – who else? – Tony Blair. The DDC won production of the engine to be used in a new diesel-powered Jaguar, a 'stunning ... luxury sports coupe ... bristl[ing] with innovative features ....'[5] Meanwhile, an 'independent UK poll' voted for Ford as the 'top car company' in a list of 'responsible corporate citizens'. According to a local paper, the survey 'represents ... companies ... which are working to improve the way that business affects society'[6] – a somewhat bizarre choice given how Ford had recently 'affected' Dagenham and its workforce.

Yet press and company propaganda continued to squeeze the maximum kudos out of the decimated Dagenham site. The local papers helped, with optimism exuding from their reports as early as February 2002; 'Carmaking may have finished but the expertise remains,' beamed the *Barking and Dagenham Recorder*, noting that 'Seventy years of vehicle manufacture ... has resulted in an impressive concentration of skills, knowledge and experience at Dagenham' to be enshrined in the new Centre for Manufacturing Excellence, which was expected to be 'operational' by early 2003.[7] Three months later, the same paper featured a resolutely smiling Vince Passfield, the Engine Plant convenor, cheek by jowl with Stamping Plant manager Lee Turner.

Not everyone was so positive about Ford's impact on the area. Confronted with Ford sponsorship signs on local roundabouts, one worker who had lost his job because of the PTA closure was incandescent: 'When I saw a sign on the roundabout ... which said "London Borough of Barking and

Dagenham – Sponsored by Ford", I could hardly believe it. This borough has nothing to thank Ford for, it's an insult to the people of Barking and Dagenham. When Ford stopped car assembly, this had a terrible knock-on effect in the community .... I'm not the only one to be upset by these sponsorship signs – a lot of my friends have been asking what the hell's it all about?'[8] This worker had been employed not by the PTA but at Excel, a company which like so many in the area was hit by the backwash from the plant closure.

Built-In Racism

Nor was the cleansed and 'modernised' environment of post-PTA Dagenham free from the racism which had disfigured its predecessor. In 2003, 1107 loyalist Roger Dillon brought a tribunal case against Fords on the basis of racist recruitment policies which had affected him personally as a Black worker. As the evidence showed, this discrimination was literally 'built into' the structure of the plant; the better jobs were advertised on only one side of the Dagenham estate – the South side – meaning that workers on the less desirable North Estate, where a much greater proportion of Black workers were employed, never saw them. Roger's case was clinched by a map which starkly illustrates the physical divide in the plant between the site's North and South Estates. Like so many Black workers, Roger had been deprived of opportunities by this 'ghettoisation'; as his lawyer commented, 'This is as close to my understanding of institutionalised racism as you could get'.[9] Ford was forced to shell out £2,500 to Roger in 'compensation', and was yet again shamed in the media for another – literally concrete – example of blatant racism; as the West Indian *Voice* put it,[10] the company had become embroiled in a 'ghetto' row. Even more importantly, the outcome of Roger's tribunal case meant workers on the North Estate could now apply for all jobs on the South Estate.

Yet the TGWU had refused to provide legal representation to Roger because of possible accusations of favouritism by some of the Engine Plant 'old guard' – indicating that, in Roger's words, 'You're looking at a system put in place by the Engine Plant TGWU and supported or certainly tolerated by TGWU Region One'. Opposition to Roger personally and politically among Engine Plant workplace union leaders was shown in their later refusal to allow Roger to represent Fords Dagenham when he became a TGWU official; they threatened to join the GMB if Roger was to be the official covering the site. As Roger pointed out, this effective boycott meant that the plant 'could blow up in the future [over racism] and there would be no Black officials to sort it out'.

As is clear from the previous chapter, it was the union leadership in the Engine Plant which had created the possibility of such disputes in the first place through a poisonous mixture of nepotism and racism. Nor did this go unassisted by management – or even that much-respected body, the Commission for Racial Equality. In Roger's words, 'The CRE was in bed with the Ford Motor Company – they were wined and dined ....' For example, the CRE, while aware of the North/South Estate discrepancy on jobs, had never moved to change it.

As Roger mournfully reflected, 'The company spent millions on Equal Opportunities – but they never changed ... they were just ticking the box. It's harder now for a Black person to claim discrimination than ever – the worker could lose their job, because if they can't prove it in law they can be disciplined for [making a] malicious accusation. So we've got the "rights" we wanted but we can't use them, because the consequence could be to lose your job.'

In this sense and others, the Equal Opportunities policies so hard fought for by 1107 activists had been neatly outflanked by Ford's 'Human Resources' professionals with politically-correct policies on 'diversity management'. Ford had appointed a Diversity Manager as early as February 2000 with responsibility for 'improving the record of promoting Black and Asian candidates – and women – within Ford UK', while a similar post had been 'created solely for Dagenham ... [along with] "diversity committees" to focus on the interests of staff from ethnic minorities at each of Ford UK's 23 plants'.[11] Yet Roger shrugged off the idea that much had changed: 'The policy documents [on diversity/Equal Opportunities] are used as cover.'

Nevertheless, the company's self-satisfied adoption of what it called 'the diversity commitment to its employees' was confirmed with an increasing number of awards, while the company continues to be depicted in Human Resource Management literature as the acme of 'Diversity Management' (as opposed to genuine equal opportunities). A 2010 company publication entitled *Diversity@Ford* reported that the company had 'once again honoured the Diversity commitment of its employees with the Chairman's Leadership Awards for Diversity .... Award categories were: Leading the Way; Valuing a Diverse Workforce; Building a Respectful and Inclusive Workforce',[12] etc. etc. A succession of smug-looking, sleek and almost entirely white managers smiled from its glossy pages – but little had changed in the grimy world of Dagenham's Engine Plant, or indeed the high-tech and highly polished Dagenham Diesel Centre.

Lions Led By Donkeys

Top-level workplace union thinking went along the same 'positive' lines in the early post-PTA years. In 2003, Amicus[13] convenor Passfield assured a local paper that he had 'never known the relationship between the management and the unions to be as good as it is now'.[14] This assessment was based on a highly 'cooperative' union-management relationship a long way from the approach of ex-PTA militants. Almost from the beginning of the post-PTA workplace regime, 1107 activists were critical of the Engine Plant leadership now inflicted upon them. In one leaflet headed 'Lions Led By Donkeys',[15] dissident activists severely criticised the 'in-plant union', commenting: 'In the past two years we have had a number of issues that have been dealt with in a most disgraceful and unprofessional manner and it has been said that a number of our representatives, in particular the leadership, are unapproachable, defensive, disorganised, arrogant and disrespectful to the views of its members.' The leaflet goes on to list a number of accusations against the in-plant union leadership, including 'changing the long-standing practice of Company service for no apparent reason', which had resulted in a plant 'divided by different seniority rules'. The recent acquisition of the DV engine, however welcome, had come 'without any information by our trade union leadership of the cost to our work conditions .... The arrogance displayed by the union leadership would not be tolerated in other [workplaces] where there would be a full and open discussion ... and in many cases even a vote.'

On the same theme of workplace union democracy – or the lack of it – the leaflet noted that shop steward elections had been postponed to January of that year 'in breach of union rules and policy'. Further, although a vote to reject that year's pay offer had taken place 'many weeks ago' the 1107 activists complained that 'not one leaflet ... from the Shop Stewards' Committee has appeared to ... explain ... the current position, or what can be achieved by a postal industrial ballot.' Finally, 'The biggest crime of all was to allow the Company to take on a large number of contract [temporary] workers without a provision to make at least some of them full time at some point in the future. We now have to watch people who have become our friends and colleagues leave without even a promise of a future call back when the need arises.' As 1107-ers emphasised, temporary working had never been permitted in the PTA.

On the loss of the Ferry Service – a penny-pinching action causing enormous inconvenience to workers living on the south side of the River Thames – the leaflet notes, 'Lack of communication to the workforce meant that a number of people gave up the fight because they could see that the union was not organised and in fact some Stewards had given up arguing against the loss ....' Although Amicus and the TGWU had launched a legal challenge to the decision, this made no difference to the company, which was adamant that the service would end on 30 January 2004.

Whatever the concrete issues – and they were by no means minor – the central message of this leaflet was the lack of workplace union democracy and accountability associated with the current workplace leadership. As the activists' statement concludes, 'Whether ... this is incompetence or arrogance ... doesn't matter. What is clear is that <u>something is wrong</u> and there needs to be a change, starting with the Shop Stewards who have not ... put the members first ... <u>In many cases we have ... elected people who do not understand that they're there to serve us and that they have a number of responsibilities to us ... We all deserve better</u>'.[16] It was clear that opposition to the drastic lack of workplace democracy in the post-PTA plants was stirring significant levels of discontent.

'No More Untouchables!'

The heading of another (also undated) leaflet was to the point: 'BETTER UNION DEMOCRACY IN THE ENGINE PLANT'. As the text pointed out, 'The Assembly people are the majority in the Engine Plant but they have only eight Stewards including the two new Lion [engine] Stewards. This means only eight votes. Assembly and Machine Shop Production are ¾ of the hourly paid people, but are outvoted by Trades and Indirect. ¼ outvotes ¾.'

This was an old complaint in the Engine Plant (see above) and contrasted painfully with the equitable shopfloor representation provided in the PTA: 'The old rule for the Assemblies was: over 100 people per shift = 2 Stewards. Over 200 per shift = 3 Stewards etc. This needs to be re-introduced .... The corrupt system of block votes against areas and shifts needs to be abolished. Each area and each shift should vote for its Rep so that the TU Rep is well known to their people and answerable to them ....'

As the text insisted, 'The corrupt system of having a full-time JWC hidden away in an office needs to be stopped ... we [only] need a full-time Convenor .... The rest of the JWC should work on the job and be released for TU work and meetings.' The writers called for 'A working JWC more in touch with the people and more answerable to them ...' and suggested a return to a PTA-style system in which 'Each area [would] elect their Stewards then the workforce could elect the convenor and 2 Deputies ... THE LEADING PEOPLE WOULD THEN BE DIRECTLY ANSWERABLE TO THE WORKFORCE. <u>NO MORE UNTOUCHABLES</u>.' It was an ABC of effective, democratic and participative workplace union organisation.

Yet the JWC's – staggering – 'defence' for their member-shy behaviour was that 'they dress and act in a professional manner which means they should have an air-conditioned office with an ensuite WC and shower, with FORD TV and all mod cons as well as a private car park'. Jim Brinklow's 1980s description of senior stewards as 'suited and booted the same [as management]' is surely trumped by this description. Although the oppositionists comment generously that 'They may be well entitled to all this for a modern union who would expect to receive the same standards as management', they also point out, only too accurately, that 'this approach leads to losing touch with the majority of the workforce'.[17]

Much of the 1107ers' criticism is backed up in a *Socialist Worker* article that summer by Mick Jones, who described himself as 'an assembly line worker of 30 years' standing at the Ford Engine Plant, Dagenham Plant' who had 'taken part in many struggles for better conditions'. The writer alleges that 'Our present Joint Works Committee has been secretly discussing a "deal" with the plant management [which will mean] the union [will] accept speed-ups, ever-increasing workloads ..., the abolition of local agreements on the movement of labour and allocation of overtime, etc. .... Every worker will be expected to demonstrate 100 per cent efficiency and if they ... cannot ... will be put in the "capability" process to get rid of them ... [T]his has been ... recommended for acceptance by the stewards' committee without ever asking the shop floor workers ... pressure [has been] put on the few stewards who have opposed it .... So why have they gone along with it? Because of a vague promise of a new engine coming to the plant ....'[18]

In September 2004 a group of stewards and workers from both Amicus and the TGWU wrote to Dagenham Engine Plant managers and union officers pleading for 'change [in] the system under which the present trade union is working and ... how Shop Stewards, JWC, Convenors and Deputy Convenors are elected. We assembly workers feel we have no representation, since if we want to raise any grievance the JWC does not allow us to do so.' Part of the reason for this was that while 'the majority of the workforce are assembly workers, the majority of the Shop Stewards are from the skilled side, therefore, they do not give much thought to our representation.' The writers noted that 'We would like to elect Convenors, Deputy Convenors and [the Joint Works Committee] directly from the shop floor, so that ... they have been elected by the majority of the workers. At present, this is not the case .... We feel that the current trade union system is a failure that does not give equal representation, since people sitting on the [committee] have not been elected by the majority of the workers. They are making their own rules …. When anyone wants to raise [an issue] through an agreed grievance procedure to highlight an issue to the company and trade union, they are not allowed to do so ….'

Democracy Not Dictatorship …

Just over a year later, divisions between stewards on the North and South estates were potentially overcome by the setting-up of a 'Joint Estates' shop stewards' committee – but very little had changed. According to a political leaflet, no shopfloor meetings were being held between the two estates; more to the point, steward elections were still being held 'on the old format' whereby for example 'over 170 workers on a line like the Puma have 1 steward and elsewhere 1 steward represents 5 workers …. The balance of Stewards between assembly, machining, indirect [worker]s and trades [skilled workers] needs addressing in favour of assembly people.' These comments suggests that the imbalance in the 'old' Engine Plant described by Ted Amos in Chapter Five was still in place –also that management was complicit with this system: 'It seems that there have been attempts to prevent new candidates for stewards from being released from their jobs to 'canvas'.'[19]

The bulletin suggests that 'The election of the convenor [and] JWC – the leading Stewards – also needs looking at. The in-plant leadership needs to be accountable and answerable to the majority, not beyond their reach. These days openness and Democracy rights are key issues as never before, both individually and collectively.'

The same syndrome was noted in an 1107 Branch Bulletin issued in early 2005, which reported that branch representatives were involved in a dispute with the Engine Plant JWC over 'the lack of assembly [workers'] representation and the injustice of the majority of workers not having a majority vote'. The leaflet continued, 'The … most important issue raised by the 1107 was the Lack Of Shop Floor Consultation by either the management or the JWC'. While it might have been in line with management logic not to consult the shop floor, clearly the opposite applied when it came to their senior shopfloor representatives. As the leaflet continued, 'This is still an outstanding disgrace …. **The people who have to do the work need to know all about it and agree to what's to be done.** For the 1107 to raise these issues and [to question] 'limited outsourcing' for our future and 600 jobs, is ***right and proper.*** For Stewards to take decisions without consulting their members is ***wrong*** … Our union movement should be known for **Democracy not Dictatorship**' (emphasis in original).

It was a classic statement of the need for direct democracy and accountability by workplace representatives, ending with the three-fold demand:

> 'We need to be informed and consulted
> We need agreements we can trust
> We need one person one vote Democracy'.[20]

But it was, alas, ignored. In fact this injustice was never redressed; even in late 2012, one self-described 'moderate' assembly-line worker could comment 'The convenor and them are stuck in the office – you don't see them at all – they don't come down.'

The branch continued to fight this extraordinary lack of basic shopfloor democracy. An undated 1/1107 Ford Central Branch Bulletin concerning 'The DV Engine and 600 jobs' quoted a joint union statement that 'We got … close to 1 hour off Lynx and Puma engines. Enough for [management] to recommend to … Detroit … that the DV engines should come to Dagenham in 2007 – then we will get a _Piece Of Paper_ guaranteeing us the engine and the 600 jobs'. But, as the bulletin noted, '(Ford) Jag in Coventry was promised job security and a good future on a _Piece Of Paper_. **Averly plant, Croydon plant, the P.T.A. Dagenham** etc. All had promises _On Paper_ and look what happened …

'It was the JWC who said **No to any out sourcing** (or there would be no Ford workers left in the engine plant … **remember**). But the JWC when their bluff was called agreed to this outsourcing'.[21]

This leaflet points to the craven kow-towing of the plant 'leadership' to any so-called pledges of new engines, etc, coming from the masters of job provision in Detroit. Yet such pledges – unless written down, as the branch pointed out – had little value other than to keep the job-hungry JWC in line.

Useless Qualification

By contrast to the grim reality revealed in the activists' critique, Ford's propaganda machine was relentlessly sunny-side-up, emphasising a 'socially conscious' approach at Dagenham which included an 'extended skills programme' alleged to have 'created a team of more confident, better-equipped staff.' As an example, the training manager commented that 'in the past Ford had struggled to recruit suitable team leaders from the factory floor, but the company is now seeing a much larger number of applicants for these roles ….'[22] The 'team' was now, it seemed, well and truly in harness.

Yet grim reality surfaced when the company was 'forced' not to renew the contracts of temporary workers in October 2008, while also announcing 'a total of 21 days without production in October, November and December' which would 'affect … around 2,500 employees'.[23] A week later, the _Mirror_ reported 4,500 jobs to be 'at risk' in the Dagenham plant,[24] while workers were to be put on a three-day week. The shine was indeed coming off the Dagenham Dream; the disastrous 'credit crunch' which had erupted throughout the capitalist world was rapidly encroaching into the car industry – and, as always, workers were the sacrificial victims.

Yet shop floor militancy at Dagenham was not dead. In early February 2009, hundreds of workers in the Body Plant and Press Shop downed tools after the company pulled back from an agreed pay deal and imposed a pay freeze instead. One union official described the atmosphere in the plant as 'incendiary', adding that 'workers at the body and stamping plant simply refused to carry on working – they were absolutely furious ....' As he continued, 'For years they've been told that the way to safeguard their pay and jobs was to become more efficient. But those efficiency gains have now become the basis for making people redundant'.[25]

'A dispute that has to be won'

Spring 2009 brought more class-struggle embarrassment for Fords when workers at the ex-Ford parts supplier Visteon exploded in resistance on hearing that their three factories – in Basildon, Belfast and Enfield – were to be closed down. Workers at Belfast and Enfield occupied their plants, and 1107 activists visited both sites to show their support. Mick Gosling, the 1107 stalwart victimised by Fords in 1989, was a strong supporter of the occupation; as he told a reporter, 'This dispute is having an electrifying effect on people. It is galvanising other workers .... This is a dispute that has to be won'.[26]

The *Morning Star* reported that 'Hundreds of people rallied at the Visteon car parts factory [in Enfield] to support workers ... occupying the site since being sacked last week ... [including] workers from Ford's Dagenham plant .... Unite[27] regional officer Steve Hart said: 'Nothing can stop our solidarity ... This union will not stop in its support for our members'.[28] Unfortunately Hart's optimism was to be undermined, at least in relation to official backing for the occupation.

One Enfield worker provided a vivid description of the excitement of occupation – and the let-down of Unite's cautious response:

> We went down to the plant .... We found a side entrance and gained entry very easily .... At the beginning it was incredibly exciting – a real buzz .... Taking back that little bit of control after having everything taken away from us – and the thing is we knew we had nothing to lose ... and so "We can't lose – we can only win."
>
> 'But ... the vast majority of us were disappointed with the initial

backing we were getting from our [Unite] national officials and district officials …. A lot of us would have expected [their support] to be more public. It was the illegality – that's the reason they held back …. Basically … a deal was struck that in response to all charges being dropped we had to agree to leave the site. The majority of us were very disappointed with this – we saw the occupation as our trump card, and I still to this day believe that it was …

It's hard to say who argued most for staying in … I can think of a number of women in their 50s that wanted to stay who maybe I wouldn't have expected to have wanted to carry on with the occupation … I think a lot of people's views have changed [now] … this whole dispute has opened up our eyes and we're just aware more of what's going on … and I think we all look on it quite differently … But the mechanics of the dispute, the way KPMG behaved, really shocked people … I think the biggest shock for most of us was just the cold hard brutality of it from the very start.[29]

In the Front Line, Last to Know …

By contrast to Unite's cautious approach to insurgent workers' illegal activities, a new 'Organising Strategy',[30] launched during the run-up to the TGWU-Amicus merger, seemed to offer a more energetic, ground-up approach to union revival. Yet the reality seemed to offer a raw deal for the union's more established members. Asked about the new approach in 2008,[31] 1107-er Terry Turner responded, 'Have I heard about the organising strategy? The last thing I heard from [Unite] was to tell me I could have a personal say in whether or not I took the union magazine ….' As opposed to being 'organised', Terry commented gloomily, 'We're about as divorced from [the union] as we can be – In the front line and always the last to know. We were expecting our union official to turn up to a branch meeting and we found out on the second or third call that he wasn't our district official any more. We seem to be as far away from the process as you possibly can be.'

As active 1107 members, 'We're getting it from the members all the time – "What's the union doing? What's the union doing about it?" And I can't tell them because I don't know. We just cannot find out. We can't get full-timers down – where we are, absolutely never. Trade unions but no shop stewards – that's where we are now.'

As shown above, the current JWC was as much at fault: 'The Works Committee isn't representative. They're just not doing anything ….' It seemed impossible simply to contact senior stewards: 'They have so many different phone numbers and they're all switched off. Whether [the rep] knows about [the problem] or not – he's[32] not getting back. Been here all his working life but it's the one place he's never there.'

Though Terry had put himself forward as steward, 'I wasn't allowed to stand ... Management called me one afternoon – "We're not allowing you to stand". "None of your business". "We believe it is." '

This serious allegation could nail only one suspect: 'It could be only one person, the convenor.' Why this united management-union opposition? 'Because of the branch, because I'm ex-PTA. The PTA was the conscience of the Ford estate ... the golden age of trade unionism – a committee of 50 stewards – you could go to any of them and they'd do the job.' Things had started to go downhill when the PTA shut down: 'Out of the whole stewards committee, six were left [at the new site]. It's just a different planet. A totally different way of working, a different world ... I would even go as far as to say it doesn't justify trade unionism.'

Terry noted that 'We're actually losing people [from the union] and they're not doing anything about it.' Ford workers were still '100% in the union ... 70% of workers are in the T&G. But it's a shrinking percentage – more people are joining the GMB ... because Unite isn't taking responsibility .... I think for the T&G it's "If it ain't broke don't fix it ..." There used to be a 30,000 strong workforce with 25,000 of them in the T&G, and it wasn't taken for granted – but they started to be and ever since have been.' As part of this bizarre scenario, 'Unite has been letting the GMB get away with allowing dual membership' with an 'exodus of [JWC] stewards into the GMB purely as an attempt to escape accountability.'

This complex dynamic arose from the Amicus-TGWU merger, bringing stewards into Unite who might not meet the TGWU stewards' higher standards of internal union democracy. 'The GMB has emerged as the major force because once Unite was formed, it gave no one in Amicus a place to hide – there was nowhere they couldn't be held to account. For a while they were going to URTU or the works committee – then they decamped to the GMB so that you could never call them to account for their actions – failing to represent people, scheming against people.'

Two years later, Roger Dillon's comments echoed Terry's view of Unite's increasing neglect of its workplace membership: 'The trade union promotes the Organising Model – the membership "looks after itself" – the union wouldn't put union officials in the plant because it "runs itself". So there's no more official involvement in the plant.' Not surprisingly, given the problems outlined above, distrust of the union in the Engine Plant lingered, with many workers viewing the plant union organisation as 'corrupt'; also, not surprisingly in the context of the 1990s scandals, as racist. This had had the unfortunate effect of far fewer Asian workers coming forward to fill shop steward positions.

At a branch meeting In October 2010, 1107 stalwart Pete Singh reminisced: 'From [the PTA] I learned so much – the races stuck together [and understood that] in the end the enemy is the boss … .In that plant we used to do things in a different way.' Pete now seemed worn down by the experience of representing often 'apathetic' workers in the Engine Plant. Other 1107-ers echoed Roger's comment that current Dagenham workers had little interest in becoming stewards themselves: 'Why should I be like him?' – referring to a corrupt or ineffective steward – was a common comment, and not without foundation: 'The [current] stewards get into a comfort zone.' As Pete Singh added, 'I had Steve Riley, I had [naming two other active stewards] – we don't have none of that.' Jim Brinklow added to the criticism: 'This [plant] union – they ain't got a clue – they ain't like us.' Production workers were said to have 'no voice' in the Engine Plant.

The problems could be linked to the Engine Plant's long tradition of 'moderation'. As 1107 activist Allan Martin noted in a 2011 interview, even before the PTA closure 'There was never any resistance in the Engine Plant from the JWC – their position then was always "If we don't [accept this change] someone else will …" And [now] we've got the chance of this engine, this new product coming into the plant … so [they'll say] If you make these concessions …. The philosophy is always We'll say Yes yes yes and then when it comes to it we'll [fight] … but of course that never really works.' In fact, working conditions in the Engine Plant now were 'Tough, very tough … on these new-style assembly lines [workers are] being monitored. Like a supermarket check-out worker – the amount of items you put through is monitored – so is this. "Over-cycling", they call it. If you over-cycle certain items they'll ask you why did you take that long.'

At a branch meeting in November 2011, other 1107 members added to this portrait of work intensification via ever-more sophisticated systems. As Terry Turner recalled, 'In the '70s and '80s, [if] you built the daily schedule before say four pm, the line stopped – then the next day you got a free cup of tea. Whereas now if you do that you just keep going, keep going, keep going, and you set the rod for your own back for the next day …. The work isn't too fast-paced, but there's always a subtle trade-off between speed and quantity. The slower the speed, the more you have to do. There's a critical point where the speed is too much, and every time that point's reached you're allowed extra time to get used to it and adjust – and then it becomes standard.' In this sense, '"Management by stress"[33] is still going on ….' Pete Singh noted the impact of 'teamworking': 'If you've got say seven people in a group and six of them come in and work on a regular basis and the seventh one is ill ... they don't want him as part of the team because the other six have to do their work .... that's a part of *kaizan* ["constant improvement"]'. Such changes in work organisation, summed up under the title of 'Lean Production', were now becoming universal in the car industry and indeed elsewhere.[34]

Yet there was little resistance, at least at this point, among the beleaguered workers of post-PTA Dagenham. As Roger Dillon noted, discussing the different levels of militancy in the engine plant and the PTA, 'One of the reasons [PTA workers] got militant was they were at the bottom of the pile – [they were] like caged animals.' Yet, at the time, the shared suffering had overcome ethnic differences: 'We pulled whole swathes of Asian workers with us.' The very pressure of work on the assembly line had encouraged class struggle and solidarity. Ron Doel recalled 'From that [PTA] plant I learnt so much about race – the races struck together – in the end the enemy is the boss.' Now, with the PTA closed for almost ten years, stewards had 'got into a comfort zone', as Pete Singh put it. Yet workers were very far from being 'comfortable' – 'All the production jobs are tough because you're working under the spotlight... very tough. The money's reasonable ... but gone are the days when you could get a job here and be secure .... They were employing temporary contract people and they got rid of all of them when recession hit.' This insecurity was in sharp contrast to the PTA days, when, as Jim Brinklow recalled, 'We never let in temps.'

Such insecurities were breeding wider problems; as the 'noughties' drew to a close, a different threat loomed in the Dagenham area. The BNP (British National Party), which had been gaining support steadily since the PTA closure, now had more councillors than any other local authority in the country. Disillusionment with Labour was widespread; one voter summed it up: 'This area has always been Labour but this lot are not the sort of Labour I grew up with'.[35] Yet, as one reporter commented, 'the underlying problems here are simple enough. Local life used to revolve around the massive Ford car works, which once employed 50,000, but is now home to a diesel engine plant staffed by only 2000'.[36]

But despite all New Labour's crimes, in the 2010 General Election the constituency was won back decisively for Labour MP Margaret Hodge – with a considerable amount of help from her friends in Unite 1/1107. As well as ex-District official Steve Hart, the forces galvanising the local Labour Party's 'Hope Not Hate' campaign included the usual suspects from the branch: Jim Brinklow, Roger Dillon, Ron Doel, Rod Finlayson, Allan and Mavis Martin, Pete Singh and many more.

'Lowering wages for new ... '

But within a year of the victory against the BNP, Ford activists were embroiled in conflict over a very twenty-first-century issue – pensions. As sympathetic GMB official Justin Bowden explained, 'At the moment up to 75% of [Ford workers'] pension is linked to RPI [but] the government's changed the price indexation measure for public sector workers to the CPI,[37] and the way the Ford pension scheme is written makes reference to the government's indexation measure so they are now arguing ... that they have to pay CPI. It's worth £450m to them, this change ....'

On 16 March 2011, 'hundreds of angry pensioners' demonstrated outside a meeting between union officials and the company's UK Human Resources director. Although an offer for current staff was made at the meeting, it did not cover the 30,000 ex-Ford workers who draw a company pension. UNITE official Roger Maddison pledged that 'Unite will not stand idly by while a company with billions attempts to rob workers and vulnerable pensioners of potentially thousands of pounds'.[38]

By the autumn, conflict was again brewing over this issue – and raising the spectre of strike action. In late October 2011, a Ford newsletter announced a 6 per cent pay rise for 2011-12 with a possible 2 per cent in the second year. But the sting in the tail of the (comparatively) high pay rise was less than good news on pensions – and more. From 1 January 2013, the Hourly Paid Contributory Pension Scheme was to be closed to new members. Not only that, but 'The Company proposed distinct Standard Grade Rates for new employees hired on or after 1 April 2012'. The announcement, slipped in at the very end of the glossy supplement, was followed by the comment, 'This proposal does not affect existing employees.' But a scribbled note by an 1107 activist, 'Lowering wages for new [workers]' was an eloquent expression of the injustice that had taken place.

On 9 November 2011, an official Unite bulletin quoted a journalist's comment: 'Ford union mulls strike action in final salary pension dispute'.[39] Unite was threatening the action 'in protest at what it claims is the company's intention to close its final salary pension scheme to new entrants' – a claim 'strenuously refut[ed] by Fords.' As a union spokesman put it, 'If the company are not prepared to recognise our members want the final salary scheme to remain, then maybe it will come to a point where there will be a ballot for strike action .... We are saying it is the thin end of the wedge. Obviously there is always space to negotiate, but the basic proposal from the company is unacceptable.' The breakdown in talks had followed the rejection of the company 'offer' the previous day by the hourly-paid workers affected, prompting Unite national officer Roger Maddison to comment

'We call upon Ford management to restart negotiations ... rather than demanding changes to longstanding agreements that could lead to Ford's first strike since the 1970s.' As this history has shown, it would be far from Dagenham's 'first strike since the 1970s', but the statement nevertheless underlined the seriousness of the issue.

Sure enough, in April 2012 conflict broke out when Ford finally came clean with its plans to close the final salary pension scheme to 'new starts' and lower the new rates from an RPI-based to CPI-based calculation. Furious Unite officials served notice of a strike ballot of its 2,500 members at Ford UK; Roger Maddox warned that 'Ford faces the very real prospect of a strike. Unite will not stand by and allow Ford to create a two-tier workforce on pay and pensions ...'.[40]

And in fact, in June that year Fords Dagenham workers did indeed strike against the company's threats to reduce their pension from an RPI to a CPI calculation. This was now an ever-increasing threat for workers – as one striker put it, 'It seems like the whole country is in a race to the bottom on pensions ....' US-style, the company was announcing its plans unilaterally, refusing to discuss them with trade union representatives; one rep accused Fords of 'Willie Walsh-style negotiating', referring to the British Airways boss's refusal to talk to unions two years before.[41]

PostFordism?

Yet underlying insecurities in the plant were likely to undermine any sustained militancy. As Terry Turner reported later that year, 'Dagenham is in competition with Turkey, with Rumania, with Cologne for the [new] engine – will we get it? I don't know – if not it'll ring the death knell for the plant .... We're optimistic in the branch that there will still be engine plant work in Dagenham. If they don't get the new engine, I've no idea what will happen.'

It was not long until – brutally – Ford workers across Britain and Europe were to find out. That October, the first shock was the closure of Ford's Genk plant, once the 'efficient' rival to Dagenham; a tabloid newspaper, showing pictures of weeping, hugging workers, reported 'Ford bosses have asked to meet the union leaders of its British workforce after announcing the closure of its Belgian factory with the loss of 4,300 jobs yesterday .... The ominous request has sparked fears over the future of the car giant's Transit van factory in Soton'.[42] And Southampton, which still produced Transit vans, was indeed next for the chop. The company argued that it was facing a 'glut in capacity' caused by the 20 per cent fall in demand in western Europe since 2007. The Ford axe of Genk and Southampton sparked widespread media and political condemnation. Less publicised was the closure, announced at the same time, of the Dagenham Press Shop.

1107: An Alternative Venue for the Disgruntled

But before even this major blow to Ford's luckless workforce, a still more fundamental threat was growing – a threat to 1107's very existence. Unite was moving to merge all its branches at Dagenham, posing the question of who would control the new 'super-branch'. At first 1107-ers were confident; Terry Turner commented that

> The 1107 branch's purpose is as an alternative venue for the disgruntled. Theoretically that's threatened by the merger – but we can mobilise people .... When Dagenham was a huge estate the only place you could really find out what was going on was the 1107 branch – it was the only place you could get to the truth, basically. That went on till the PTA closure .... Now new workers are "inducted" into the union by the convenor and that doesn't get them to take much notice of the branch. But when people have turned up to the [1107] branch with a problem they haven't been let down.
>
> 'We will have a larger branch and let's hope it's the right kind of branch with new vigour and new purpose. I would always say a workplace branch was a good idea – but it depends on who's running it. Whoever does run it or get in can't be "running it" and not turning up. Some branches on the Dagenham estate have never been quorate; 1107 always has been ... The PTA closure took a lot of the effective trade unionism out of Dagenham ... But I think that can come back. If the new branch gets up and running the way we want it to, there are things we can do – the current works committee members can't be there for ever. There should be a stage when a steward can have credentials withdrawn if they're particularly useless. If the steward suddenly realises they can be called to account by UNITE they'll jump ship ....

Yet Terry's optimism was to be sadly undermined. In early Autumn 2012, I received a typically mordant text: 'Sorry about not being in touch about the branch but after extensive enquiries I have found out we no longer exist.' It was a very 21st-century way to announce that a trade union branch born out of fierce struggle in the 1940s and built throughout a 'Fordist' twentieth century had been merged into bureaucratic anonymity as, of all things, 'Unite LE OOO1'.

As it turned out, Ford Dagenham management's paid 'release' of a large number of workers had allowed the vote for control of the newly merged branch to go in favour of the Engine Plant elements the 1107ers had spent so many years fighting. As Ron Doel put it at a gathering of 1107 stalwarts in November 2012, 'There was a solid united front between management and the JWC – people were paid[43] to attend the meeting.'

And so it was that, on 3 September 2012, the 1107-ers lost their battle for genuine workplace trade union representation and democracy in what was left of the historic Dagenham plant – at least for the time being. It was a depressingly predictable outcome for a struggle spent so long on the back foot: as one 1107-er commented, 'For the 10 years since the PTA closed we've been fighting at a distance'. For the whole period between the PTA closure and today's postmodern, post-Fordist Dagenham, the 1107-ers had, as Rod Finlayson put it, 'been trying to make inroads into the Engine Plant shop stewards' committee and failing.'

According to the activists, the TGWU had 'never got to grips with the hard right' in the pre-PTA closure Engine Plant. Echoing Ted Amos' complaint (see Chapter Five) of disproportionate workplace representation, one 1107er commented, 'Maintenance and services was running the whole show – six [skilled] workers with one steward versus 200 [semi-skilled] with one steward …. It all stems from that. [Johnny] Davies operated by placing people – he worked with management to reduce militancy.' Jim Brinklow agreed; 'The structure in the Engine Plant was very clever from a right-wing point of view. To break [it] would take some organising – and management was on their side ….'

The discussion at this informal gathering covered the domination of ex-Amicus members in the current plant organisation, historically mirroring AEU and right-wing TGWU control of the Engine Plant. As Ron Doel put it, 'The Engine Plant haven't embraced the T&G since the [PTA] closure.' In the PTA, by contrast, 'The canteen rep had the same status on the PTA JWC as any other steward. There was no "them and us".' The management-assisted victory of union 'moderates' over the activist leadership of a historic branch was – at least for now – a tragic defeat for the principles of representative equality, class unity and workplace union democracy upheld for so many years by the workplace-based leaders of TGWU/Unite 1/1107.

'They don't come down'

But the last word on the post-PTA regime must come from a self-described 'non-political' worker, interviewed in December 2012, who had worked at Dagenham since the late 1980s. Though a strong 1107 supporter, she had been unable to vote for 1107: 'The shifts meant no one could come to the meeting when 1107 was defeated.' As noted above, the same obstacles did not apply to supporters of the victorious faction, who had been 'paid' to attend.

This worker, who asked not to be named, was as critical of the JWC as the 1107 activists; commenting on the recent closure of the Press Shop, she reported, 'The convenor was aware but we heard nothing – we saw it on the TV news – the convenor has not come out to say anything. They stab you in the back and then say you have to agree it.'

Of Rod Finlayson, her steward until he retired, she commented 'Anything he knows he'll tell you', but 'since he left five years ago they don't tell you nothing.' The union was not as strong as it had been in the '80s: 'Even if they don't like [something] they don't come fighting back .... The union these days don't come back and feed you with anything – they negotiate and that's it. Everything's gone quiet these days. They have a meeting and then they don't come back [to us]. The convenor and them are stuck in the office – you don't see them at all – they don't come down ....'

When I visited the plant in May 2012, the dark figures of the stewards lurking in the union office had confirmed this distance from 'the floor'. It seemed that the union-management collaboration strategy launched in the late 1980s had achieved its malign ends; Jim Brinklow had been right to be enraged at the shop steward who had cooperated in joint 'scissors-and-paper' games.

Yet the reaction of the 1107 veterans astounded me with its stoicism. As Jim Brinklow put it, 'You got to keep on going'; Ron Doel's reaction was 'We'll keep fighting.' At my last meeting with the 1107 activists before concluding this book, the discussion revolved around mobilising support and organising to regain leadership from the largely semi-retired opposition.

Perhaps the lesson to be drawn from the resolute 1107ers is that it never is 'the end'. The oppressed and apparently defeated workers of the 1930s and '40s rose up – in both Britain and America – to combat injustice in the only way workers can or ever could: withdrawing their labour and seizing the means of production. Paradoxically, we can take heart from the pessimistic pronouncements of earlier labour historians that 'Many of the big motor firms refuse to recognise any sort of combination'[44] – and we can laugh, in retrospect, at the complacent predictions of early 1960s sociologists regarding an 'affluent' working class who would never do anything as old-fashioned as rebel against their paymasters.[45]

Two decades or so later, Cole's assessment of car workers must have seemed almost laughable, while the smug assumptions of Goldthorpe et al were themselves blown out of the water by a furious strike over appalling factory conditions. Today, forty years after the 1968-74 'upsurge' which tore apart these forecasts, we are confronted again by an apparently defeated working class of which the few remaining Dagenham workers form only too apprehensive a part. Yet history must warn us against making predictions. The story of Ford and its workers tells us, above all, never to second-guess what will happen in the future – and never, ever to lose hope.

NOTES

1. Cf Sheila Cohen, *Ramparts of Resistance: Why Workers Lost Their Power and How to Get It Back*, London: Pluto, 2006, especially Chapter 7.
2. Daniel Trilling, '10 Myths of the Far Right', *Guardian G2*, 13 September 2012, p. 6.
3. A description echoing US Ford workers in the 1930s, who called the Ford plant 'Alcatraz' (cf Phillip Bonosky, *Brother Bill McKie: Building the Union at Ford*, New York: International Publishers, 2000, p. 29).
4. 'Wind turbines', *Essex Chronicle*, 29 August 2003, p. 2.
5. 'Bristling with innovative design ideas', *The Journal*, 13 September 2003.
6. 'Ford top "responsible citizens"', *Essex Chronicle*, Motoring Supplement 28 April 2005, p. 13.
7. 'Driving forward into 21st Century', *Barking and Dagenham Recorder*, 28 February 2002, p. 42.
8. Julie Russell, 'Going round the bend over signs', *Barking and Dagenham Post*, 6 November 2002, p. 2.
9. Clinton Manning, 'The Ford Ghetto', *Daily Mirror*, 28 March 2003, p. 25.
10. *The Voice*, 7 April 2003, p. 10.
11. Greg John, 'Ford recruits the army in drive to combat racism' *The Independent*, 21 February 2000, p. 8.
12. *Diversity@Ford*, December 2010/January 2011, pp. 2-3.
13. AMICUS was the new title of the engineering workers' union, which had now merged with a number of other unions including from the print and power industries.
14. 'Ford's clean break', *Barking and Dagenham Recorder*, 12 June 2003, p. 40.
15. Undated, but almost certainly late 2003-4.
16. 'LIONS LED BY DONKEYS', anonymous, nd.
17. 'BETTER UNION DEMOCRACY in the Engine Plant', nd.
18. Mick Jones, 'Rotten deal at Dagenham?' *Socialist Worker*, 31 July 2004, p. 14.
19. Workers' Fight, 'Ford Dagenham', 1 November 2005.
20. T&G 1/1107 FORD CENTRAL Branch Bulletin (emphasis in original) nd. circa 2005.
21. T&G 1/1107 Ford Central Branch Bulletin (emphasis in original) nd. *circa* 2006.
22. Matthew Goodman, 'The right skills to banish our labour ills', *Sunday Times*, 25 May 2008, p. 14.
23. Ken Gibson, 'Industry facing a bumpy road' *The Sun* (Motors Section), 14 November 2008, p. 6.

24 Graham Hiscott, 'Motor Bosses: Give us a Bail-Out Too ... ' *The Mirror*, 20 November 2008, p. 15.
25 'Ford bosses are rewarding us with kick in teeth', *Socialist Worker*, 14 February 2009, p. 2.
26 Sadie Robinson, 'Workers' action has Visteon on the run', *Socialist Worker*, 28 April 2009, p. .
27 In 2007, Amicus and the TGWU had merged to form UNITE.
28 'Unions rally for scrapped Ford workers', *Morning Star*, 6 April 2009, p. ??.
29 Phil Wilson, 'We Can Only Win', *Solidarity* Summer 2009, p. ??.
30 Cf Sharon Graham, 'Organising out of decline – the rebuilding of the UK and Ireland shop stewards' movement', Union Ideas Network (uin.org.uk/content/view/236/125/, 2006.
31 See 'Opening the Pandora's Box: The Paradox of Institutionalised Organising', by Sheila Cohen, in Gregor Gall (ed.), *The Future of Union Organising: Building for Tomorrow*, London: Palgrave Macmillan, 2009.
32 The JWC was still all-male.
33 Mike Parker and Jane Slaughter, *Working Smart: A Union Guide to Participation Programs and Reengineering*, Detroit: Labor Notes, 1994 (www.labornotes.org).
34 See Ken Murphy, 'Making more cars than ever' in Sheila Cohen (ed) *What's Happening? The Truth About Work*, London: TU Publications, 2008, pp109-112.
35 Anna Pukas, 'Fascists who are after your vote', *The Express*, 23 May 2009, p. 34.
36 John Harris, 'The Battle for Barking', *Guardian Weekend*, 13 March 2010, p. 22.
37 The RPI (Retail Price Index), unlike the Consumer Price Index, includes housing in its calculation of inflation and therefore provides a more 'generous' pension.
38 'Ford in pension cuts row', *Workplace Report*, March 2011, p. 4.
39 Simon Warburton, *just-auto*, 9 November 2011.
40 'Ford strike threat over pensions and pay' Dan Milmo, *Guardian*, 26 April 2012, p. 26.
41 'Unions strike together to stop Ford bosses' attacks', *Socialist Worker*, 23 June 2012, p. 19.
42 Jayne Atherton, 'Ford hatchet men leave Brussels for British showdown' *Metro*, 25 October 2012, p. 59.
43 In other words, kept on the payroll as though still at work.
44 G.D.H. Cole, *British Trade Unionism Today: A Survey*, London: Methuen, 1945, p. 108.
45 J.H. Goldthorpe, D. Lockwood et al, *The Affluent Worker: Industrial Attitudes and Behaviour*, Cambridge: Cambridge University Press, 1968.

Bibliography

BOOKS, JOURNALS AND PAMPHLETS

Huw Beynon, *Working For Ford*, Harmondsworth: Penguin, 1973

Phillip Bonosky, *Brother Bill McKie: Building the Union at Ford*, New York: International Publishers, 2000.

David Burgess-Wise, *Ford at Dagenham: The Rise and Fall of Detroit in Europe*, Derby: Breedon Books, 2007

Lord Cameron *Report of a Court of Inquiry* Cmnd 131, HMSO 1957.

Barbara Castle, *The Castle Diaries*, London: Weidenfeld and Nicolson 1984

Tony Cliff, *The Employers' Offensive: Productivity Deals and How to Fight Them*, London: Pluto Press, 1970

Sheila Cohen, 'You Are The Union' Workers' Educational Association Studies For Trade Unionists Vol. 14, No. 53, April1988.

_, *Ramparts of Resistance: Why Workers Lost Their Power and How to Get It Back*, London: Pluto, 2006

_, 'Left Agency and Class Action: The Paradox of Workplace Radicalism', *Capital and Class*, Vol 35, Number 3, 2011.

G.D.H. Cole, *British Trade Unionism Today: A Survey*, London: Methuen, 1945

Peter Collier and David Horowitz, *The Fords: An American Epic*, London: Futura, 1987

Fred Creamer, 'Riot', in *Life's Too Short: True stories about Life at Work*, Bantam Books 2010.

Richard Croucher, *Engineers at War 1939-1945*, Merlin, 1980.

Liz Fekete, 'Black workers at Fords car plant challenge racism at the workplace', Institute of Race Relations, 1 March 1997.

Henry Ford, *My Life and Work*, New York: Doubleday, 1923

Patricia Fosh and Edmund Heery (eds), *Trade Unions and their Members*, London: Macmillan, 1990.

Mike Freeman, *Taking Control*, London: Junius, 1984

Henry Friedman, 'Multi-Plant Working and Trade Union Organisation', WEA Studies for Trade Unionists, Volume 2, Number 8, December 1976, p. 9.

Henry Friedman and Sander Meredeen, *The Dynamics of Industrial Conflict: Lessons from Ford*, London: Croom Helm 1980.

J.F.B. Goodman and T.G. Whittingham, *Shop Stewards*, London: Pan, 1969

Kevin Halpin, *Memoirs of a Militant*, Glasgow: Praxis Press 2012

Dave Lyddon, 'The car industry, 1945-79: shop stewards and workplace unionism' in Chris Wrigley ed. *A History of British Industrial Relations 1939-1979*, Cheltenham: Edward Elger, 1996.

David Marsden, Timothy Morris, Paul Willman and Stephen Wood, *The Car Industry: labour Relations and Industrial Adjustment*, London: Tavistock Publications, 1985

John Mathews, *Ford Strike*, London: Panther Books, 1972. Andrew Murray, *A New Labour Nightmare*, Verso 2003.

Allan Nevins, *Henry Ford: The Times, The Man, the Company*, New York: Charles Scribner, 1957

Bernie Passingham and Danny Connors, in *Ford Shop Stewards on Industrial Democracy*, Institute for Workers' Control Pamphlet No. 54, October 1977, p. 15.

People Management, '100 Years of Ford', 20 November 2003.

Colin Pond, 'The Growth of Trade Unions at Fords', Thesis for Diploma in Industrial Relations and Trade Union Studies, Middlesex Polytechnic, 1978.

_, 'The Growth of White-Collar Unions at Ford Motor Company', Middlesex Polytechnic, BA Business Studies Final Year Project, Manpower Studies, 1982-3 (TUC Library)

Red Notes 'Workers' Struggles and the Development of Ford in Britain', 1976 (TUC Library)

Yvonne Roberts, *Mad About Women: Can There Ever Be Fair Play Between the Sexes?* London: Virago Press, 1992.

Upton Sinclair, *The Flivver King: A Story of Ford-America*, Chicago: Charles H. Kerr, 1984

Graham Turner, *The Car Makers*, Harmondsworth: Penguin, 1964

Steven Tolliday and Jonathan Zeitlin, *Industrial Relations in the Age of Fordism*, Oxford: Berg Publishers, 1992, p. 104.

Graham Turner, *The Car Makers*, Harmondsworth: Penguin, 1964.

H.A. Turner, Garfield Clack and Geoffrey Roberts, *Labour Relations in the Motor Industry*, London: Allen and Unwin, 1967

Ken Weller and Ernie Stanton, *What Happened at Fords*, London: Solidarity

Mira Wilkins and Frank Ernest Hill, *American Business Abroad: Ford on Six Continents*, New York: Cambridge University Press, 2011

Barry Wilkinson and Nick Oliver, 'Obstacles to Japanisation: The Case of Ford UK', *Employee Relations* 1990 (12) (1).

FILMS

Greg Dropkin (Dir.), *Making The Grade*, Open Eye Video and Animation Workshop, 1985.

Chris Searle (Dir) *The People's Flag*, Film Four, Platform Films, London, 1987.

MAGAZINES and NEWSPAPERS

Daily Worker, Morning Star, Red Notes, Socialist Worker, Solidarity, Trade Union News: Available from respectively Marx Memorial Library, Socialist Worker archives, personal collection of Ken Weller, TUC Library.

Mainstream national newspapers eg *Daily Mirror, Financial Times, Guardian, Times:* Available from British Library (newspaper archive) and internet sources.

Local newspapers eg *Barking and Dagenham Recorder, Dagenham Post, Essex Chronicle*: available from Valence House Museum and Library Collections, Becontree, Essex.

INTERVIEWS

Ed Blissett and **Justin Bowden**, current and ex-GMB officials, Ford's Dagenham, December 2011 and February 2012.

Dora Challingsworth, senior steward and **Sheila Douglas**, sewing machinists and TGWU 667 activists, May 2011.

Henry Coleman (retired plumber at Dagenham), interview recorded for the Eastside Community Heritage Project in 1999; interviewed by SC December 2010.

Fred Creamer, TGWU 667 activist in Body Plant, March 2012

Jon Cruddas, MP for Dagenham and Rainham, July 2010.

Johnny Davies, ex-deputy Convenor and 1107 member in the Chassis/Engine plant, interviewed May and June 2010.

Joe Gordon and **Steve Riley**, interviewed as part of the Workplace Trade Union Democracy project, 1986-88.

Kevin Halpin, AEU activist and ex-PTA convenor, December 2010.

Margaret Hodge, MP for Barking and Dagenham (telephone), October 2012.

Bernie Passingham, Rover Plant convenor (retired), June 2010, July 2010.

Eddie Prevost, PTA worker in late 1950s, November 2011.

Sabby Sagall, *Socialist Worker* reporter, June 2010.

"Samantha", granddaughter of Ford worker, recorded for the Eastside Community Heritage Project (see Acknowledgements) in 1999.

Terry Turner, TGWU/Unite 1107, July 2008, as part of research into the union's Organising Strategy, published as Sheila Cohen, 'Opening Pandora's Box: the Paradox of Institutionalised Organising' in Gregor Gall, ed. *The Future of Union Organising: Building for Tomorrow*, Palgrave Macmillan, 2009.

Maisie Watson, wartime Dagenham worker, April 2011.

Keith Gould, TGWU/Unite steward, PTA, February 2012.

Mick Hadgraft, EPIU activist in Body Plant, December 2011.

Steve Hart, TGWU/Unite official at Dagenham, February 2011 and December 2011.

Graham Stevenson, TGWU/Unite official and historian, on internal TGWU issues in the 1980s and '90s, October 2011.

Steve Turner, TGWU/Unite official at Dagenham, November 2011.

Ken Weller, TGWU steward in 'Body-in-White' plant, March 2010.

All other post-1980s TGWU/Unite 1/1107 activists as follows:

Ted Amos (Engine Plant steward) February 2011

Frankie Bland (Engine Plant), April 2011

Jim Brinklow (PTA, 1107 Chair) March 2010, January 2011, March 2012.

Matt Conklin (PTA steward), January 2011.

Alan Deyna-Jones (PTA steward), November 2010.

Roger Dillon (PTA steward) May 2010, June 2010, September 2011,

November 2012.

Ron Doel (PTA, 1107 Branch Secretary) May 2010, November 2011.

Rod Finlayson (PTA Steward), June 2010, November 2011.

Joe Gordon, (ex-PTA Convenor), November 2010.

Mick Gosling (PTA steward: victimised), June 2010, May 2011, February 2012.

Berlyne Hamilton (PTA steward) January 2011.

Janet Marlow (PTA) November 2011.

Allan Martin (Engine Plant steward), Feb/March 2011.

Mavis Martin (Engine Plant), Feb/March 2011

Al Richards (Engine Plant steward), November 2010.

Pete Singh (PTA steward) June and July 2010.

Trevor Tansley (Engine Plant) December 2011.

Terry Turner (PTA) October 2010, November 2011, April 2012.

INDEX

1107 (TGWU/Unite 1/1107) 4, 44-5, 49, 53, 55, 59, 66, 71-2, 111, 119-20, 122-6, 129, 132-4, 140, 142-4, 146, 151, 157, 164, 167, 172, 175-6, 158, 169,178, 181, 198, 201, 207, 211-12
35-hour week 121, 159

Accountability 3, 42, 45, 50, 52, 199, 205
Activists, workplace 5, 31, 53, 79, 101, 129, 142, 198
Adams, Jack 158, 169
AEF 88-9, 94-5
AEU 61-3
'After Japan' 135, 143-4, 151
American Federation of Labor (AFL) 13, 15
Amicus 198-9, 200, 205
Amos, Ted (1107 activist), 72, 76, 77, 80, 134, 138, 146, 157, 211
Andon boards 26
Anti-unionism 43, 60
Anti-union laws 6, 132, 146
Asian workers 120, 175, 206-7
Assembly line 1,2,4,9,11,18,24,26, 49, 51, 71, 76, 80, 92, 126, 199-201, 207
ASTMS 124, 141
AUEW 71, 128
Automation 72, 151

Ballots 77, 108, 126, 147
Beadle, Colin 104, 109
'Bellringer' 55, 60-62, 70
Bennett, Harry 13-18
Bevin, Ernest 31-2, 34

Beynon, Huw 10, 31, 81, 90, 95
Birch, Reg 104-5
Black stewards,workers 120, 139, 197
Blair, Tony 177, 184, 186, 195
Blakeman, Leslie 74, 92
Body, Jeff 183, 185, 188
Body Plant 77, 102-3, 111
Boland, Rosie 86, 89-90
Briggs Bodies 15, 24, 31, 35, 44, 46-8, 51-3, 55-62, 64
Brinklow, Jim 3, 31, 132, 133, 140-2, 144, 148-9, 152, 165, 167, 169, 194, 200, 206-8, 211-12 (1107 activist)
Bureaucratisation 60, 79, 114, 116, 146

Callaghan, Jim 113, 125
Cameron Inquiry 63-4, 81
Carr, Robert 105-6
Castle, Barbara 87, 92, 94, 113
Challingsworth, Dora 134, 137-8
Class 7-9, 63, 78, 132, 207, 211
'Class warfare' 63, 78
Coleman, Henry 23, 26
Cologne plant 103, 179, 185, 179
Combine, Ford national 127, 135
Commission for Racial Equality 182-3, 197
Communist Party (at Dagenham)14, 36, 51, 63, 76, 78
Conklin, Matt (1107 activist) 170, 174, 186-7, 190
Congress of Industrial Organisations (CIO), 16-17
Connors, Danny (Convenor, Body plant) 116, 121, 123-4,

INDEX 221

Conservative government 63, 132, 146
Contracting-out 149, 164, 168, 172
Convenors 82, 85, 95, 108, 110, 113, 121, 124-5, 170, 200
Convenors, facilities for 82, 114
Cooperation (union-management) 74, 81-2, 114, 133, 154, 157, 175, 177, 194, 198, 212
Cork (as Ford location) 20, 21
Cortina 109, 125
Crèche 3, 173
Cruddas, Jon MP, 7
Custom and practice 84, 149

Dagenham, Dagenham plant 22-3, 29, 31-2, 42, 120-1, 127, 172, 179, 184, 187, 203
Dagenham Diesel Centre (DDC) 195, 197
Davies, John 71, 95, 111, 122, 146, 157, 211
Democracy, trade union 201, 205
Depression (at work) 4, 5, 65
Detroit 10, 153
Deyna-Jones Alan (1107 activist) 112, 143
Diesel engines 185-6
Dillon, Roger (1107 activist) 86, 126, 132, 167, 174, 177, 186, 190, 196, 205, 207-8
Direct democracy 52-3, 77
Discrimination 119, 197
'Diversity Policy' 6, 175, 183, 197
Dockers 93, 127
Doughty Inquiry, Report 34-5, 47
Dual power 43, 72
DV engine 198, 202

'Efficiency' 114, 164
Electricians (EETPU, EPIU, ETU) 163
'Employee Involvement' 114, 139, 144, 150, 157, 168-9
Engine Plant 36, 144, 166, 176, 180, 185, 195-9, 200, 211
Equal Opportunities (workplace) 6, 120, 140-1, 165, 168, 174, 182, 184, 197
Equal pay 7, 86, 89, 90, 107, 137
Ethnic minorities, monitoring 141, 175
Evans, Moss (TGWU) 106, 120
Excel 9, 196
Exploitation 5, 90, 194

Feather, Vic 31, 35, 41, 106
Ferry 28, 198
Fiesta 172, 179, 186, 190
Finlayson, Rod (1107 activist) 128, 133, 136, 180, 208, 211-2
Five dollar day 12, 20
Flexibility of labour 28, 84, 143, 146, 149-50, 153, 159, 163
Ford, Clara 21-22
Ford Central Branch 3, 122
Ford, Edsel 12, 14, 22
Ford, Henry 1, 10, 14, 16, 18, 23, 52
Fordism 1, 3-4, 7, 8, 10, 11, 19, 22, 56, 86
Ford Model T 10, 11, 21, 23
Ford National Joint Negotiating Committee (FNJNC) 35, 44, 47, 53, 56, 58-9, 60-62, 71, 74-5, 83-4, 92-6, 102, 107-8, 113-6, 125, 134, 163, 173
Ford Shop Stewards' Committee 74, 88, 134, 136, 145
Ford Worker 14, 29, 50
Ford Workers' Combine 7, 56, 97, 105, 127, 135
Ford Workers' Group 127, 135, 145
Foundry 77, 83, 102-4, 121
Francis, Bill 74-6
Fraud News 134, 136, 145
Friedman, Henry 47, 52, 55, 61, 65, 85, 91, 116
Full-time union officials 50, 58, 73, 118, 121, 124-5, 145, 204

Gender, sexism 88, 91 138, 176
Genk (Ford plant) 7, 44, 127, 136, 150, 156-7, 209-10
Germany 7, 97, 100, 114-5
GMB 46, 71, 80, 205

222 NOTORIOUSLY MILITANT

Gordon, Joe (1107 activist) 136-7, 139, 141, 144, 149-50, 152-3, 168
Gosling, Mick (1107 activist) 3, 6, 119, 134-5, 137, 142, 152-5, 165
Gould, Keith 186-7
Grades, grading 28, 86, 90, 136
Greater London Council (GLC) 138-9
Group leaders 150, 154

Hadgraft, Mick 133, 189
Halewood plant 79, 80, 90, 97, 104, 113, 136, 138, 170-1, 177, 187
Halpin, Kevin 41, 46, 49, 52, 55, 57, 59, 66, 75, 79
Hamilton, Berlyne 108, 113, 117, 182
Harrison, Harry 176, 180
Harroway, Sid 32, 93-5, 102, 104, 108, 124
Harry, Jupiter 120, 126
Hart, Steve 46, 77, 114, 120, 122, 126-7, 132, 139, 165, 187, 203, 207
Health and safety 23, 31, 34, 64, 114, 158
Heath, Edward (PM) 106, 113
Hodge, Margaret MP 188, 207
Hours of work 35, 56-7, 72, 158, 172, 184

Incomes policy 84, 113
Industrial action 43, 63, 15
Industrial Relations Act 103
Industrial Relations Bill 102, 105, 107
Inflation 102, 113, 122
Institute for Workers' Control (IWC) 93, 95, 123
International organisation 7, 128, 136

Jackson, Ken (AUEW/Amicus) 179, 186
Job cuts 139, 169
Job loss 158, 170-1
Joint Shop Stewards' Committee 81, 88, 108
Joint Works Committee (JWC) 56, 81, 88, 103, 115, 124
Jones, Jack 27, 106-7, 113-4, 120, 122

'Just-in-Time' (*Kaizan*) 135-6, 151-2, 173, 207

Keeley, Les 74-5, 81, 83
Kelsey-Hayes wheel plant 16, 24, 31, 61, 139

Labour government 82, 89, 113
Lathorne, Ernie 28
Layoffs 26, 91, 111, 116, 119, 121, 172
Layoff pay 95, 108, 116, 121, 170
'Lead operators' 149-50
'Lean Production' 187, 207
Leary, Ned 133, 155
Lockouts, 42, 75
Longworth, Jack 28-9

Maddison, Roger 208-9
Management 2, 56, 60, 67, 72, 77, 82, 133, 156, 169, 180
Management aggression 133, 169, 207
Marlow, Janet 166, 188
Martin, Allan 3, 134, 144, 154, 165, 189, 206, 208
Martin, Mavis 138, 208
Marx, Karl 4, 66, 78, 80
Mass meetings 109-10, 126, 165, 188
May 1968 87
McLoughlin, Johnny 62-3
McCrae, Jock (Body Plant convenor) 78, 102
Measured Day Work (MDW) 106, 109
Membership education 4, 68, 85
Membership involvement 4, 52, 147
Meredeen, Sander 83, 87, 116
Merit pay 41, 81
Militants, militancy 28, 49, 66-7, 77, 81, 109, 110, 112, 125-6, 158, 169, 179
Miners, miners' strikes 113, 137, 143, 151, 168
Mobility of labour 59-60, 64, 145, 149
'Modern Operating Agreement' 183, 186
Morris, Bill 175-6, 183, 186-7
Multi-unionism 46
Murphy, Mick 106, 122, 124, 151-2

Nasser, Jacques 172, 182-3
National Ford Convenors' Committee 110, 170
National Labor Relations Act (NLRA) 15, 17-18
National Union of Vehicle Builders (NUVB), 31-2, 46, 86, 88
'New Labour' 184, 187, 207-8
New technology 133, 139
Nissan 152, 158
North Estate, South Estate 183-4, 195
'Notoriously Militant' 152, 153

O'Callaghan, Lil 89-90
Occupations 17, 35, 41-2, 109, 111, 116-7, 203-4
O'Flynn, Dennis 96
Organising (trade union) 31, 66, 81, 156, 204
Overtime 26, 71, 96, 163, 173, 200
Overtime bans 70, 87, 110, 116, 151

Paint sprayers 58, 83-4
Paint Trim and Assembly plant (PTA) 1, 2, 49, 65, 67, 70, 71, 74, 76, 77, 92, 103, 110, 117, 122, 125-6, 135, 151, 156, 176, 178, 183-6, 188-9, 191, 194-6, 205, 207
Parity 56, 92, 95-6, 101, 105, 120
Parma, Sukhit 180, 182-3
'Partnership' 115, 184
Part-time working 165-6
Passfield, Vince 195, 198
Passingham, Bernie 34, 50, 53, 81, 85, 87, 110
Pay freeze 110, 128, 170, 203
Penalty clauses 92-6, 102, 127-8
Pensions 208-9
Perry, Perceval Lea Dewhurst (First Baron Perry) 20-21, 24, 29
Picketing 29, 43, 121-2
Piecework 26, 47, 59, 64, 96
Policies (trade union) 4, 147, 196
Politics In workplace) 2, 63, 78, 91-2, 128-9, 142, 146, 167
'PostFordism' 94, 193-4, 211

Postal workers 106-7
Press, role of 104, 195
Press Shop 113, 139, 202, 210
Procedure 43-5, 47, 57-8, 63-4, 73, 110, 114-5, 133, 177
Productivity 11, 56, 57, 84, 96, 109, 115, 125, 127, 133, 184
Productivity deals 84, 92, 94
Profitability 65, 90-1, 96, 111, 157-8
Propaganda, management 144, 202
PTA closure 158, 164, 189, 196
PTA stewards 70, 74, 121-2, 151, 156, 159, 167

Quality circles 135, 143-4, 157, 178, 195

Racism 6, 120, 140, 175-6, 180-1, 183, 196, 206
Ramsey, Bob 96, 102-5, 112, 115
Rank and file 15, 47, 52, 65, 91, 122, 127, 145-6
Redundancies 59-61, 74, 169, 170-2, 189, 190
Regrading 85, 89, 119
Shift work 5, 36, 38, 58, 72-4
Resistance 72, 91, 159, 170, 207
Richards, Alf (1107 activist) 119, 173-4
Riley, Steve 1, 61, 64-5,67-8, 70, 72, 74-6, 78-9, 80-84, 91, 133-4, 139, 142, 145, 147-8, 153, 157, 163-5, 167-8, 173-5, 177, 179, 182, 184, 186-7, 206
Riots 118-9, 179
River Plant 62, 86, 125, 129

Sackings 60, 119
Safety 23, 31, 24, 64, 114, 158
Scanlon, Hugh 94, 107
Semi-skilled workers 45, 70, 90
Sewing machinists 58, 82-3, 85-89, 90, 136, 139
Sexual abuse, harassment 141, 166
Sexual orientation policy 176
Shift work 5, 59, 79, 84, 89, 127, 157-8, 163, 179
'Shop floor' 70, 96, 110, 115, 178

Shop meetings 50, 75
Shop steward elections 150, 198, 200, 201-2
Shop stewards, shop stewards' committee 4, 31, 34, 40, 41, 45, 46, 48, 50, 52, 56-9, 60, 64, 65, 70, 74, 77-9, 81, 84, 85, 89, 93, 95, 108, 110, 114-5, 121, 123, 125, 134, 145, 147, 150, 157, 198, 199, 201
Shorter working week 66, 169, 173
Short time 60, 170
Sierra 134, 136, 156-8
Singh, Pete (1107 activist) 2, 128, 133, 144-5, 148, 173, 186, 206-7
Skilled workers 36, 48, 200
Social Contract 113-4, 120, 122
Solidarity 6, 7, 60, 64, 79, 91, 93, 116, 128, 132, 142, 183, 207
Sorenson, Charles 11, 18, 20
South Africa 7, 142-3
Southampton plant 127, 210
Speed-up 5, 11, 30, 33, 35, 48, 51-2, 65, 71-3, 76-7, 81, 114, 117, 125, 135, 200, 206
Standardisation (Briggs and Fords) 59, 61, 64, 67
'Strings' 150, 153-4, 165, 158, 163
Swansea plant 104, 116

Tansley, Trevor 5, 176
Taylorism 7, 9-11
Tea breaks 57, 16-4
'Teamworking' 143, 178, 178, 203
Temporary workers 151, 157, 202, 207
Thatcher, Margaret 107, 132, 148, 152-3
Three-day week 170, 202, 205
Three-year deals 106, 151
Time rate 47, 59, 66, 96
Todd, Ron 111, 190
Toolmakers 83, 84
Toyota 158, 173
Trade union bureaucracy 3, 60, 114
Trade union officials 50, 58, 118, 121, 125, 145, 204
Trade union recognition 29, 32, 34, 36, 40-1
Trafford Park 19-21, 24, 28
Transfer of labour 45, 71, 80, 149
Transport and General Workers' Union (TGWU) 27, 30, 41, 46, 50, 71, 78, 83, 94, 106, 122, 142, 147, 158, 170, 175, 176, 180, 187, 196, 199, 200
Trim Shop 86, 89
Truck Fleet 71, 141, 171
TUC 29-31, 41, 102, 107, 113
TULRA (Trade Union and Labour Relations Act) 1974 114, 123
Turner, Steve 6, 135, 142, 176, 178-9, 180, 188
Turner, Terry 2-3, 138, 142, 165, 168, 191, 204, 206, 209-10
Two-year deals 107, 152

Unconstitutional action 95, 133, 162
Under Pressure 155, 163, 179, 182
Union as institution 177, 194
Union officials, 50, 58, 118, 121, 125, 145, 204
'union within the Union' 53, 60
Unite 203-4, 208, 211
Unite LE OOO1 211
United Auto Workers (UAW) 16, 17, 106
Unofficial action 62, 64, 66, 70, 73, 81, 91-2, 103, 113, 128, 140, 154
URTU (United Road Transport Union) 175, 205

Vauxhall motors 46, 60, 92, 105
Vending machines 163-4
Victimisation 74, 165
Visteon occupation 203-4

Wages 87-8, 90, 96, 103, 122, 172
Wage cuts 28, 29
Watson, Maisie 33-40
What Happened At Fords 91
Weller, Ken 79, 81, 91
'Whiting out' of photos 174
Williams, Winston 111-2

'Winter of Discontent' 113-4, 126, 128
Women workers 2, 6, 12, 33-4, 48, 50, 84, 88, 90, 138, 165-6, 168
Woodley, Tony 177, 189
Workers' control 96, 178
Work intensification 26, 114, 139, 178, 194, 206
Working conditions 58, 67, 158, 206
Workload 71, 117, 123, 200
Workplace representation 41, 43-4, 202
Workplace union 1, 45, 56, 76, 132, 156-7, 198-9
Workplace union democracy 1, 45, 52, 56, 60, 76-7, 96, 123, 132, 156-7, 198-9, 201, 205, 211
Wray, Dave 123-4

Also available from the Merlin Press

Alan Campbell, Nina Fishman, John McIlroy, Editors
THE POST-WAR COMPROMISE: British Trade Unions and Industrial Politics, 1945–64
This text focuses on the politics of trade unionism – not only unions' relations with political parties and the state but also on the politics of workplace conflict and industrial action. Broad perspectives on trade union organising, and on the parameters of the post-war industrial environment, with case studies on particular fields: union relations with the Labour Party, international politics productivity, major strikes and key groups of workers. For anyone that aspires to recreate these high points in our struggle, these books will be valuable reading. *Morning Star*
360 pages, 978 0 85036 601 3 Paperback £18.95

John McIlroy, Nina Fishman, Alan Campbell, Editors
THE HIGH TIDE OF BRITISH TRADE UNIONISM: Trade Unions & Industrial Politics, 1964–79
The years 1964–79 constitute an exciting, turbulent period in labour history: a period, when the Transport Workers' leader, Jack Jones, appeared to be more powerful than the prime minister, with unions running the country into the ground and the 'Winter of Discontent' paving the way for Thatcherism.
'their publication in paperback is most welcome, making them more affordable and hopefully more widely read. In addition the new introduction by John McIlroy is sharp, incisive and engaging, explaining the strength and limits of union power during the period.' *Labour Research*. For anyone that aspires to recreate these high points in our struggle, these books will be valuable reading. *Morning Star*
408 pages, 978 0 85036 602 0 Paperback £18.95

Joyce L. Kornbluh, Editor
With a new preface by Daniel Gross, Introduction by Fred Thompson
REBEL VOICES An IWW Anthology THIRD EDITION
The biggest and best source on IWW history, fiction, songs, art and lore.
'Not even the doughtiest of capitalism's defenders can read these pages without understanding how much glory and nobility there was in the IWW story...' — *NY Times Book Review*
'an indispensable collection of documents for the history of the American

labour movement' – *Times Literary Supplement*
Illustrated With Contemporary Cartoons & Graphics
467 pages, 50 illustrations 978 0 85036 651 8 Paperback £22.50

Mary Davis, Editor
CLASS AND GENDER IN BRITISH LABOUR HISTORY: Renewing the Debate (or starting it?)
Capitalism constructs gender and gender constructs the development of capitalism: this is a central theme in this collection of essays.

'These essays certainly renew, or restart, the debate about gender in labour history, opening up, sometimes tantalizingly, avenues of research which demand to be taken further.' *Labour History Review.*
231pp 978 0 85036 668 6 Pbk £16.95

Griselda Carr
PIT WOMEN: Coal Communities in Northern England in the Early 20th Century
This book focuses on family life and on the coal communities of Yorkshire and the North East. It provides interesting perspectives on relations between women and men, on how girls grew up and on the culture of these communities. 'an inspiring book. It provokes anger at the treatment meted out to generations of mining families' *North East History*
180 pages, 978 0 85036 495 8 Paperback £12.95

Leo Panitch & Colin Leys, Editors
WORKING CLASSES, GLOBAL REALITIES
Socialist Register 2001 examines the concept and the reality of class as it effects workers at the beginning of the 21st Century.
'an excellent collection' Bill Fletcher, *Against The Current*
403pp 978 0 85036 490 6 Pbk £16.95

Chris Mcguffie
WORKING IN METAL: Management and Labour in the Metal Industries of Europe and the USA 1890-1914.
Traces the history of the dramatic transformation of industrial life at the beginning of the century in four countries – Britain, France, Germany and the USA.
340 pages, 978 0 85036 312 8 Hardback £17.50

www.merlinpress.co.uk